Narratives of Neglect

CRIME ETHNOGRAPHY SERIES

Series editors: Dick Hobbs and Geoffrey Pearson

Published titles

Holding Your Square: streetlife, masculinities and violence, by Christopher W. Mullins

Narratives of Neglect: Community, regeneration and the governance of security, by Jacqui Karn

Narratives of Neglect
Community, regeneration and the governance of security

Jacqui Karn

WILLAN
PUBLISHING

Published by

Willan Publishing
Culmcott House
Mill Street, Uffculme
Cullompton, Devon
EX15 3AT, UK
Tel: +44(0)1884 840337
Fax: +44(0)1884 840251
e-mail: info@willanpublishing.co.uk
website: www.willanpublishing.co.uk

Published simultaneously in the USA and Canada by

Willan Publishing
c/o ISBS, 920 NE 58th Ave, Suite 300,
Portland, Oregon 97213-3786, USA
Tel: +001(0)503 287 3093
Fax: +001(0)503 280 8832
e-mail: info@isbs.com
website: www.isbs.com

First published 2007

Hardback
ISBN: 978 1-84392-195-0

British Library Cataloguing-in-Publication Data

A catalogue record for this book is available from the British Library

Project managed by Deer Park Productions, Tavistock, Devon
Typeset by GCS, Leighton Buzzard, Bedfordshire
Printed and bound by T.J. International Ltd, Padstow, Cornwall

To the memory of my mother.
For the stories she told.

Contents

Acknowledgements

My thanks go firstly to the residents of the estates in which I conducted this research for their warm welcome, time and frank advice. Though in order to preserve confidentiality I cannot name the area or the individuals, I would, in particular, like to thank those I have called Pat, James, Henry, Deb and Rob. Likewise my thanks go to the professional staff working there, who again I cannot name, who gave me their time, interest and put up with my presence at meetings. Special thanks are due to the staff at the youth centre who allowed me to hang around for weeks. Thanks also to Peter Chi Man Chan for translation and to Nicola Moran for help in emergencies.

My special gratitude goes to Ian Loader and Evi Girling for their enthusiasm, advice and occasional thick skins. My thanks also go to all in the Criminology Department at Keele University and those at the Mannheim Centre for Criminology, the London School of Economics, for comments and support. I am also grateful to Richard Sparks and Adam Crawford for tactful but challenging criticism and timely encouragement to publish. Further thanks to Tim Newburn and Dick Hobbs for guidance during the editing process. I also want to thank the Economic and Social Research Council for financial support during the course of the PhD (R00429934240) and for funding me as a Postdoctoral Fellow (PTA-026-27-057) which gave me the space to edit this for publication.

I also owe a huge debt of gratitude to Evangeline, Bill and Katharine for unwavering friendship, love and support. Similarly to Ceri, Andy, Meg, Jo, Sal, Sarah and Lisa for providing light relief. Thanks also to Deborah and Julia for carrying on their friendship to the next generation.

Jacqui Karn
jacqui.karn1@btinternet.com

Part I

Introducing an Ethnography

Chapter 1

Introducing the estate

Throughout the book I will be exploring the ways in which both residents and professionals went about making sense of the changes that had already occurred, and those that were continuing to take place, on a small, multiple-deprived council estate on the edge of Manchester city centre. The estate having declined in appearance, reputation and population, the city had secured approval for its demolition and rebuilding in conjunction with private developers. In contrast to its stigmatised present, it was hoped that this future would be a model of sustainable city centre living. As well as a record of the responses to these changes, this book is in part an attempt to build 'a locally sensitive sociology of sensibilities about crime' that reflect the local experience of wider (global) social changes (Girling *et al*. 2000: 12; Taylor *et al*. 1996). I hope to explore the ways in which crime figures as a problem amongst others within wider understandings of the trajectories of the estate and its place (and that of its residents) in the world.

In particular I will draw attention to the relationship between the constitution of problems, responses to change and relationships with authorities and residents' sense of social position. I will explore the ways in which these relationships with authorities impact on residents' sense of insecurity and are influenced by their understandings of social inequality. This emphasis on relationships between residents and authorities, and their respective understandings of local problems, structures the book. The title, *Narratives of Neglect*, refers to this central strand running through the book, of the ways in which residents and professionals understood the decline of the area and its apparent neglect by those variously seen to be responsible for its maintenance and control. An exploration of these narratives amongst residents and professionals provides the context for discussion of the capacity for communities to influence regeneration and the local governance of security through participation processes.

I will explore the concepts, questions and policy context that form the background to this research in Chapters 2 and 3. However, I want here to begin by giving some impression of the area (which I have renamed Millton)[1] and 'the estate' on which I focus and of what was entailed in undertaking the ethnography there.

Millton and 'the estate'

Millton is a small area on the borders of Manchester city centre, but its poverty stands in marked contrast to the growing prosperity of the city centre's renaissance. It is divided almost in half by a canal. On one side of this 'the estate' is made up of low-rise late-1970s council housing in a circular but confusing layout. On the other side of the canal stand the crumbling historic warehouses of Manchester's industrial revolution. Once the most densely populated area of Manchester (Kidd and Wyke 1993), this area is now largely abandoned, but crowned with World Heritage status, and slowly being revamped to provide loft-style living accommodation. The area has been dubbed an 'urban village' and its history rewritten as an

View of nineteenth-century warehouses overlooking the canal (line of trees) from a now demolished part of the estate

Boarded-up houses on the estate with old warehouses overlooking in the background

Italian enclave,[2] while the mundane and abandoned estate stands as its antithesis.

The estate, when full, housed 270 households but by the time I began my fieldwork it was almost a third empty and when I left the site 18 months later[3] there were only 75 households remaining. It stood as a warning of failure and was considered by marketing managers as a threat to the promotion of the area's future.

Blocking a view of the estate from the nearby main road (not shown) squat some square, plastic-coated chain retail stores and their car parks, reflecting the impact on the area of a wider shift in employment and the economy. Even though only yards from it, the estate is invisible from the road, hidden and literally excluded from access to the flows of traffic. This view became, to me, very symbolic of some of the dramatic economic, historical and social changes that had taken place over the last century and their impact on those least able to survive them. That this place had changed and lost much of its life and population was constantly impressed upon me by that view.

The estate is cut off from another main road by a grassy bank. This greenness of the landscape, particularly as more and more of the estate has been demolished, might seem peaceful to some, though deserted to others. It could even appear suburban, except that with the boarded-up windows and burned-out roofs of empty houses (obviously, from their architecture, council-owned), it lacks the prosperity of suburbia.

View from a demolished portion of the estate of old mills on the right and the back of retail outlets on the left

The statistics about the estate are starkly telling. Ward figures from the 2001 census (www.statistics.gov.uk) give some idea of deprivation, though they are distorted as they also cover the city centre. Millton lies in one of the most deprived wards in the city, though the ward includes some of the wealthiest newcomers to city centre living. In the last census 10 per cent of the ward's population were permanently sick or disabled, with 20 per cent in all reporting a limiting long-term illness. (The health of the estate's residents, in particular, was identified as being of concern as long ago as 1998, having the highest premature death rate (before 65) in the city at two and a half times the national average (Griffiths 1998)). Five per cent of the ward's population were unemployed, and of these 13 per cent had never worked and a further 37 per cent had been unemployed for over two years. Though a third of those living in the ward were students, another 30 per cent had no qualifications at all. Two thirds did not own a car.

The estate's fortunes mirrored that of the surrounding residential area which had lost 12.9 per cent of its population between 1991 and 1999. Those in that wider area who were in work tended to be in low-paid work, in 1996 receiving an average weekly income of £163.30 (compared to a city average of £190), and in 1999 over half of all households were in receipt of housing benefit or income support. The deprivation rates for the ward, when broken down to exclude

The 'leafy' green hills at the centre of the estate. Sites of earlier demolition

the city centre, present some of the most deprived in the country according to its Local Action Partnership.[4]

The estate had a local reputation for crime and street drug dealing. The local crime audit for 1998/99, for example, identified it as a 'hotspot' for local fears about crime. Though there had been attempts to improve security by blocking alleyways, putting up high fences and some selective demolition, local officials had characterised it as 'criminogenic'. A police crackdown on street dealing around five years earlier, and the closure and then demolition of the shop on the estate more recently, had reduced and moved on some of the disorder associated with the estate[5] but the circular design of the estate continued to be seen as a stumbling block to improving it (Manchester Housing, October 1999).

Nevertheless, the estate's position at the edge of the city centre made it a prime location for redevelopment. Partnership with private developers offered an opportunity to rebuild the area, restructure the population and housing market and secure investment in the wider area. This represented in many ways a new stage in the history of this small place, which had repeatedly been a site of changing governance, whether of industrial investment and then disinvestment, of early twentieth-century community movements, such as a Settlement House in the area, or of social welfare resources and then their removal. It offered a fascinating case study of participation in governance in the context of that history.

First encounters

I first came across this estate through some research I did there for a master's degree. After I had expressed an interest in 'vigilantism', a magistrate on the course mentioned a protest[6] about a supposed paedophile on the estate that had occurred some years previously and put me in touch with a local community activist. From him I began to snowball into the area and learn about local politics beyond this event, in particular, the level of activity amongst residents to improve the area and stop the closure of facilities. Campaigns to save the hospital and local primary school, a Tenants' Association and Single Regeneration Budget (SRB) funding for local development had all been organised by community activists. The two latter had been banned and taken over by council officers respectively, due to financial mismanagement, restricting representation to authorities and heightening resentment of 'the Council'.[7] This gave me an impression of the capacity for organisation in the area and of the fraught relationships with authorities, especially on 'the estate', the site of the protest. One of the women involved in the paedophile protest left me with the sense that her anger and frustration with the housing of a paedophile on the estate was as much to do with this wider context of the governance of the area as it was with the risks he posed to children. As much as moral outrage (Abrahams 1998) the protest was an example of an attempt to hold authorities to account. Although vigilantism now takes a back seat in the analysis, this past was a constant reminder of an aspect of community which warned against romanticisation and informed my interest in relations with authorities.

Early experiences on 'the estate' made me very aware of how suspicious residents could be of outsiders and how close knit some relationships were. A baulked attempt to interview young people on the estate at this time had ended in shouts of 'I'm not a grass' and running off, and a conversation I had had with the local shop owner got back to my original contact remarkably fast. As one of these early contacts confessed to me over two years later, she had at that time suspected me of being a 'police spy'.

Returning a year later, in the hopes of beginning more ethnographic fieldwork on the estate, I found that the Council had announced plans for the area's regeneration. This announcement made the estate a useful case study of the impact of changes in urban policy and of the way in which residents interpreted them. Intending only to test the water as to whether I could snowball from my previous contacts, I received a surprisingly enthusiastic welcome. Time enough had elapsed, it seemed, for me to be deemed to a degree trustworthy.

This renewed contact began a process of meeting people and attending meetings as one contact invited me to observe and participate (taking minutes) in a tenants' association that five of them were setting up. They were doing so in the light of the regeneration proposals and the announcement of plans to establish a 'residents' steering group' of six residents chosen by the Council.[8] These residents had demanded an election and had set up this tenants' group at the suggestion of a local councillor. This period gave me insight into the squabbles and politics of the place as this group and an opposing group of residents ran an energetic election campaign, door knocking and getting forms filled in and posted. Once the election results were announced (with three members from each group elected) the opposing camps met to organise a 'clean-up day' (to clear up rubbish and replant flower beds, in conjunction with a local environmental voluntary organisation), in an effort to heal the breach. I observed that meeting and then the first residents' steering group meetings. Aware of how tense these would be, and not being an elected member, I observed them as unobtrusively as possible. All this propelled me into a series of meetings and an awareness of politics between residents, of gossip and networks that gave me unique opportunities to observe an otherwise very closed estate.

The sudden shift in trajectory towards a focus on regeneration meant that I was as ignorant of the process as residents, which gave me an insight into the confusions and anxieties created by this position of ignorance, especially for those faced with the responsibility of representing and negotiating the future for the whole estate. My focus during this period turned to this communication between the 'community' and authorities and, in particular, how residents and professionals made sense of each other.

Early impressions

This early contact was mainly with residents through meetings and public events and I took a defensively sympathetic view of the place, mixed with a little fear of it. Overcoming this sense of trepidation was a part of getting acquainted with the area and as much about allaying my own nervousness as that of other people. My early impressions of the estate were informed by my encounters with resident activists and those they introduced me to during tenants' association meetings, residents' steering group meetings with the regeneration company, 'clean-up' days and visits to other regeneration projects. At that time I was concerned with getting my face known and meeting people – important both for making people aware of what I was doing,

View of the mainly closed pub and demolished shop at the heart of the estate

and for hearing local gossip and gaining an awareness of friendship circles. It was a period that impressed me with how close-knit the area was and acquainted me with the established families of the area and those who were seen as representative of and belonging to a nostalgic image of Millton and the estate. It was also a period when gossip and stories began to give me an inkling of the exclusiveness of these networks and identified individuals who tended to be pointed out for criticism by other residents. I spent upwards of six months observing these events and meetings and establishing relationships with a few key informants.

However, my fieldwork was dramatically altered after a period of illness which had meant that I had had no contact with residents for two months. On returning, though welcomed back, I was given the news that I was no longer to have access to residents' steering group meetings, which I had been observing, and that the tenants' association had been disbanded. Though this exclusion was upsetting I was reassured when I heard that some residents had argued for me and the debate had become so heated they had had to hold a vote.[9] A more positive outcome was that they gave me formal permission as a group to interview on the estate. I already had a lot of material from those early meetings so this freed me to spend more time elsewhere. Although I was returned to a position of relative outsider, I was also extricated from the politics of the consultation process, and this came as a bit of a relief. Having observed the politics between the residents, and fallen foul of it myself, I had learned some valuable lessons about the divisions on the estate. I began to gain a sense of the power relations, intimacies and disputes, exclusions and understandings of belonging amongst residents. I was, however, now faced with the difficulties inherent in conducting ethnographic fieldwork in a place that was both abandoned and defended.

Ethnography in an abandoned place

The two main problems in researching the area were the residents' suspicion of outsiders, or their nervousness about being seen as a 'grass', and also the lack of places to meet people and 'hang around', as ethnographers are often advised to do (e.g. Hammersley and Atkinson 1995). Although there were several pubs in the immediate area, two were closed and two only opened intermittently. The shop, though a meeting point in the early days of the research, had closed down and was demolished soon after. Other than the windswept grassed areas where houses had been demolished there were no real public spaces in which to hang about and the weather often made it difficult and fruitless to spend time outside.

Loitering about in this way was both impractical and could look suspicious so I went to some lengths to find pretexts for being on the estate.[10] I posted leaflets about my research and took photographs both alone and in conjunction with resident guides. Finding ways of wandering with purpose in public spaces gave me a strong sense of the spaces on this estate, of the dark corners, bright gardens, fences and alleyways which feature heavily in people's descriptions.

Having met a lot of residents through meetings and events I began to follow up that contact by interviewing them in their homes.[11] The period of getting to know people had been essential for me to become a familiar face on the estate, and although it would be an exaggeration to suggest that I was known to all residents, there were occasions on which residents mentioned me knowing someone, or having been asked about me. I initially used a strategy of 'snowballing' asking residents to introduce me to others,[12] a common strategy to overcome some of the difficulties posed by accessing a 'hard-to-reach' population suspicious of outsiders (Hancock 2000; Lee 1993; Merry 1981). However, this could, I realised, limit the scope of the research as few networks would lead to the most actively excluded, nor to those least involved. It could create a distorted impression of cohesiveness. Purposeful interviewing of more isolated residents revealed some contradictions to an impression of cohesion which more established residents were keen to convey. Dependence

A typical alleyway, overlooked by the former hospital.

on the latter to introduce me to others would have meant that I was continually recommended to talk to particular 'old families' and established members of the community.

It was never going to be possible to be considered totally trustworthy in the context of fears of being seen as a 'grass' and of people's concerns about outsiders. One of the residents with whom I was most frequently in contact said that 'the jury was still out' months after he had met me and he still expected to see me in court one day as a witness. Yet some whom I had only just met talked openly about their illegal activities (one interview actually took place whilst the interviewee was on the way into the city centre to go shoplifting), chatting about their prison experiences and the inconvenience of so many cameras in the area. After I had spent two years researching on the estate a resident from one of the established families claimed that people now thought I was 'all right', but this also reflected her claim to be able to talk for all. I overheard some of the young people at the youth centre say that one of the large 'criminal' families in the area had said that I was 'all right', but the telling response of the boy to whom this was said was 'Yes, but I don't like [that family].' Trust did not necessarily increase with time and intimacy. For some loyalty was important, a quality increasingly difficult to demonstrate when at odds with the need to show neutrality at public events. One of the residents I knew best told me less and less about her personal life and began to treat me more as a colleague than confidante. Yet others who met me for the first time as a stranger told me things I could never have expected.

There was a sense of the confessional in some of the interviews, of off-loading on a stranger. One man, for example, I only met because I had arranged to interview someone else who was then not in. He happened to be in his garden and invited me in when I asked him if he would be interviewed. I was there for two and a half hours while he gave me his life story. Of more importance than establishing trusting relationships was the ability to foster 'rapport' (Oakley 1986), respect and confidence with participants, which had more to do with interview style than embeddedness in the community.[13] People were then willing to extend a surprising level of frank openness and confidence.

Though there were pragmatic reasons for my focus on interviews, they also reflect a style of ethnography adapted to researching British culture where, as Hockey (2002: 210) puts it, 'the weather is dire and everything interesting seems to be going on behind closed doors.' With such privatised lives and limited access to public spaces, for residents as well as for myself, interviewing people in their houses gave me far greater insight into their lives and friendship circles, family life and understandings than observation in more public areas allowed. In this sense the interview perhaps represents 'a culturally appropriate form of participation' in Britain (Hockey 2002: 210) and, in particular, in estates with so few public resources. These visits prompted tours to view the repairs not done in their houses, the bars on their windows and the views from those windows. I witnessed reactions to noises outside and was able to situate the spaces of their home in relation to the rest of the estate. Some residents brought out photographs of family or boxes with memorabilia from childhood. In some cases they displayed their ornaments with pride and concern that they had not dusted, in others we sat on the only two chairs in the house in an empty, dirty room showing off a video collection. People cried and told me secrets, confessing to a stranger things they would not to someone that they would continue to see. The 'hidden intimacies' of interviewing (Hockey 2002) admitted me into a private world of individuals as well as into their public relationships as community members.

As I realised the extent to which young people were seen as a problem, I decided to spend time at the local youth centre where I observed and conducted focus groups. Focus groups were very difficult to carry out, with children coming in and out, slamming doors, shouting, playing computer games, hitting each other and bursting into song. Even so, the stories they told, arguments they had with each other, the songs, shouts and silences all made for some fascinating insights. I visited the centre twice a week for at least three months, and began to get a very strong sense of the dynamics of the youth centre. Gaining a real insight into the experiences of these young people would have entailed a much more concerted effort to establish myself with them than I had time for. However, some of the focus groups and conversations I held while hanging about with them are incorporated in an attempt to include young voices.[14]

Interviewing professionals

Only when I had been interviewing residents for over six months did I begin interviewing professionals involved in the local governance and regeneration of the area. I interviewed 35 of these professionals. They included the private developer team, regeneration agency staff (both regeneration company and former SRB officers), housing authority[15] and housing association officials, local police, community safety and neighbourhood warden managers, youth workers and community and voluntary group workers, councillors and consultants employed by the private developer.

My decision to access this estate through residents put me in a strange position with agency staff, some of whom were confused as to how I had come to be researching there and a few, when they found out, were rather dismissive or defensive. Although this could make access to professionals difficult, it also made some less guarded. Interviewing professionals in their offices rarely yielded the same insight into the individuals interviewed as would be gained from interviewing them in their own homes. However, offices often gave clues as to the status within the organisation of the person being interviewed. Limited time made available also reflected status and it often required persistence to gain access. Once contacted though, the majority of the professionals were friendly and actively interested.

There were other insights to be gained from the offices and work spaces of the professionals: mugs bearing the logo of a local private security company were present in the offices of police, community safety and regeneration officers, indicating wider relationships of organisations involved in local policing. These work spaces were of course qualitatively different from those of residents houses, as were the interviews themselves.

Before I turn to an exploration of residents' and professionals' understandings, I shall devote the rest of Part 1 to exploring the policy and academic debates that form the context for regeneration and governance of the estate, and that drive the research and analysis. Chapter 2 will focus on the implications of changes in governance for questions of citizen participation in the local governance of security and regeneration, and situates these questions within broader debates within criminology and urban studies. Chapter 3 then explores issues around the constitution of 'local problems' and attributions of blame, and outlines their conception as an expression of 'habituated' understandings.

Notes

1 I have renamed the area 'Millton' and refer to the small estate on which I focused as 'the estate' in order to preserve anonymity for participants.
2 This historical description draws on a small but visible minority of Italian immigrants who arrived in the nineteenth century, some of whose descendants are still present. However, the description forms part of the marketing of the area for European investment as an Italian Quarter, perhaps considered more romantic than focusing on the Irish majority.
3 In total I spent 18 months in the field, from January 2001 to September 2002.
4 I did not have access to these figures.
5 Details of offences for the period 2000 to 2002 saw incidents on the estate halve in that time. Recorded incidents of 'juvenile nuisance' fell from 26 in 2000 to six in 2002, for example, and 'recovered stolen vehicles' numbered 29 in 2000, 12 by 2002. (Thanks to Greater Manchester Police, North Manchester Division for providing this information.)
6 This term reflects descriptions of the event, not an apologist interpretation to imply sympathy for attacks (Evans 2003).
7 This reference to the 'Council' reflects the way in which residents referred to local authorities as a generic body.
8 The 'Residents' Steering Group' was to act as a representative body in partnership with the Regeneration Company (Local Authority regeneration body) to ensure 'community consultation' in the planning process.
9 This exclusion may have been more to do with my perceived status as 'on the side of' the tenants' association group and, in particular, close to a resident distrusted by one of the other residents.
10 Though this varied, I averaged about three days a week, sometimes going there every day.
11 I interviewed half the households remaining at the end of my fieldwork (just over a third of those there at the start). In doing so I tried to capture as comprehensive a picture as I could of the range of background, age,

gender and ethnicity. I was not attempting proportionality or a statistical sampling but a subjective reflection of the variety of experiences of those living there.

12 I often 'snowballed' on to people without mentioning who had passed me on, to allow relative confidentiality for both sides.

13 See Appendix 1 for an account of my approach to interviewing. I only had two definite refusals and two who were clearly avoiding me.

14 I briefly contemplated interviewing children of residents (and did interview those of a resident I knew well) but considered the methodological and ethical questions beyond the scope of this project (Greig and Taylor 1999).

15 Unfortunately, the team leader of local housing management refused access. There was no way to get round this problem and as there was no way to telephone her (a centralised system made accessing individuals impossible except through e-mail), no way to persuade her in a more personal way.

Chapter 2

Governing urban communities

Having given a broad description of the estate, I want in this chapter to turn to some of the debates and questions about the governance of urban communities that my research there inevitably touched on, and that frame those raised throughout the book. My particular interest is in the participation of citizens in local governance, particularly of security. The events and trajectory of the estate gave me the opportunity to observe the engagement of residents in the process of consultation leading up to the regeneration of the area. Though this might be seen as a distinct issue, in practice regeneration blurred with the governance of security in important ways, reflecting wider trends in urban governance.

Participation in local governance was not new to the area and had been part of previous attempts to regenerate the area. Most significantly, recent Single Regeneration Budget (SRB) projects had made fairly successful attempts to build on the existing levels of community activism and voluntary sector activity to involve more residents in service delivery and community events. There was a degree of grass-roots activism on which authorities drew in wider regeneration projects in the area, though not without friction at times. The Local Action Partnership (LAP), set up to address crime and disorder in the area, had also initiated consultation with residents but had then suspended the process until agencies felt they could improve their practices enough to be able to deliver on residents' demands. This suspension and focus on enforcement was an important reflection of approaches to the governance of security that I will come back to shortly. In practice these officials, engaged in

SRB projects, the LAP and a newer 'regeneration company'[1] worked closely together, sharing an agenda for the area's improvement.

Much of this activity, however, related to the areas surrounding 'the estate', and the new proposals for rebuild represented the first time that residents had been involved in a process targeted specifically to the estate itself. Consultation with residents was intended initially to focus on 'masterplanning' (designing the layout and infrastructure of the area) but inevitably touched on wider issues of local governance. Invited into early meetings by residents, I was presented with a unique opportunity to gain insight into a participatory process and residents' responses to it. This focus on participation has a particular currency because of the centrality of participatory processes within government policy. It also strikes at key concerns in academic debates around public policy as to the accountability of local services.

There are several ways in which citizen participation has gained ground as an aspect of governance. Though more recently associated with New Labour, citizen involvement in local governance has a long history. It became, however, a particular concern in urban regeneration within policies of the Conservative government under John Major (Atkinson and Cope 1997; Imrie and Raco 2003; Jones 2003). In the context of criticisms of the failure of past interventions, imposed by top-down approaches to development, the need for participation of citizens was stressed as a means to mobilise support and draw on local knowledge and experience to improve the efficiency and chances of successful outcomes of regeneration. This view has, however, tended to conceive of participating citizens as consumers in communication with providers rather than seeing them in political terms (Young 2000). Similar understandings of participation have also been noted in structures for citizen involvement in policing (Loader 2000). More recent understandings of participation have acquired further connotations by being coupled with a New Labour language of 'community' involvement that I want to explore in some detail.

Community participation

Community is a contradictory and slippery concept, so over-used as to be somewhat useless for sociological analysis yet with an everyday currency that suggests a political and sociological salience to identities and social networks beyond the rhetoric. It is the vagueness of the term and its versatility for the creation of common identities that lends it political potency (Anderson 1983). Community can, of course, have multiple meanings and characteristics whether they are political, religious, professional or residential, and can mean different things in different cultures (Lacey and Zedner 1995; Massey 1994).

Despite these definitional problems, 'community' lies at the heart of New Labour public policy and is transcribed into policies to tackle multiple problems from health and social exclusion to urban decline and crime. Communities are assumed to be capable of informal social control and of providing social support, a capacity that is understood to have declined with economic and structural change, and also to be the means of re-including those excluded or estranged from social institutions. It is thereby hoped that this 'community capacity' will provide the means to address crime and restore order and a sense of security and mutual support, particularly in areas of social exclusion.[2] In effect communities represent a social institution that it is hoped will be able to cushion the worst effects of market economics (Bauman 2001; Jessop 2002) and act as a mediating institution between state and individual, offering a focus for a 'Third Way' of minimal regulation (Giddens 1998). It is this focus on empowering vulnerable communities and addressing social exclusion that gives this discourse a particular New Labour flavour (Kearns 2003). It is hoped that building strong communities will provide support, widen opportunities and foster a kind of informal control, particularly in areas that have suffered from fragmentation, unemployment and a range of problems of crime and disorder. However, communities are thereby contradictorily envisioned as both the means of achieving policy goals, the object of regeneration (Atkinson 2000) and the end to which policy is aiming (Crawford 1997; Nelken 1994).

For this reason the aims of participation, to foster and build on 'community', can also be somewhat vague; sometimes used to suggest people's engagement in community events, at other times to mean a more formal, semi-political involvement in local decision-making processes. The 'community capacity' it is hoped to engender is increasingly termed 'social capital', a concept I shall return to later. Viewed in such a beneficial light participation, like community, can tend both to be described as the means of creating strong communities and to be seen as an end in itself (Crawford 1997; Newburn 2002).

This Third Way politics provides a vision of a new democratic state (Giddens 1998) that it is hoped will be created through forms of citizen participation to fill the gap created by the crisis of welfare and re-engage 'hard-to-reach' groups. It aims to rebuild trust in mainstream democratic institutions and 'recalibrate the legitimacy expectations of the public' away from a reliance on the state (Crawford 1997: 47). Building communities will, it is hoped, encourage local self-governance and the involvement of community members in local governance. This is sometimes referred to as promoting 'active citizenship' (www.homeoffice.gov.uk) and is apparent within the drive to create 'sustainable communities' (ODPM 2000).[3]

Equally importantly, communities are imbued with the status of being representative of a moral consensus, particularly around crime and disorder. This stems from a Communitarian influence on New Labour which calls for a renewed emphasis on the moral responsibility of citizens to their communities (Etzioni 1993). Communities, along with other civil institutions, such as families and schools, are seen to embody common values through which social order can be maintained and expressed. This gives the language of community a moral dimension and community participation can become conceived as the mobilisation of the 'moral voice' of community, particularly around issues of crime and disorder.

Much of the language of strengthening communities in areas of social exclusion is geared around issues of confronting crime, disorder and fear of crime. Neglected in the past, the impact of crime and disorder on such communities is highlighted as a problem that can undermine the creation of supportive, strong communities; fear of crime for this reason is described as a problem in itself. Equally, there is understood to have been a loss of faith in the police and other local authorities. These understandings have particularly driven a 'reassurance agenda', aiming to reduce the fear of crime and re-emphasising the need for a visible policing presence. It is hoped that reassuring communities will also encourage more community interaction and cooperation with local agencies. This understanding of the role of crime and the fear of crime in hampering the building of strong communities and community–authority relations is key to the way issues of security and reassurance have become so central to local governance, not only those engaged in the governance of security but in urban governance more widely. Participation, as the means to build these strong, safe and supportive communities and good relations with agencies, lies at the heart of public policy.

However, with the range of ways in which participation is conceived and the breadth of ways in which it is hoped to be beneficial, one cannot help but question whether what is hoped for is realistic and what, in practice, the goals and outcomes of community participation turn out to be. This research gave the opportunity to explore how both residents and professionals viewed one such process. The questions that I will be most concerned with here are: what impact citizens can have on local decision- and policy-making through 'consultation' with governing bodies; and what role they can play in crime control. The next section is devoted to exploring barriers to participation in urban governance and the governance of security created by policy discourses and practices. I will then turn to questions around the role of communities in crime control, particularly whether they have a capacity to informally control crime. These provide the context for a shift in perspective and approach to these issues that I will outline in Chapter 3.

Barriers to participation

I want here to focus on the way that centralising policy discourses and trends in local governance, embodied in professional understandings, present barriers to participation of citizens in decision-making. They make decision-making processes a very top-down affair when lay participants find them difficult to challenge.

A neo-liberal turn

Both urban policy and crime control are formed in the context of a particular discursive script about governance that has developed since the late 1970s. This script sets some parameters around what is thinkable in policy-making and informs the changing ways in which local governance is organised. Crucially, it emphasises the limited capacity of the state. For crime control this entails a move away from an emphasis on the state monopoly of security (Garland 1995, 2001; Johnston and Shearing 2003; O'Malley 1999; Rose 2000) in the face of a failure of state agencies to check rising crime rates or rehabilitate offenders. While intermediate institutions of family and community are understood to have declined, state agencies cannot fill the gap to maintain control alone. Policies of urban regeneration offer a similarly sorry tale of urban disorder and the inability of state institutions to cope in the face of the decline of these institutions of informal social control. Both criminal justice and urban policy discourses in this sense echo a wider pattern in policy thinking, attributing loss of control to the decline of those intervening social institutions, to human agency rather than to changing economic or global structures (Hastings 1999; Stone 1988). This focuses policies to counter this loss of control on communities and families rather than addressing structural shifts which are constituted as inevitable (Stone 1988).

This understanding of the limited capacity of the state and the need to strengthen intermediate structures of social control and support is, of course, reflected in the focus on 'community' that I have already discussed. There are, however, two parallel trends in thinking about governance that emerge from this script: the state's moderated role in supporting markets, and the need for state agencies to work in partnership with other sectors. This emphasis on market dynamics has been characterised as marking a 'neo-liberal' turn within public policies (Harvey 1996; Jessop 2002).

This turn is particularly apparent in urban policy, emphasising the role of urban governments in the promotion of cities in a global market-place, local authorities acting not just in partnership with business (Cox 1993) but as one themselves, as 'entrepreneurial cities' (Hall and Hubbard 1996). City strategies set about reinventing their image in order to compete with other European cities, rather than simply national, and try to turn around what are characterised as failed markets in the inner city. Manchester is often used as an example of an entrepreneurial city. Regeneration of the city centre to attract investors, and residents to live there and, more recently, in surrounding areas, was placed at the forefront of the city's corporate strategy (Manchester City Council 2001). The proposals for the future redevelopment of 'the estate' exemplify this understanding of city competitiveness and stress its location as ideal for a new form of city-centre living.

> The transformation of this great British city into a major European regional capital is well underway … Manchester is acknowledged as a 24-hour city, indeed it was one of the first cities to re-embrace the concept of city-centre living. (New Manchester Ltd 2000)

Similarly, an emphasis within regeneration policies on restoring market conditions, rather than welfare (Jessop 2002), arguably reduces the aims of regeneration to short-term intervention in order to produce and promote a self-sustaining market balance (Atkinson 2000). These aims to promote places or cities to a wider market represent an agenda that could easily override local concerns.

The neo-liberal turn is also to a degree apparent in the way that security has come to play such a central role in public policy as a 'market-supporting' activity (Crawford 1997). Deeply politicised, and perhaps better described as exhibiting a neo-conservatism, crime control has become a key feature of local governance but these changes are apparent in the pluralisation of policing away from state monopoly and in the spread of responsibilities for confronting crime across all public services.[4]

The implications for accountability of these changes in governance, particularly of partnership structures, have been the subject of much controversy amongst critics of both urban policy and criminal justice. Attention has tended to be focused on the reduced role of the state to one of 'steering' policy, but leaving the 'rowing' (provision of services) to other bodies over whom they have limited control (Osborne and Gaebler 1992). Dispersed governance to the private and voluntary sector (Crawford 1997, 2001, 2003b; Johnston and Shearing 2003; Shearing and Stenning 1987), for example, uses long-leash controls of targets and training that provide questionable control (Jones and Newburn 1998; Loader 2000). More focused on potentially unaccountable partnerships between city governments and the private sector, sometimes termed 'growth coalitions', critics of urban policy have warned of the shared interests of state and private sectors in promoting growth, potentially at the expense of other concerns (Jessop 1997; Logan and Molotch 1987; Quilley 1999; Ward 2003).

Of course, one of the other outcomes of this partnership approach has also been the inclusion of communities as another partner. However, this both implies equality between partners that does not recognise relative powerlessness of communities and, in practice, brings representatives into partnerships dominated by professionals and professional understandings. Despite concerns about the loss of state control, and so of accountability of partnerships and dispersed governance arrangements, it is the attempts of governments to steer through auditing, targets and funding stipulations, and locally also through professional relationships and understandings, that implies a more centralising tendency than these concerns would suggest. Ironically, managerial arrangements for accountability also have the potential to limit local sensitivity and discretionary implementation of central policy. In the face of the politics of partnership, managerialism and professional discourses, it is questionable what capacity communities have to influence local decision-making.

The promotional and security roles of local governing arrangements supporting healthy local markets, in particular, provide, alongside that of supporting vulnerable communities, the basis for a discursive coherence between those involved in the local governance of security and regeneration. It provides a powerful justification for policies that is difficult to challenge. I will go into these policies in more detail.

Renaissance of cities and sustainable communities

Policies to promote a 'renaissance of cities' represent the first attempt to create a coherent urban policy in the UK since the late 1970s. Heavily influenced by US developments (particularly in Baltimore and Detroit) 'renaissance' spells out some of the challenges facing Britain's post-industrial cities and outlines principles for their renewal. These policies emphasise the need to create attractive and safe cities capable of drawing people to live and invest in them. Crucially, this renaissance hopes to counter the exodus from city centres and surrounding areas.

In addition to a characteristically neo-liberal discourse of market competition and image-making, New Labour's urban renaissance also introduces an environmental agenda to regeneration of urban areas, emphasising development of brown field sites and density of construction to reduce reliance on the car. The emphasis on increasing density is also proposed as a counter to the loss of population in urban centres, to sustain services and businesses in those centres and, as a consequence, to reduce crime by increasing social interaction in public spaces (Imrie and Raco 2003). The emphasis on density of urban form is particularly characteristic of the Urban Task Force report (DETR 1999) which echoes a rather utopian strain to architectural and planning discourses, offering density, Lees (2003) argues, almost as the 'magic cure-all' for urban environmental and social ills. Since this is coupled with a focus on attracting new and more prosperous residents to create areas with more of a social mix, this agenda has been closely associated with gentrification (Imrie and Raco 2003; Lees 2003; MacLeod and Ward 2002), potentially putting the interests of new, more wealthy newcomers above those of existing residents.

Particularly in areas that have been characterised as failed markets because of inappropriate or unpopular housing, proposals for increasing density and attracting wealthier owner-occupiers necessitate demolition, which can be threatening and deeply controversial for existing residents. Such proposals may reinforce a sense of powerlessness to control the changes taking place, and residents may become hostile to outsiders and newcomers (Foster 1999). This is particularly apparent when existing residents may be envisaged as a minority of the future population.

Though associated with gentrification, the input of the Social Exclusion Unit in the Urban White Paper (DETR 2000) ensured that 'social mixing' became framed as a means to address concentrations of deprivation and social exclusion in urban areas (Lees 2003). This intervention also introduced an emphasis on mixing ethnic backgrounds and a celebration of diversity. However, a tendency to focus attention on council housing estates as the sites of concentrated deprivation, rather than including deprivation within areas of low-income home ownership, for example, has tended to discursively blur issues of concentrated poverty with concentrations of tenure (Lee and Murie 1999). Mixed *tenure* development is therefore frequently presented as a means to achieve this social mix and counter the 'residualisation' of council housing as a tenure of last choice. This reinforces the emphasis on the need to attract owner-occupiers into areas of council housing, heightening a sense of difference between existing tenants and newcomers. Coupled with the trend towards transfer of social housing to housing associations, some of the major decisions about the future of the area being regenerated can appear to have been made prior to consultation. Certainly these principles for development are difficult for residents to challenge, especially when embodied in funding proposals and city strategies.

As in the development prospectus above, notions of successful areas of city-centre living often envisage bustling developments of 24-hour activity and conspicuous consumption at odds with an emphasis on environmental sustainability (Imrie and Raco 2003). The creation of 'sustainable communities' is also informed by an understanding of the need to create sustainable *markets* that both attract population and investment minimizing the need for future state intervention and *retain* population. However, this entails a particular vision of what makes places attractive that tends to skirt over differences in taste, income and exclusionary practices. Again the development prospectus for 'the estate' exemplified the concerns dominating policies of 'renaissance' and 'sustainable communities' within its outline of the goals of the new development. These were to achieve:

> a ... community that is safe, inclusive and diverse, within a high quality environment, ... [that] offers a vibrant and viable area that will not require ongoing subsidy to sustain it. ([New] Manchester Ltd. 2000)

Despite these laudable aims it is questionable how much these notions of creating successful places really address problems of social inequality and social exclusion that the 'sustainable communities' agenda hopes to confront. Such developments may not address but simply mask inequality.

The 'sustainable communities' agenda is also informed by Communitarian understandings promoting the development of strong, self-governing communities, closely associated with an emphasis on community participation (Imrie and Raco 2003). Sustainability, for example, is defined, within the guidelines for the development of the estate as 'embodying the key concepts [of] social equity, community participation and the notion of a sustainable community as a dynamic self-maintaining system' (DETR 2000; ODPM 2000). Participation is linked to the sustainability of an area as a means to encourage self-governance by building relationships both between communities and local authorities/service providers and within communities themselves. Implicitly, sustainability is also used in reference to building *safe* communities that can deal with or prevent problems of crime, disorder and environmental decay that could otherwise contribute to their decline. In this way security has become a central issue for lasting regeneration. Addressing crime and disorder in areas of social exclusion has to some extent become reframed as an attempt to address inequality of security and improve vulnerable people's quality of life.

Nevertheless, what is apparent within these policy proposals is a tendency to make some assumptions about the nature of community demands both for the type of place they wish to live and for security. In effect community views are taken rather as a given, as something common to most people. Policies leave little room for negotiating change or addressing the potential to override and alienate communities. This begs the question of what the role of community participation can, in practice, signify. Moreover, where objections to regeneration policies, particularly to demolition, may be seen as understandable, if regrettable, by professionals, there is even less room for dissent in the face of policies of crime control which are justified as fulfilling the legitimate demands of any 'community'. My concern is that this legitimates policies that seem to contradict a goal of social inclusion, and prioritises the pursuit of security at the expense of concerns for justice. I will now turn to the trends in the local governance of security, and the professional understandings that inform them, that again potentially represent a barrier to meaningful local participation. Though security is approached as another area of policy, I want to emphasise the blurred boundaries between these aspects of local governance which in practice are often complementary.

The local governance of security

Focused on the identification of 'hot spots', risky or at risk individuals and 'criminogenic' situations, the technologies and strategies of crime prevention and community safety have been characterised as a governance of risk management (Garland 2001; O'Malley 1999). Such techniques and the emphasis on prevention, in the context of scepticism about the possibilities of rehabilitation, appear to have few other goals than incapacitation or exclusion of those who are deemed to put others at risk (Beck 1992; Ericson and Haggerty 1997; Feeley and Simon 1996; Garland 2001; O'Malley 1999). Such policies aim simply to reduce exposure to risks in the name of protecting the community, while exercising control of risky populations (Johnston and Shearing 2003) and inadvertently expanding the disciplinary power of the state (Feeley and Simon 1996; Garland 2001). This preventative pursuit of security has in this way also been particularly associated with exclusionary forms of governance and has been the subject of polemic on what these trends augur for the future.

Gated communities and 'zero-tolerance' policing are often cited as exemplars of a dystopian future created by this governance of risks, ever-widening surveillance, inequity and exclusivity (Crawford 2003a; Davis 1990; Harvey 1996; Johnston and Shearing 2003; MacLeod and Ward 2002; Smith 1996; Young 1999). Particularly associated with developments in the US, Brazil and South Africa, they appear to symbolise a widening gap in wealth and in access to security and increasingly exclusionary forms of governance. Gated communities represent safe havens for those who can afford them, removing themselves from exposure to risks (Johnston and Shearing 2003), while those who cannot are exposed to increased risks and intrusive policing. 'Zero-tolerance' policing of city centres is used as a parallel example of a form of risk management of public space, emphasising prevention and the identification (and exclusion) of risky people. Commonly associated with New York, 'zero-tolerance' policing was justified there through Wilson and Kelling's theory of 'broken windows' (Wilson and Kelling 1982) which called for the policing of minor offences to prevent the likelihood of future crime. Its preventative focus, and particularly a use of anticipatory punishment, has been characterised as an extreme example of risk management, sacrificing concerns for justice for provision of security (Johnston and Shearing 2003; Davis, 1990).

Similar accusations of exclusionary practices have been levelled by critics of gentrification-led regeneration. Attempts to 'clean up' areas during and preceding regeneration have been seen as attempts to exclude undesirables, putting the desire to attract investment above the welfare of vulnerable groups, particularly of the homeless, beggars (Smith 1996) and street sellers (Duneier 1999). Such practices have been characterised as a form of market-driven moral authoritarianism, effectively a 'moral governance of an underclass' (Haworth and Manzi 1999), justified in terms of improving people's 'quality of life' but rooted in an understanding of competition between places.

What links these debates about the nature and effects of urban regeneration to those of the governance of security is a tendency to polarise between a neo-liberal vision of future utopias built around a notion of community, prosperity and safety, and a critical counter-position highlighting the exclusionary or authoritarian control of excluded groups (MacLeod and Ward 2002; Newburn 2001). However, this tendency to polarise positions, imagining utopias and dystopias, may be rather counterproductive to local analysis and distorts some of the questions raised by local circumstances (MacLeod and Ward 2002: Walklate and Evans 1999). These examples, often drawn from US contexts, also take little account of New Labour policy goals to address social exclusion, of protecting, supporting and improving the environment of vulnerable communities.

Nevertheless there are parallels in the UK context that have particular implications for citizen participation in the local governance of security. While New York-style 'zero tolerance' policing has not found such enthusiastic proponents amongst public police in the UK, the influence of the 'broken windows' understanding of crime and disorder has been widespread. Wilson and Kelling's (1982) suggestion was that signs of disorder (broken windows) hinder social control mechanisms by communicating social and physical decline and creating fear. Disorderly appearance and minor offences are linked to more serious offences because of a consequent reduction in capacity to control (Kelling 2001). Extending this further, Skogan (1990) linked disorder to incivility which, he argued, contributes to this communication of social breakdown. The fears created by such visual and behavioural signs contribute to a further withdrawal from relationships with neighbours or active participation in control, resulting in further disorder, spiralling out of control.

This thinking has contributed particularly to an emphasis on the need for the management of public spaces to reduce signs of disorder, as well as to improve the image and appearance of places. The influence of this approach is apparent in the preventative work done by crime and disorder partnerships, and especially in the introduction of neighbourhood wardens whose remit includes tackling signs of disorder. Introduced under the auspices of the Social Exclusion Unit, and responding to a reassurance agenda in policing, these schemes illustrate the blurring of lines between policies of urban management and the governance of security. The call to tackle 'anti-social behaviour' also echoes these understandings, tackling behaviour contributing to people's fears. Participation is, within this context, rather a passive affair, largely limited to reporting problems for authorities to address. There is again a focus on agency enforcement and prevention of risky behaviour though dressed in a language of supporting fearful communities.

Similarly, while the development of gated communities in the UK is not nearly as widespread as in the United States (Newburn 2001; Crawford 2003a), some of the contractual neighbourhood and tenancy agreements within the social housing sector are reminiscent of attempts to control behaviour within such developments (Crawford 2003a). Since this is such a large sector in the UK, and often the object of regeneration or market renewal, these contracts are a significant means of control. Although legitimised as consensual rules of inclusion, this 'contractual governance' is a form of 'consent encircled by coercion' (Crawford 2003a: 500), particularly by the threat of eviction (Burney 1999). It is in itself a form of risk management, preventing behaviour that could contribute to an escalation in crime or decline.

Agreements about acceptable conduct and a focus on the management of disorderly behaviours, although framed by this language of risk, also appear to echo some of the more paternalistic styles of local government of post-war Britain and have a tendency both to pathologise the poor and to constitute behaviour within a discourse of moral conduct. Though these contemporary developments have emerged from very different circumstances and political pressures, there are some parallels to this attempt at moral reform. Informed by Communitarian understandings, there is an emphasis on instilling a sense of responsibility to the community. Importantly, the management of behaviour is described as part of an attempt to help communities 'take back control' of their areas. People are encouraged to take responsibility for their area and their own behaviour (Haggerty 2003).

Moving away from a notion of desert, pathology or structural/ social conditions, the stress is on people's choices, their willingness

29

and ability to self-control (Hunt 2003). This recalibrates the governance of risks to stress the responsibility of individuals for their own behaviour and exposure to risks (Haggerty 2003). Those unwilling to take responsibility for themselves are by the same token both immoral, because culpable (irresponsible), and risky. This is a much more morally loaded understanding behind the governance of security than a language of risk might imply. Attempts to address behaviour are based on assumptions of universal notions of acceptable conduct. This again limits participation to mobilisation of community support for authority intervention around issues of crime and disorder, of garnering the 'moral voice' of community in Communitarian terms (Etzioni 1993).

Despite the language of active participation, these trends in crime control policy imply a rather passive role for communities, as informants for enforcement agencies and providing support for intervention to address disruptive and illegal behaviour. How much community members are encouraged to participate in local problem-solving is questionable, let alone how far local authorities really envisage communities as able to control crime through more informal social controls. There is an implication that crime and disorder need to be tackled *before* communities can be created and transformed. Building 'social capital' will then provide the social support and informal control necessary to maintain that position of security. This is key to notions of regeneration to rebuild communities and reduce crime and disorder in the long term.

I want now to explore this quality of 'community' (social capital) in addressing the second of my core questions: that of how far communities can realistically be expected to be able to contribute to crime control; whether communities have a capacity to informally control, and whether increasing 'social capital' presents a viable foundation for crime control.

The role of communities in crime control

Much academic debate around community involvement in crime control has focused on the capacities of urban communities to informally control crime. This reflects a long tradition in criminology, drawing on Durkheimian notions of 'organic' communities with strong social bonds, common values and a goal of security. This is a conception of community that is echoed in Communitarian understandings and in current government policy. It is, furthermore, apparent in a resurgence of interest in 'social disorganisation' theories; sometimes confusingly referred to as 'environmental' theories of crime.

Social disorganisation theories

These theories essentially point to the fragmentation of urban communities and increasing individualisation as a contributory factor to high crime rates in urban areas. Social disorganisation models drew on Chicago School observations of patterns of urban crime rates (Park and Burgess 1924) to predict a relationship between poverty, heterogeneity in ethnic composition and population mobility as factors contributing to social breakdown (Shaw and McKay 1942). Chicago School understandings stressed the invasion and succession of immigrants within inner city areas through a model of competition for desirable space and housing. Once able to afford it, people would move to suburbs of greater stability and safety. Later social disorganisation theories stressed the role of community and family relationships as a constraint on behaviour, and a means of creating norms and values through socialisation contributory to informal social control. They similarly argued that in areas where those relationships would be more difficult to cement, crime rates would be expected to be higher. A focus on socialisation has tended to concentrate attention on the control of young people within families and neighbourhoods (Bursik and Gramsmick 1993; Suttles 1972). Family structures in particular are understood to provide close and stable ties that mitigate against the destabilising influence of poverty and heterogeneity of communities. However, studies of high crime communities have highlighted the impact of structural changes wrought by mass male unemployment and shifts to service industry, temporary and part-time employment and changing gender relations that have arguably reduced social cohesion and capacity for informal control (Campbell 1993; Hunter 1995; Massey 1994).

Nevertheless, recent studies concerned with these issues have pointed to the 'collective efficacy' of communities (Sampson, Raudenbush and Earls 1997; Sampson and Raudenbush 1999). Some also report a negative correlation between organisational involvement and crime rates (Skogan and Maxfield 1981; Skogan 1990) and fear of crime (Hope 1995). Rather than fragmentation some important ethnographic studies of deprived urban areas have also stressed the resilience of such communities and their capacity for informal control (Foster 1995; Walklate and Evans 1999). These studies have contributed to calls for policies to encourage greater civic engagement and state support for community organisations to confront crime (Foster 1995; Hope 1995; Lewis and Salem 1986; Skogan and Maxfield 1981; Skogan 1990). Others have also pointed to the capacity, if sometimes oppressive, within communities for informal justice (Braithwaite and Daly, 1994; Girling, Loader and Sparks, 1998; McEvoy and Mika, 2002; Walklate, 2002; Walklate and Evans, 1999).

This research emphasis on community capacity for crime control shares much in common with calls to build 'social capital' to tackle social exclusion. Though often vaguely conceived within policy discourses (Kearns 2003), the need to build 'social capital' has been proposed across many areas of social policy from health and employment to grass-roots politicisation. The close link to concepts of community has created the context for its application to crime control. The coherence between Communitarian understandings of community and the norm-creating capacity of social networks implicitly ties the creation of 'social capital' within policies to a moral authoritarianism, unintended in its sociological conceptualisation (Field 2003). Social capital provides an intellectual language to describe the resources with which deprived communities are broadly understood to have coped in the past and that they have, to a degree, lost. The concept offers a means to explore the qualities of 'community' that are assumed to contribute to a capacity for crime control.

Social capital

Attributed in particular to Bourdieu, Coleman and Putnam (Field 2003), social capital has been variously described as: one of several forms of capital (economic, cultural and symbolic amongst others) providing resources within various 'fields' of relationships and knowledge production within which power relationships are contested (Bourdieu 2000); as a set of resources amongst the relatively disadvantaged within family and community social relationships that complement human capital and can support educational achievement (Coleman 1990); and as a societal resource contributing to collective action by fostering norms of reciprocity and trust (Putnam 1993). Putnam and Coleman have been particularly influential because of their application of this resource to disadvantaged groups.

While I do not want to diminish the significance of social support networks for social policy, some of the flaws within the concept of social capital highlight some reasons for caution in an increased role for communities in crime control. In particular, Putnam's dominant version of social capital shares with social disorganisation theories a functionalism, assuming that communities have a common goal of security. The reliance within policy debates on Putnam's formulation of the concept, which draws heavily on a rational choice understanding of relationships, also makes too ready an assumption that relationships engender and are characterised by trust and reciprocity. This has prompted criticisms of an over-emphasis on the 'bright side' of social capital (Field 2003). I want here to draw attention to the 'dark side' of social capital that has particular relevance for thinking about the role of 'community' in crime control.

The 'dark side' of social capital

Stable but high-crime neighbourhoods presented problematic anomalies for social disorganisation theories, and tended to be explained as having deviant norms (see Bursick and Gramsmick (1993) for an extensive review). Such communities have been variously described as tolerating juvenile delinquency because they protected residents from newcomers and outsiders (Suttles 1972); as protecting criminal activity through oppressive enforcement of local rules of trustworthiness and non-cooperation with state authorities (Power and Tunstall 1997; Walklate and Evans 1999); and as having cultures of machismo (Bourgois 1996; Campbell 1993; Young 1999). These explanations importantly point to a darker side of social capital that can compound the harmful effects of social and economic change within communities though demonstrating a capacity for informal control. Limited prospects of achieving status and capital outside of the area or through legal means may tie young men to these networks and activities. Such studies highlight the way in which networks can produce effects beyond and contradictory to a goal of safety.

Ironically, the combination of changes in employment structure and limited access to networks beyond neighbourhood may increase reliance on local networks, not only for a sense of security but also for status. This may compound the effects of spatial fixity for such communities when they have fewer resources to cope with globalised change (Bauman 1998; O'Bryrne 1997) and cause a turn inwards into 'defended' communities hostile to outsiders (Castells 1997). There are important reasons to question the assumed communal drive to ensure security rather than, say, maintain boundaries or social status. Status may be conferred by notions of strength, including violence and dangerousness, hardly conducive to security. Rather than assuming relationships of trust and reciprocity these studies point to the importance of power dynamics within communities. This emphasises a rather different vision of communities which may have both an oppressive capacity for informal control and criminality. This has far more resonance with Bourdieu's notion of social capital within particular 'fields' governed by power relationships.

Most importantly, studies of close-knit communities have also pointed to their exclusionary potential. A rosy vision of informal control does not address the articulation of community in contrast to culturally constituted 'others' and outsiders (Douglas 1992; Elias and Scotson 1965; Keith and Pile 1993), who may be isolated or victimised. Perceptions of others' dangerousness may be led by racial stereotypes (Merry 1981; Suttles 1972) or be conceived as such because of their status as officials (Walklate and Evans 1999) or length of residence (Elias and Scotson 1965). These visions of dangerousness hinder relationships of trust, dividing communities along cultural lines (Merry 1981) and can be used to justify exclusionary responses (Suttles 1972; Keith and Pile 1993).

There is no guarantee that close association produces more trusting, reciprocal and peaceful relationships. Baumgartner (Baumgartner 1988), for example, in her comparison of middle- and working-class areas in the US, emphasised the degree to which middle-class suburban residents avoided contact and confrontation with neighbours. Their networks were less spatially fixed and their financial resources made mutual support less important. While working-class areas did have closer and mutually supportive structures of neighbourly contact, this could also, however, bring people into confrontation. Brent (Brent 1997) goes so far as to suggest that a focus on disputes would be more relevant to the social relationships within deprived areas of Britain than a more romanticised notion of community and, ironically, such disputes lay at the heart of concerns to address 'anti-social behaviour' in social housing.

In reviewing this 'dark side' of social capital and community I do not want to resort to the same dystopianism that I criticised earlier. There need be no either/or of supportive or oppressive relationships. Community is inclusive and exclusive, conformist and supportive, preventative of crime and conducive to it. Qualities of relationships made through social networks are likely to be much more complex than simply creative of trust and reciprocity. What dominant concepts of social capital and community capacity for order lack is a means of conceptualising crucial power dynamics.

A tendency to see community capacity as wholly beneficial, to only see the 'bright side' of relationships, means that proposals to increase community capacity appear to skirt over the exclusionary potential of communities and cultural conceptions of dangerousness and trustworthiness. There is too easy an assumption of shared norms and values, of common perspectives and goals in addressing issues of security. In re-emphasising the dark side of social capital and community I want to highlight conflict, power dynamics and the way in which people constitute dangers and problems, which I think need to be at the core of debates about the participation of communities in crime control. I want to shift the focus of debate away from social networks and draw attention instead to the way crime, disorder and other local problems are constituted. This is to refocus on the way problems, and crime in particular, are politicised rather than on the resources for politicisation.

In this way I want to challenge some of the assumptions within debates about the role of communities in crime control that there are societal norms of behaviour. This emphasis will also question 'broken windows' assumptions that there are universal readings of 'signs of disorder' that have so influenced policy. Rather, people may have very different perceptions of seriousness of offence (Lewis and Salem 1986) and very different responses to disorder or incivility (Girling *et al*. 2000). This stresses questions of how people can participate in the local governance of security beyond reporting.

I also want to move away from a focus on the internal dynamics of communities and their capacity for informal control, and concentrate instead on the constitution of local problems and relationships with authorities, especially in the context of changes taking place in governing relationships. For areas that have had poor relationships with local authorities, conflict with these bodies may be central to a sense of inability to confront crime and disorder, may compound a sense of insecurity and powerlessness, and even legitimise other forms of 'informal control'.

In engaging citizens in local governance there is a need to acknowledge and counter exclusionary reactions and to respond in ways that do not simply endorse them. Equally there is a need to respond to crime and disorder in ways that do not assume a demand for punitive enforcement. It is doubtful whether crime and disorder is really an issue around which to build inclusive or tolerant communities (Crawford 1997). While a focus on mobilising support for exclusionary measures may appeal to those with more punitive views, it is equally capable of alienating others. This danger is, I want to suggest, particularly true for those whose experiences of exclusion inform a sense of vulnerability to such measures. Engaging such communities not only has to address the demand for security but also respond to a deep sense of injustice also embodied in the accusations of neglect through which this demand is made.

The research questions that inform this enquiry will therefore address three core issues: firstly, the way in which local problems are variously constituted by residents; secondly, the ways in which these lay narratives resonate with, or are found dissonant with, understandings and expectations of professionals engaged in local governance; thirdly, the implications of differing constitution and explanations of local problems for the ways in which communication between these various positions is played out in participation. In particular I want to address the effects of resonance and dissonance between understandings and the ways in which preconceptions can be confirmed and reinforced. This raises important issues for potential exclusion of certain perspectives even when sitting at the same table.

Notes

1   Local authority regeneration body.
2   'Social exclusion' also often has a rather vague meaning. Though tied to notions of poverty, relative deprivation and marginalisation, the term is used in various ways to mean slightly differing things. The dominant use of this term tends to be in reference to exclusion from paid work (Levitas 1998). However, it is also used in relation to insufficient means to participate in community life. This sense of social exclusion as incapacity to participate also emphasises exclusion as the result of ill-health or disability, providing a much broader meaning to the term (Burchardt, Le Grand and Piachaud 2002) and encompassing a sense of exclusion from some citizenship rights (Ratcliffe 1999). Exclusion is also used in relation to spatial boundaries and exclusion of particular groups and areas from services and the sense that they are marginalised in some way from the rest of society (Sibley 1995; Young 1999). In this sense social exclusion is also related to exclusionary, discriminatory social practices. Though vague, 'social exclusion' can encompass a range of causes and experiences of exclusion from mainstream society and is a useful shorthand, one that I will be using in its broadest sense throughout the book.
3   This is central to the renamed Department for Communities and Local Government, sustainability also refers to an environmental agenda within generation policies but is also used in relation to 'sustainable' places with levels of crime and disorder that do not drive people away.
4   The Crime and Disorder Act 1998 (Section 17) made prevention issues a consideration in all areas of policy development.

Chapter 3

Constituting local problems

In the chapters that follow I will be exploring the way residents talked about the estate, its decline or changes they had seen and the problems they describe. I want to unpack the ways that residents differ in their explanations of and identification of problems on the estate. This is an attempt to examine differing world views amongst residents and the various interpretations of change that they bring to participatory processes. Although crime, disorder and threatening behaviour are central to the way residents talked about the problems on the estate, my emphasis is on the way residents identify problems and explain change more generally. It is in the way that crime and disorder are constituted as problems with which I am interested; how they are explained within the framework of other understandings of the world, their role as symbolic signifiers of change and as issues around which to mobilise action. This chapter outlines the theoretical approach that I have taken. Before I begin to outline this approach I want first to clarify the way in which it differs from other debates about public responses to crime and disorder.

Fearful responses

The most influential of these debates about public responses in recent years has focused on public fears about crime. The product of surveys tempting a comparison between likelihood of victimisation and levels of fear, debates have hinged around the irrationality/rationality of fear of crime (Mirlees-Black and Allen 1998). Fear appears to outstrip the reality. This has contributed to policy attention on reassurance of the public. Fear, for the reasons I have already outlined in Chapter 2, is constituted as a problem in itself.

This policy emphasis on the impact of fear also echoes a left realist demand for a recognition of differential experiences of victimisation, and so levels of fear, of certain groups in society (especially generational (Bursik and Gramsmick 1993), minority ethnic (Merry 1981) and gender (Stanko 1990); see also Payne (2001) for a review). This research has stressed the way people manage their exposure to dangers in accordance with experience, whether real or vicarious, of victimisation and harassment. The emphasis on 'coping strategies' rightly stresses the impact of such fears on people's quality of life. The research stresses the rationality of fears, though victimisation rates may reflect the success of risk avoidance (Stanko 1990).

Another approach to this issue of public fears outstripping levels of victimisation, however, has called into question just what 'fear' is being measured in these surveys. This psychoanalytic approach has suggested the displacement of wider anxieties about people's lives, deaths and trajectories on to more knowable and actionable fear of crime (Hollway and Jefferson 2000; Hollway and Jefferson 1997; Lupton and Tulloch 1999). This research attempts to sensitively analyse what people's descriptions of their fears reveal about their wider sense of insecurity. Though in no way contradicting the impact of anxiety on people's quality of life, this approach suggests varying responses because of different thresholds of anxiety. It questions whether crime is the cause of the fear, though the fear is expressed in these terms.

This approach draws attention to wider causes of anxiety in people's lives, echoing some more sociological observations about the nature of insecurity and the demand for security in post-modern societies (Bauman 2001; Castells 1997; Giddens 1991). An understanding that we are living through an 'age of insecurity' has been influential in political and academic circles, an observation stressing the impact of social conditions productive of a sense of 'ontological insecurity' (Giddens 1991). Certainly it has been an age of some significant and rapid social changes – in gender relations, class structure, employment and consumption in particular – that have had a profound impact on the way status and social position are signified. An awareness of the fragility of social position may contribute to anxiety levels, to a sense of insecurity and vulnerability and a search for a sense of security and stability in a changing world (Bauman 2001). The impact of these social changes and a sense of powerlessness to control them may be expressed through fears about crime (Smith 1986) and heighten anxieties (Girling, Loader and Sparks 2000; Tylor and Boeckmann 1997). In this sense 'fear of crime' may be more indicative of wider experiences of insecurity and of responses to social change than to crime.

Questioning the significance of 'fear of crime' separates issues of the cause of social insecurity from the way it is expressed. This is not to diminish the impact on their lives of people's fears, nor to write them off as irrational or unjustified. Rather this approach provides the context for some valuable debates about the way crime is talked about and what meanings are attached to crime.

The meaning of crime talk

Crime talk can, it has been suggested, act as a locally meaningful way of making sense of the impact of social change (Girling, Loader and Sparks 2000; Taylor and Jamieson 1996; Taylor, Evans and Fraser 1996). It is 'bound up in a context of meaning and significance, involving the use of metaphors and narratives about social change' (Sparks 1997: 131). Indeed, Girling *et al.* (2000) suggest that local sensibilities about crime reflect more significant conversations about conceptions of order, of 'the way things are these days'. Crime talk can, they suggest, reflect a sense of powerlessness to control such changes locally and feed a punitive demand for tough criminal justice responses.

The value of these approaches is to draw attention to the way people interpret crime and disorder, rather than focusing on their emotional response. Crime can be an almost symbolic issue around which to make judgements about the state of the world, about what is happening to the place where you live and, by implication, what prospects this could portend for your own life. An event may elicit a range of responses reflecting differences in how people interpret its significance. Assessments of the meaning and seriousness of an apparently mundane problem such as youth disorder, for example, may depend upon judgements about what the young people are like, where they are from, what relationship the person has with them or their parents or whether they have children themselves (Girling *et al.* 2000). These judgements are in themselves part and parcel of the way people make sense of the world. Crime talk in this way may say more about the person expressing their views and their understandings of 'the way things are' than it does about their personal experience of crime and victimisation.

Attention to the meanings attached to crime talk brings into relief a particular problem with 'broken windows' assertions of the impact of crime and disorder as signs of decline. Wilson and Kelling (1982) argued that disorder is interpreted as a sign that 'no one cares' and so prompts people to see little point in trying to maintain their properties themselves. Disorder, they suggest, signifies decline and heightens fearfulness. This makes an assumption of universal responses to crime and disorder that recognition of differing interpretations calls into question. Talk about disorder, such as environmental decay, rubbish or graffiti, may act in a similar way to other crime talk, as an indication of 'the way things are these days', and of the fortunes of the place. In this sense it may indeed indicate negative change and be talked about in such terms. Nevertheless, crime and disorder may be interpreted in very different ways by different people. Disorder does not necessarily signify further criminality and may not necessarily be interpreted as a sign that neighbours do not care for the area. It might just as importantly, for example, signify poor maintenance and inequality of service delivery.

Interpretations say much about how people view the nature of the social order. In particular I want to draw attention to the way crime and disorder may be talked about in terms of injustice, inequality and relations with local authorities. These are again bound up with understandings of 'the way things are'. How inequality and the responses of authorities are explained, draws on the way people make sense of the world and their position in it more generally. This is a particularly important aspect of the potential meanings attached to crime and disorder in areas of social exclusion where people may be in regular contact with authorities of one sort or another and conscious of stigma and prejudice (Sennett 2005). Furthermore, the way crime talk is engaged with assessments of the responses of governing agencies arguably reflects more widespread cultural conceptions of order, and expectations of government action to resolve social problems. Providing security represents the most basic role of governments, and crime talk is necessarily engaged with the failure of authorities to provide order. It is a powerful stick with which to beat governments.

Expectations of governments, it has been suggested, have shifted since the introduction of the welfare state when it took on responsibility for finding solutions to a wider array of social problems (Della Porta and Diani 1999; Hacking 2003; Pitch 1995). If crime and disorder are indicative of wider concerns about 'the way things are these days', they are also potentially symbolic of a failure of governments to fulfil their promises of resolving wider social problems. A demand to address crime and disorder does not necessarily represent a simple demand for more punitive measures. What is important is what problems crime and disorder are understood to be indicative of. Are they, for example, seen as an indication of a decline in moral values, of community breakdown, of the presence of dangerous outsiders, of lack of protection or of inequality? How crime is constituted as a problem is central to understanding public responses to it and what expectations citizens bring to participatory processes. The concern with emotional responses to crime and disorder, though an important recognition of its impact on people's lives, has tended to depoliticise them. I want here to refocus attention on the way crime and disorder is politicised by exploring how they are constituted as problems.

In this focus on problem constitution I am of course building on a social constructionist tradition which addressed how social problems are identified in particular ways. Crimes, and groups associated with them, have been the subject of 'moral panics' inspiring punitive responses (Cohen 1973; Hall *et al.* 1978). As with these approaches I want to recognise the terms in which problems are described and the way they mobilise a political response. However, my approach to problem constitution is informed by a rather different perspective that I want now to outline in more detail.

Accounting for change

My abiding concern throughout this book is with how residents and professionals account for change. Professionals, of course, use some very clear professional scripts for making sense of the changes they identify on the estate, informed by some of the policy approaches outlined in Chapter 2. Though less clearly elicited, residents also produce accounts of the area and of changes they have seen in living there that use some equally significant explanatory scripts which I will be attempting to make more explicit. Though I will be exploring professional scripts from a similar perspective I want here to outline the theoretical approach I have taken to residents' accounts.

My focus throughout will be on residents' accounts of the area, what changes they have seen, why they think things have changed and who they hold responsible for those changes and for addressing them. At a time of impending change and uncertainty about the future of the estate, understandings of decline and change implicit within these conversations had a particular urgency and immediacy. Crime, disorder and issues of security play a significant role in these accounts but my concern is less with how residents talk about crime, disorder and security than on the role these problems play in their stories of change. I use this word 'stories' deliberately, again not to belittle the emotional impact and reality of crime and disorder, but because I want to take a step back from this emotive foreground in debates about responses to crime and concentrate on everyday meaning-making and the way people create narratives that make sense of change and its causes.

Narrative, causation and habitus

I want to draw on an understanding of people as story-tellers, using stories to make sense of our lives and the world around us (Lieblich, Tuval-Mashiach and Zilber 1998; Linde 1993). This approach builds on observations of the way individuals use narratives to produce and maintain a sense of coherence of experience and meaning or purpose in life (Bourdieu 2000b; Josselson and Lieblich 1999; Linde 1993) to defend against what Sennett (1998) might call a sense of 'drift' (see also Lieblich, Tuval-Mashiach and Zilber 1998; Linde 1993). Narratives include significant characters, dramatic episodes, a moral to the tale and, most importantly, use causal logics and shared cultural assumptions about the world to create meaningful accounts. Looking at residents' accounts as narratives provides a tool for analysis of differing causal explanations for change revealed in the way they identify and explain problems or describe significant events and characters. 'Problems' are constituted through these causal explanations for change.

Understandings of causation are rooted in particular visions of 'the way things are'. However, these are not simply individualised attempts to make sense of the world but use learned cultural causal logics and reflect background and experience (Linde 1993). In this way they say much about the person using them and can reflect experiences of social position. Although individual experiences and situations varied enormously amongst residents, I want to draw out some commonalities between them that reveal particular visions of and explanations for 'the way things are'. In describing these narratives of change I hope to build a picture of similarities in causal explanations stemming from broadly similar experiences of position in the world and in the place they live. By distinguishing these narratives from one another I do not mean to suggest different 'types' of people and, though lines of difference may reflect wider social categories and experience, particularly of gender, ethnicity and age, I have not grouped people in this way but have instead tried to distinguish between particular ways of talking about the estate.

I have explicitly linked these causal explanations to Bourdieu's notion of 'habitus'. This concept describes the ways in which experiences springing from culture and social position 'habituate' people to and within entrenched interpretations of the world and practices (Bourdieu 2000a; Bourdieu and Wacquant 1992). These causal narratives, I want to suggest, are formed and reinforced by experiences of social position (Bourdieu 2000). Because entrenched in experience, 'habituated' understandings may become more so, as with each experience people find confirmation of the applicability of their understanding. Difficult to shift, these 'dispositions' are only likely to change with some fundamental change in position. The appeal of Bourdieu's notion of habitus is in its provision of a means to root ways of thinking in the structured nature of experience without being deterministic nor exposed to the charge of relativism that haunts Foucauldian and biographical approaches (Bourdieu 2000b; Flick 1998; Rimstead 1997; Wetherell 2001).

Habitus as a concept offers the capacity to incorporate and elaborate the creativity and diversity of individual experience within the constraints placed upon us by position and experience, predisposing us towards the world. I have implicitly linked this understanding of habitus to people's use of particular causal narratives which are assumed to be natural (Bourdieu 2000b; Bourdieu and Wacquant 1992; Linde 1993). I want to use this notion of habitus, in particular, to analyse the impacts of attempts to communicate between people of differing world views, which is crucial for understanding miscommunications during participation.

Differences between narratives used by residents are in this way intended to illustrate some differences in experience and position from which they stem. These narratives of change can say as much about the person using them as they do about the changes themselves. Likewise, the way people identify problems, explain their impact and causes and so on reveals, in using these explanations, as much about the person describing them as it does about what problems there are. For this reason people may also talk about very different problems though living in the same place.

In order to piece together this constitution of local problems I want in particular to focus on the way residents variously attributed blame, a process bound up with understandings of causation. In this I will be drawing closely on Mary Douglas's cultural theory of the constitution of danger.

Blame, danger and defilement

Douglas's thesis focuses on different societies' explanations for misfortune and attribution of blame (Douglas 1966, 1992). The key to this work is the emphasis she puts on the impact of social bonds and structures on explanations for misfortune. Dangers, she suggests, are culturally constituted as a threat to valued social institutions, for example to religion, and blame attributed in ways that reaffirm the value of these institutions. She distinguishes between four types of society differentiated by the strengths or weaknesses of 'grid-group' relationships (Vaughan 2002). 'Group' refers to the boundaries erected between the group and the outside world, while 'grid' relates to the social distinctions and rules that are used to limit the ways in which people behave towards one another. A society with strong group and grid relationships, for example, will tend to blame misfortune on outsiders and on the breach of rules governing behaviour (taboos). They will present dangers as a threat to the group and the values governing them, reinforcing and enforcing those boundaries and rules (Douglas 1986; Douglas 1966).

While Douglas's *Purity and Danger* (1966) developed this thesis in relation to tribal societies and sacred texts (in particular, the Old Testament), her later book *Risk and Blame* (1992) extended her thesis to modern (post-) industrialised societies, stressing the similarity of the way in which 'risks' are identified as a threat to individuals and individual liberty, to the valued social institution of individualised societies. The importance is not whether such risks are real but how they are politicised. Identification of threats or risks are a means of mobilising a response and holding authorities to account in a way that reflects the values of the society in which they are voiced.

Though there are some problems with these generalised cultural distinctions, Douglas's theory draws attention to the way negative changes may be explained by attributing blame in ways that reflect social values and structures. She developed the thesis, famously outlined in *Purity and Danger* (1966), that group identity and boundaries of belonging are expressed in relation to dangers. Most importantly she highlighted the use of understandings of 'pollution' in explaining the dangers posed. While the group is associated with positive attributes of purity, dangers are described in terms of their ability to pollute or defile. Maintenance of group identity, particularly in the face of misfortune and change, involves the identification and reaffirmation of what is pure and what defiling. Uncleanness or dirt is 'that which must not be included' if a symbolic order is to be maintained (Douglas 1966: 41). Pollution is posited as a universal device for defining and maintaining a society's sense of who/what it is. The implication is that blame is attributed to those already culturally constituted as defiled or defiling, an explanation of change and identification of dangers that maintains a sense of a moral order. It both reflects and confirms people's understandings of 'the way things are'. In this she stresses the cultural bias in risk perception and, in particular, the way in which blame for society's ills tends to be attributed to those already unpopular and excluded.

I have drawn on this work in two important respects. Primarily I want to echo Douglas's emphasis on the role of notions of pollution and, what I will call a discourse of disgust – of dirt, defilement and disease – in the way people constitute problems through attributing blame to, and associating danger with, otherness. Secondly I want to draw on her thesis of the impact of social structure on explanations for misfortune, though I want to raise some doubts about its application to cultures and link it to notions of identity-formation and social position. I will explore these in a little more detail.

Discourses of disgust

Discourses of disgust provide a repertoire for constituting problems through notions of purity and defilement. Douglas's observations on the use of concepts of pollution in the constitution of danger highlight the way it is used to explain their impact on the group. The potential to corrupt, invade or defile signifies the wider implications of the threat. Dangers as diverse as water pollution and incest are understood through such language as both 'literal and figurative filth', having both a symbolic and material impact on those who experience their effects (Hacking 2003). They are presented through this language as a threat not only to individuals but also to the moral order.

An association of dangers with the symbolic significance of the defilement of purity is a powerful political weapon. It expresses moral outrage, justified both in terms of material and symbolic threat. Child murderers and paedophiles represent the ultimate danger in this regard; defilement of purity (children) is coupled with extremely harmful outcome. Such people are a potent symbol of danger and moral corruption, of negative social change. The symbolic potential and outcome of these dangers outweighs any consideration of calculated risk and encourages a precautionary response (Haggerty 2003). Such dangers are politicised as a threat to society, and indicative of change, a 'sign of the times', expressed as a danger to children. References to these wider moral, as well as material, implications of this danger express the unacceptability of 'the way things are these days'.

Discourses of disgust in this way signify the impact, extent and seriousness of a problem. The rhetoric of pollution and defilement has a cultural resonance and symbolic power. So, for example, the danger posed by drivers to children is given a symbolic resonance when coupled with the polluting influence of alcohol around which responses to the problem are mobilised (Hacking 2003). This risk is constituted as the use of alcohol when driving, not by the number of cars on the road which increases the likelihood of accidents. The rhetoric of pollution gives this problem a political resonance and is constituted as a moral problem of drink driving.

These observations on the role of a language of pollution in the constitution of dangers draws attention to the way problems are politicised. Such language is used to mobilise a response. In these terms there may indeed be some 'signal crimes', as Innes (2004) calls them, that are widely accepted as an indication of crisis, that 'the way things are' is unacceptable. However, it is the terms in which these crimes or events are constituted as a threat (e.g. to innocent children or the elderly) that gives them significance as much as the crime itself.

Blaming 'others'

Perhaps most important, however, is the way in which discourses of disgust – of pollution, defilement and disease – associate danger with otherness. They are used to describe or identify 'others', constitute them as a danger and blame them for change. The attributes of groups are identified in these terms as both 'other' and dangerous. This is most apparent amongst racialised conceptions of otherness, whereby minority groups and immigrants are described and denigrated in these terms, particularly as invading and spreading (Keith and Pile 1993; Sibley 1995; Riggins 1997). Their otherness may also be signified by associating groups with dirt or disease, with animals (denying humanity), with immorality, irrational violence and any number of negative attributes contrasted to the supposedly positive qualities of the majority (Helleiner and Szuchewycz 1997; Sibley 1995; Riggins 1997).

These attributes of otherness may also be applied to other denigrated groups who may thereby be described as dangerous. Though these may not include racialised understandings of difference, there is still a tendency to describe their dangerousness in terms of defilement, disease and dirt, with attributes in contrast to notions of purity and innocence (Sibley 1995). Notions of otherness may also, for example, be constituted along moral boundaries, associating certain behaviours with moral corruption. Women, for example, can be described in terms of a dangerous otherness when they breach these boundaries of behaviour. Prostitutes, single and teenage mothers can tend to be described in these ways as indicative of a societal moral decay. They threaten conceptions of moral purity, female sexual respectability and the two-parent family. They can be cited as symbolic of social changes for which they are also blamed.

Some figures also become cast as other because of their morally borderline status with regard to their capacity to take responsibility for themselves (Sibley 1995; Walkerdine 2001). The dangerousness of 'others' is bound up with notions of culpability informed by cultural (and legal) conceptions of capacity to take responsibility for actions. In particular, young people, drug addicts and the mentally ill present difficult judgements about culpability, as to whether they can control themselves, make judgements of right and wrong, whether they are to blame or not. Teenagers, for example, at the border of adulthood, are difficult to determine as to age, maturity and responsibility for their own actions. While small children may symbolise vulnerable purity and innocence (though also the reverse, of untamed wildness and corrupted innocence), teenagers occupy a more ambiguous status. The behaviour of young people again can be presented as indicative of societal trajectory (James and James 2001; James 2000; Valentine 1996; Walkerdine 2001).

These judgements of otherness, of capacity and culpability, are particularly susceptible to changing cultural conceptions of personal responsibility. These conceptions are arguably shifting towards an increased emphasis on personal responsibility for one's actions, a shift attributing blame to individuals for exposing themselves to risk (Haggerty 2003; Hunt 2003). This judgement of responsibility of the actor is particularly important in how blame is attributed. So, for example, if a drug is considered addictive beyond capacity to self-control, an addict might be seen as driven by the drug to commit their offence. This defines the problem as one of addiction. However, they may also be considered able to choose to stop, or irresponsible if they fail to respond to, or take up, help with their addiction and thereby blameworthy (Hunt 2003). This emphasis on personal responsibility is particularly true of the mentally ill who may be considered to some extent blameworthy if they fail or refuse to take medication. They are doubly mad and bad. The attribution of dangerousness (riskiness) to these increasingly culpable 'others' encourages a precautionary response – excluding or containing them prior to offence (Haggerty 2003; Hunt 2003).

Discourses of disgust are both a means of denigrating groups in society already understood to be 'other', and of describing them as dangerous. It is a language of attributing blame and justifying exclusionary responses (Sibley 1995; Riggins 1997). Following Douglas, David Sibley in his book *Geographies of Exclusion* (1995) points out the ways in which otherness and dangerousness are constituted at the boundaries of belonging – of a sense of what that society/community is and of who is included. Identifying otherness with dangerousness and dangers with 'others' – blaming 'others' – reaffirms a positive sense of the identity of the community, its values and institutions, and a sense of purity and stability during periods of rapid change (see also Bauman 2001).

This observation of the way that problems are associated with 'others', the defiled or defiling, has two important implications. Firstly, blaming 'them' for local problems or identifying 'them' as a problem coincides with distancing blame from 'us'. This may be particularly urgent amongst those living in areas of social exclusion who may be acutely aware of a tendency to be blamed and stigmatised themselves. Secondly, this attribution of blame to 'others' also mirrors power relationships, those more powerful able more successfully to denigrate those less so. Blaming 'them' reasserts the position of 'us'. Attributing blame to those already accepted as dangerous gives credence to the accusation and encourages a tendency to blame the powerless for negative change. Regeneration and participation processes heighten the importance of being accepted as a credible and blameless 'community' to be part of the future of the area, and may make the drawing of boundaries of belonging the more rigid and politicised (Kasinitz and Hillyard 1995). A sense of powerlessness in the face of change may be heightened during regeneration, and, ironically, this can result in people blaming others less powerful, such as recent immigrants, for their misfortune (Foster 1999).

The constitution of local problems not only uses a discourse of disgust to stress seriousness and mobilise a response but may also associate these problems with 'others'. In this sense the way local problems are identified (with others) may say much about the way residents view, or wish to present, themselves. Their narratives of change may act both as what Douglas would call a 'forensic resource', attributing blame and the cause of problems to others, and also reinforce a positive sense of identity in contrast to this otherness.

Identity, identification and the constitution of local problems

Douglas's cultural theory is concerned with the way blame is attributed in ways that mobilise a response, maintain the identity of a group, particularly of communities, and reinforce the bonds and rules governing social relations within it (Douglas 1986; Douglas 1966, 1992). Traitors within the group, or those in breach of rules/taboos, are as likely to be considered a danger as those outside it. Reinforcing these rules is part of the group's power dynamics, maintaining and contesting boundaries of belonging. This is crucial for thinking about the dynamics of close-knit communities and organisations, as I stressed in Chapter 2 (the 'dark side' of community).

Nevertheless, this approach, and those influenced by it, can be limited by its inherent functionalism. There is too close an association in this work between communities of place and identity. While some living in a close-knit neighbourhood may identify themselves strongly with that place, others living in the same neighbourhood may tend instead to relate themselves more closely with other equally potent 'imagined communities' (Anderson 1983). Boundaries and rules of belonging have very different attributes for different people, depending on how they identify themselves, and in this sense so do understandings of 'otherness'. I want to stress the significance of a relationship between attribution of blame and maintenance of identity in this wider sense, acknowledging the plurality of identities within contemporary British society.

If people who see themselves as part of a community of place tend to blame in particular ways, this begs the question of whether those who identify themselves with other 'communities' tend to blame differently. Instead of a community of place, might they relate to a sense of belonging to, say, a wider moral community, ethnic group, class, institution or profession? Of course, identity formation is complex and I do not want to reduce people's sense of themselves to essentialised notions of fixed identity or to only one group. More useful, especially in this instance, is an understanding of identity formation as an ongoing process whereby individuals continuously form a sense of self in contrast to others, to what they are *not* (Hall 2000). This can be both in contrast to the denigrated and powerless 'other' already discussed, but also in relation to other powerful or comparable groups with whom the person comes into contact. This ongoing process of 'identification', as Hall (2000) dubs it, is one that is part of a means of positioning oneself in the world, in relation to any number of others (see also Bourdieu 2000b).

This understanding of 'identification' suggests that how people identify 'others' may also be indicative of their experience of their position in the world, of where they see themselves in relation to others. How problems are identified (with others) may in this way also be related to people's sense of their own social position. Their identification of problems (or dangers) is, through this dynamic of blame and identification, a prism for examining people's world view, formed in part by their experience of position. Residents' narratives of change and blame in this sense offer an insight into 'habitus', their assumptions about the world and their position within it.

This provides the theoretical background to unpicking some important differences in the way residents of 'the estate' talked about the changes they had seen, problems they identified and those they blamed for them. Of course, some of these differences relate to their sense of their position within the place but I want to suggest that they also provide a glimpse into their wider understandings of their social position. This sense of position is apparent in the way they identify problems, and is echoed in their references to their sense of security, particularly of whom or of where they feel afraid. These are not 'constructed' problems but an exposition of a sense of threat and vulnerability, stressing the seriousness of problems confronting the area in terms that are meaningful within their own view of the world. The problems that residents identify may be all too apparent on the estate but it is the way that different people identify different problems and attribute blame to different groups of 'others' that I am interested in exploring. This is in an effort to refocus attention on the meanings behind the way residents talk about problems and the causal narratives that underpin their accounts.

Explaining inequality and neglect

In addition to this focus on blame, otherness and identification, I want to explore the way residents made assumptions about the nature and causes of social inequality. These understandings of 'the way things are' were particularly apparent when talking about their relationships with, and the actions (or inaction) of, local authorities. Hardly surprising in view of the condition of the estate, there was a common accusation of neglect amongst residents. What was fascinating from the point of view of unpicking causal explanations was the way they went about explaining this neglect. Talk about the failure or neglect of local authorities illustrated some of the expectations residents had of the local state and important explanations for inequality of treatment. Their differing explanations for inequality of treatment again, I want to suggest, reflect differing world views emerging from a different experience of social position (Ewick and Silbey 1999). Whether they could command the support of authorities when needed, or whether they needed them at all, was intimately bound up with understandings of their vulnerability and why they might not receive equal treatment.

Accounts of relations with authorities or of their neglect are structured by this contrast between an ideal of (legal) equality and the reality. These are fundamentally concerned with notions of legitimacy. What becomes apparent are some rather different understandings of legitimate authority, despite some common conceptions of a justice ideal, that also reflect residents' assumptions about the causes of social inequality. These understandings of legitimacy use some central causal narratives about 'the way things are' that are applied to and reinforced by wider experiences. They are the clearest reflection of residents' 'dispositions'. These causal narratives are crucial to making sense of residents' orientations to participation with governing bodies and their expectations of and reactions to the actions of agencies. Taking these differing causal narratives into account is essential in exploring what happens when professionals and residents attempt to communicate between differing world views. Their diverse assumptions and experiences of 'the way things are' inform some important problems of miscommunication between all parties.

These narratives of neglect are a common thread between residents' accounts. They embody causal explanations for 'the way things are' which are formed for many through experiences of social exclusion. Again they reveal much about the person using them, about how they tend to interpret the world, events and particularly the actions of those in authority. These understandings of neglect and social inequality are central to residents' explanations for change. In this regard blame is also attributed, by some, to authorities for a failure to tackle problems; problems identified in terms likely to mobilise a response from authorities and hold them to account, such as negligence and exposure to risks. The role of stories about crime and disorder is often not simply one stressing insecurity but is also a signifier of the failure of governing bodies to protect individuals from 'others', to fail even to provide security let alone fulfil their other promises.

Part II, *Living Here*, focuses on these residents' narratives. The chapters exploring residents' accounts follow the lines of distinction between their narratives of change. Issues of identification and belonging are explored in Chapter 4, along with residents' understandings of the trajectory of the place and their place within it. In this chapter I outline four nostalgic accounts of belonging which both illustrate the contested nature of community and act as forensic narratives tied to implicit understandings of the causes of decline. These are contrasted with two differing accounts, less entrenched in notions of decline or belonging to place, reflecting experiences of exclusion and attempts to distance themselves from the estate. Chapter 5 then consolidates these six into four to explore the ways in which conceptions of otherness, implicit in these accounts, relate to identification of local problems. Chapter 6 focuses on the ways in which understandings of the work of authorities related to residents' wider causal explanations of social inequality and notions of legitimacy. This sets the scene for understanding orientations to participation in Part IV.

Part III, *Working There*, explores professional accounts, initially, in Chapter 7, in relation to their similar use of a forensic narrative of spiralling decline in their accounts of the area's demise but also their divergent understandings of its cause. Chapter 8 focuses on the constitution of community and those excluded from it, exploring differences and similarities between private sector, housing and regeneration officers and local public police.

The two parts to the book, *Living Here* and *Working There*, invite comparison. Each part begins with an exploration of broad narratives of change that structure the accounts, such as nostalgic narratives amongst residents (Chapter 4) and narratives of spiralling decline, similarly indicative of causes, used by professionals (Chapter 7). These overall structures stress the points of coherence between professional and residents' accounts. The following chapters in both parts, however, present this coherence as a surface that belies complexity.

These underlying points of coherence and contrast provide the basis for an exploration of the effects of miscommunication and shared perspectives within the consultation process.

Part IV, thereby acts as conclusion. Chapter 9 *Participation?* provides a description of consultation meetings on which to base an exploration of the processes of miscommunication, and demonstrates how the concept of habitus aids an understanding of the misinterpretations within, and often counterproductive effects of, participation. This has important implications for wider processes of citizen participation in local governance. Though offering no answers to these questions, Chapter 10, by way of conclusion, outlines some directions towards a governance of 'just sustainability' that may present a counter-discourse to a potentially punitive pursuit of risk management in urban governance at the expense of broader concerns for justice and sustainability.

Part II

Living Here

Chapter 4

Narratives of decline and change

The meaning of place

Before looking at the way residents constitute local problems, I want
first to explore the ways in which they described the estate and
how they relate themselves (or do not) to a sense of belonging to
it. The meaning of place necessarily presents issues of how spatial
boundaries are constructed and defined by residents or imposed by
local government. While administrative boundaries may mean little to
residents in their day-to-day practices, the effects of their imposition
may be profound. At a time of spatially bounded regeneration, the
impact of change within a geographical space and its contested
identity was of heightened significance. The nature of place and its
future trajectory became part of a contested public discourse.

Equally, however, place has an importance beyond local politics.
Claims to place-based identity tend to be associated with conservative,
essentialist and nostalgic visions of lost community (Massey 1994;
Young 2001). Identity of place may act as a surrogate for the hoped
for security of community in response to wider insecurity (Bauman
2001; Davis 1979; Sennett 1998). In this sense such nostalgic narratives
may have more to do with people's responses to change, though
voiced through a relationship with place.

Nostalgic stories of decline describe the past as better, though
lost or declining, in contrast to and as a criticism of current trends
(Davis 1979). They provide a narrative form denoting coherence or
rupture with an imagined past from which a conception of a natural
identity is built (Anderson 1983). However, this identity is necessarily

created in the context of an outside, in contrast to which a conception of unity, homogeneity and belonging are created and reinforced (Douglas 1986; Hall 2000; Keith and Pile 1993).

Constituting these boundaries of belonging does not necessarily imply that they are spatial, nor do claims about the nature of a place necessarily reflect a timeless, essentialist sense of identity. Identities of place are subject to change and contest. They are constructed in relation to other places and situate their position in the world relative to them (Girling *et al.* 2000). As such, place may also act as a mirror for residents' understanding of their own position in the world and future trajectory. While they are provided with an 'ontological security' (Giddens 1991), focused around a localised sense of place, the prospect of change is potentially deeply troubling for residents who relate their sense of self-identity closely with that place.

The increased importance of the local for the provision of a sense of security in the face of global change is particularly acute for those already excluded from globalised networks, which may fix them to places in ways that exacerbate this exclusion (Castells 1997; O'Bryrne 1997). This isolation is compounded in British council estates by stigmatisation (Bauman 2001; Reynolds 1986). Place-based identity, in these terms, may be an identity of necessity, reducing a sense of being trapped. Especially when excluded from other places, either by fear, policing or an inability to participate in consumption, the sense of security and status, of being 'known', recognised or respected within a neighbourhood may make a sense of belonging to it increasingly important to a sense of self-worth and security. But, tied to a need to constantly reinforce and defend the boundaries of belonging, such a place may instead prove an oppressive one and a potentially vulnerable foundation on which to base a sense of security, adding to fears of outsiders and traitors (Bauman 2001; Sennett 1998).

In this chapter, through residents' life histories and their stories of coming to live on the estate, I provide a snapshot of the way in which they identify and position themselves in relation to this place. In particular I want to look at the significance of the use by some residents of nostalgic narratives of decline and identification of themselves as belonging to place, in contrast to those who do not use such narratives, as a means of unpacking people's orientation to change. I have differentiated between six broad narratives that provide a sense of the four emergent (dis)positions that form the basis of my analysis in Chapters 5 and 6.[1] I have characterised these narratives as: born and bred, lost values, surviving community, learning to be local, sticking it out alone and keeping a distance.

Born and bred

Those who tied their identities most closely to a nostalgic narrative of decline were those who stressed their family connections within and long-standing knowledge of the area. Often told that I should talk to one or other of these people, they were members of the 'old' families of Millton or people whose long-term residence gave them a status as established, 'authentic voices' of this place. They laid claim to antiquity of lines of belonging (Bauman 2001; Elias and Scotson 1965). One of the clearest examples of this narrative was used by Ian[2] whom I met when he approached me at a public meeting saying that I should talk to him if I wanted to know about the area. He sat me down in a corner with my tape recorder, describing the pleasures of growing up in Millton. He was keen to associate himself with a long family history in the area which he implied gave him status, one that he seemed anxious to reinforce. Millton, for him, was characterised by the people who lived there in the past, rather than now. They were the 'old Millton' people, the ones, like his family, who had lived there for six generations while the buildings changed around them.

> It's a long time we have been in Millton. Me ... mam lived in the same spot where she was lived and brought up ... Before this estate was done, right, there used to be all factories and all that and there was the best, you know, childhood you could have ... I could go in anyone's house round here. I mean, don't have to knock, the door was open, just walk in and the people, the *old* Millton people, was [slowly, emphasising each syllable loudly] absolutely brilliant. Not what we've get round here now [swinging his arm round to indicate everyone else in the room]. *These* people are not from Millton.

Ian connected himself to a better past while distancing himself from its present. His offer to introduce me to other truly Millton people (though no longer living there) involved visiting three different pubs at some distance from the estate. For Ian the true Millton was made up of the families that lived there before the estate was built and who were now gone (though even while he was saying all this he was sitting next to someone he grew up with and who still lived there).

Though she rarely spoke to him, because of her desire to distance herself from his criminal reputation and alcoholism, Ian's sister Tracy mirrored his narrative of an established circle of real Millton families. She and Ian use this nostalgic vision of Millton to draw boundaries between those who belong and those who do not. In the process they present themselves as the authoritative and authentic voices of the community, excluding a large number of their neighbours. Both hark back to a time when everyone knew one another and limit Millton people to those who lived there prior to the building of the estate. For both the problem with the present is that the newcomers are not like these 'old families'. Tracy describes this difference in terms of a lack of shared memories of growing up here but again uses memory as a vehicle for identifying those who belong:

TRACY   I loved it when I was a kid round here – it weren't like it is now – you know, like everybody knows everybody. They do now but some of them are a bit, you know, like, 'cause they don't come from round here, if you know what I mean. Like them, all the older set have been here for years, they all chat to one another … but we've not got the same in common with them as them that … I loved it round here when I was a kid.

JACQUI   What don't you think you've got in common?

TRACY   Well, no, it's not what we've not got in common, it's, I don't know, how can I say? You can't talk to them – you know, like Pat – about the old times when we was kids, 'cause she didn't live over here then. She only moved in when the houses was built.

Unable to pinpoint the difference she turns firstly to her childhood and then to the inability to share those memories with newcomers, but significantly draws on the example of a woman from a renowned 'problem family' (Pat). These descriptions of the past point to a deeply rooted and heavily invested identification of themselves as a 'Millton family'. Both, when they think about how much they like the place and their relationship with it, draw on a glowing description of an idyllic childhood[3] stressing their knowledge of and commitment to the area. They see themselves as part of this place and always will be, even if they leave. Though rooted in Millton they do not suggest that they are trapped by it. Indeed, both talk of leaving when the area is rebuilt. Instead, this nostalgic narrative differentiates them from newcomers whom they blame for the decline of the area. By presenting newcomers as to blame established residents like Ian and Tracy can maintain their deep identification of themselves with the area while distancing themselves from the cause of its decline. They defend themselves in this sense from being seen as part of the problem, or even part of this place now that it is 'like Beirut', a place alien to the Millton with which they identify themselves, an abandoned shell of what it once was. Despite this distance their claims to authenticity and authority, however, also rely on an implication that others acknowledge their status as Millton families, 'born and bred'. Their position on the estate is secure but masks other expressions of their more ambiguous status in the world outside.

Such nostalgic narratives of belonging establish Ian and Tracy as the 'authentic' voice of the area while separating them from the wider, stigmatised community (Kasinitz and Hillyard 1995). They make claims to an authentic knowledge of the area, claims that have particular power when resonant with an official discourse of 'community'.[4] Such claims to position in the new political field of consultation may be doubly strengthened at this time of change. However, the proposed introduction of newcomers into the area through its gentrification, its rebuilding and renaming, present a future even further removed from this nostalgic view of Millton. Ian and Tracy can see little place for themselves in this 'renaissance' of Millton.

Lost values

A second nostalgic narrative mirrors this emphasis on a change in the sort of people who live in Millton. Less focused on belonging, however, this change relates to the decline in respectability of the area and its residents. Jack and Sarah, a couple in their fifties, lifelong residents and until recently working locally, described this as a steady decline in 'decency'. Identifying a time when this decline began was much more difficult and less important to them.

> I think there is less decent people than there used to be all them years ago. I think it has been a natural progression, like in particular in the last five, eight years, ten years, really gone. (Jack)

Like Tracy and Ian, this couple describe a rosy (for them, respectable) past, prior to loss of 'decent' residents. However, to them it matters less where newcomers *come from* than that they *demonstrate respectability*. That they do not is indicative of a change, not only here but within wider society, of which they disapprove. To explain exactly what that trend is, Jack plunges into a nostalgic description of lost 'family values'.

JACQUI   Tell me about how it was. You say you'd like to get it back to how it was.

JACK   It is just as I said to you, I'm not talking about this estate, I'm talking about generally, any estate. I think one of the main reasons is to encourage ... the whole family values of years ago. Like my dad used to drink in the [pub] up the road ... so we used to go in there ... I'd get to know everybody, I'd have respect for the elders in there ... The kids these days ... they drink all the alcopops and then going into town from when they are 15, 16 years of age ... So whereas years ago they were content with ... playing football ... now the highlight of most of the kids' days is ... to see a car burning out. Those are the differences between 30 years ago and now.

While Sarah, like Tracy, looked back to knowing people as she walked around the area, Jack recalled the entirely male experience in the pub. The pub was a place where he felt that boys learned to respect older men. These memories may say much about the gendered separation of socialising in the area (Massey 1994). However, both Jack and Sarah's yearning for a time of being known and respected may say more about what they wish for the present than it does about the past. Getting older himself, Jack does not mix with the young and does not feel that they respect him. They both describe a sense of separation from others living in the area.

Jack bemoans the loss of a patriarchal moral authority represented within 'family values' that he associates with a more certain past (Sennett 1998) and with which he associates the pub. It is significant that the first time I met him his description of change focused on the number of single mothers bringing up sons without a father figure.[5] Sarah too goes on to use the presence of unaccompanied young children as an indication of a decline in parenting, particularly of boys, sharing this understanding of a decline in moral discipline. Theirs is a narrative of a loss of societal morality and discipline, of values and commitment in a world of immorality and instant gratification, illustrated by this contrast between the slow Sunday afternoon pint and the alcopop, the football game and the burned out car. Their struggle to maintain their 'decency' in the face of this change recalls a search for continuity with a past security through their adherence to and identification of themselves with these values (Sennett 1998). Theirs, however, is also a story of lost position both within the place and of the place itself, and is coupled with a desire to distinguish themselves from those they blame for the decline, the 'indecent'.

A similar, but distinct, narrative of lost patriarchal authority is voiced by Bob, a man in his seventies, again a lifelong resident and formerly employed in local industry. However, he differentiates between those who are 'all right' and those who are not along lines of involvement in illegality rather than decency. In describing the way the estate has run down he turns to a nostalgic memory of his local lads' club:

> I mean, I always went to a club when I was a kid, either lads' and mens' ... Well that got shut down, didn't it. They started letting *girls* in, didn't they, and all that ... so it went kaput ... because ... it's different getting lads and men together ... If a bloke tells a lad, 'Stop messing about, or else you're out ...' But if he says it to a girl it's a different entire story, you know what I mean. She'll be weeping and wailing and going bringing the parents and all sorts ... It was very strict, if you was messing about ... you had to go back and see the committee. And then they decide whether they let you go back in or you was out for good. Depends what you was doing.

Again male authority is idealised and offered as the only way to control young boys. His image of girls as somehow uncontrollable, irrational, manipulative and troublemaking, bringing in parents and preventing this exertion of authority, is very telling. In contrast, the authority he describes is rationalised, institutional, proportional to the offence and obeyed. He identifies himself with other (working) men, in contrast to women, and this account associates him with a male authority of the past, now challenged by social changes, not least in gender relations. These nostalgic narratives of lost male authority are used to account for a breakdown in control of young people. Although Bob, Jack and Sarah differ in their constitution of respectability (moral or legal), they share an understanding of a loss of male authority and loss of dignity of (male) working-class identity (Rimstead 1997).

Although Jack and Sarah's accounts distance them from other residents, they share with Bob a deep commitment to living in the area, are all heavily involved in the consultation process and intend to stay. Their life stories and trajectories are tightly bound to that of the area, both past and future, and its reputation and decline has had an enormous impact on their sense of their declining position. For Jack and Sarah this has caused them to distance themselves from others. Bob, however, voices a very different causal narrative, blaming local authorities and withdrawal of resources for decline, and stresses solidarity with other people on the estate. This narrative links him to another widespread assertion of a 'surviving community'.

A surviving community

The 'old neighbourliness' in Ian and Tracy's (born and bred) accounts is echoed in this third nostalgic narrative, in references to an era of 'open doors' and neighbours dropping in without knocking, again recalled as a time of greater security when people knew and were more welcoming of each other. However, unlike Ian and Tracy, those using this narrative do not suggest that this time pre-dated the building of the estate. Although also a claim of belonging (to the estate), it is less exclusive than amongst those 'born and bred' there. Particularly amongst women who moved to the estate when it was first built, this narrative is used to evoke a time of great optimism in contrast to its decline. For example, Doreen, now in her sixties, described those early days as idyllic compared to now:

> Oh, it was beautiful, it was really lovely, … really lovely. I mean because, there again, it was all old neighbours, or everybody knew everyone else, you know. They used to say … 'Have you got house off here yet?' and, you know, it was really lovely. It's unbelievable what trash they've brought on.

This is a tale of a time of good neighbours, when the estate was desirable. But while criticising newcomers, Doreen also stresses the continued presence of those original neighbours or their children, of a surviving community. She reserves her criticisms for the 'trash' *brought on* (by the council) since, whose malign presence has less to do with their newness than with what kind of people they are.

This narrative of a rosy past and unsavoury present is echoed amongst younger people. Take, for example, this joint description of the estate from Doreen and her daughter of 23. Kate's interruptions reinterpret her mother's account.

DOREEN   I don't know whether it's because I originated from here but people up there[6] was not like the people what was like round here. You know what I mean?

KATE   'Cause there are a lot of friendly people round here. It's a strong community, well, there was …

DOREEN   [*interrupting*] Well, it was very strong 'cause, I mean, when you've been brought up with these people round here …

KATE   [*interrupting*] … And it still is for them that had always been …

DOREEN   I mean, you've got Kath and Jane … we were brought up with them, you know what I mean, 'cause … there's still a lot of old neighbours going around.

Kate reinterprets people knowing each other as a general friendliness and links this to a notion of a strong 'community', a word that her mother never uses. In this she attaches a discourse of community to this nostalgically remembered past, linking past to present for those that belong. This retelling of the past stresses continuity as well as loss in the accounts of some younger residents (in their twenties).

This story of loss and continuity provides a sense that community is possible but is not what they have now, reinforcing an image of 'community' as an ideal state of security (Bauman 2001). This creates an impression of a cross-generational territorial, and potentially more inclusive (Back 1994), identity. However, this is a story of the survival of a community against all odds, threatened by the arrival of newcomers, 'trash' and now the gentrification of the area. Identifying themselves so closely with place, changes to it are potentially threatening not only to their image of the nature of the place but also to their position in it in the future. It is an understanding that hints at a continuing need to defend the (physical and imagined) boundaries of community.

Children playing in a still well-occupied part of the estate. Their parents described a surviving sense of community and safety around this little courtyard

Learning to be local

Some of the youngest residents, and some newer to the estate, also adopt nostalgic narratives of its past, mimicking those of older and established residents. This nostalgic history is used as a received memory of the area, newcomers sometimes using it to stress the potential for community in the vestiges of this past. These accounts suggest a process of local myth creation through which newcomers are told about the history of the area (Kasinitz and Hillyard 1995), a process that I too was being taken through. Established residents share mutual memories, knowledge of one another and stories of the place, which provide a 'cultural capital' that can exclude newcomers and maintains their position. Those who cannot engage in the memories of the area can adopt a second hand history of decline and of continuity between past and present as a means of claiming membership.

However, the use of this nostalgic narrative is widespread (Davis 1979; Massey 1994; Revill 1993; Young 2001), beyond a cultural capital (Bourdieu and Wacquant 1992) of a particular place. It evokes decline and fragmentation of community in a broader societal sense.

In a place where most people could name most of their neighbours, it is the suggestion that people do not know each other that is the real puzzle. The adoption of nostalgic accounts of its decline provide an association of identity with a positive perception of this place, distanced from its current downward trajectory. The image is often of an ideal state of security. As such, however, it presents a more problematic narrative for the young or new to the area whose experiences bear little relation to that imagined past. It can both reinforce a perception of decline and suggest continuity, potentially of decline, either way reinforcing the lines of belonging.

One striking example of this echoing of a nostalgic history of the area was in a conversation with two young men in their early twenties who, as we walked into the city centre together, talked about the way that the area had changed, repeating the story of a peaceful, welcoming past. But the past they say they are describing is only five years ago, prior to a police crackdown on dealers on the estate. Looking back at the estate from a distance, they mourned the change:

PAUL   Like, every house used to be full there and we had like a top little community around here.

JACQUI   Yeah?

PAUL   Everyone's door was always open to you but …

JIM   … Yeah, you could leave your door open and that, you know, years ago, but now you can't …

PAUL   … There's only like, hundred houses and one road what goes round it so that's our own little community – well, used to be our own little community. Just our one estate.

This description of 'open doors' is associated with a highly localised sense of safety, which relies on being known and a fear of strangers (Anderson 1990; Merry 1981). Young teenagers at the youth club – young women, in particular – expressed just such a dislike and fear of other areas where they 'don't feel comfortable with anybody' (16 years old). However, the two young men quoted above used this image of open doors within a rather different story of a change in people's treatment of one another. Rather than continuity of neighbourliness they stressed the conflicts and material jealousy dividing the estate.

Their account harks back to an imagined past when people got along 'because no one had nothing' and so no reason to envy one another or maliciously 'grass one another up'. They related this directly to a time before the influx of heroin.

Their use of a nostalgic narrative picks up on a popular discourse of security and solidarity (of open doors) imagining a past from which the problems that they attribute to the present (conflicts, jealousy and grassing) are removed. This illustrates the forensic qualities of nostalgic narratives, identifying causes for decline. The change is, for these young men, a dismal reflection of the state of wider society and a downward trend reflected in the behaviour of people around them, in particular, the younger children who behave worse, they say, than they did. They do not attempt to distance themselves from other residents, the estate's decline or this rather hopeless future but instead claim the estate is their 'manor', telling me I had come to the right people as it was *their* estate.

The use of a nostalgic narrative to describe change in relation to an imagined past from which current problems are removed is at its most extreme in the account of Winnie, a woman in her seventies, who had lived on the estate since it was built. She relates a story of a past without children.

> The whole place was empty but we moved in here and … they sent us these letters telling us we'd get one of these houses and there'd be no kids, anyone that had young children wasn't allowed in here … So we came here, no kids, you know … so it was lovely, you know, peace, it was lovely. Then the people … they started moving out and then they were filling the houses and then they were bringing them with kids and that's how the estate went to the bad.

Winnie imposes on this happy remembrance an image of a time without those she now sees as the cause of decline. This creates contradictions in her story since she also describes having been harassed by children for being Irish ('Fenian') when she first moved in, and also now knowing everyone because she has known the young ones since they were small. She also had two children herself while living there. Now very much one of the 'original' residents, she has adopted a nostalgic narrative of decline and belonging reflecting this improvement in her position. Her description both identifies children as the cause of decline and excludes them from her sense of who 'belongs'. Conjuring an imagined past, these nostalgic accounts allow a judgement of the present by contrasting it with an ideal, an ideal that can also be tied to a conception of belonging and positive sense of identity.

Though suggestive of an extant community, the sense of belonging created and expressed through these nostalgic narratives has an exclusionary effect and for some this was an oppressive place. Those who do not share these rosy memories or experiences of inclusion distance themselves from this sense of belonging. This is particularly expressed through accounts of surviving though isolated. Others distance themselves further from belonging to the estate and from association with the trajectory of the place. The following two accounts mark a distinct contrast to the preceding nostalgia.

Sticking it out alone[7]

This description of isolation is in part expressed through another narrative of belonging to a group not necessarily associated with locality. The sense of security and connection found amongst that group is contrasted with the active exclusion or abuse they have experienced from people living on the estate. Some of those who considered themselves from an ethnic minority[8] related themselves and their life stories to varying degrees with the places from which they or their families originated and other parts of the city that they have in the past felt part of, or continue to feel so now.

Dave, for example, now in his fifties, related a story of his life that began with a nostalgic account of his adolescence in Jamaica, contrasted with his experiences of racist violence in Britain. There he was respected, and even if there was violence there would be some reason for it, compared to the random and irrational violence here. This is coupled with an assertion of the injustice of this treatment of Jamaicans in the face of their loyalty to the 'Mother Country' during and after the war, drawing on a colonial discourse of commitment to Britain.[9] However, he also rejects this discourse as the product of the 'brainwashing' and innocence that led his father to move here and then made him come too. His is not a nostalgic account of post-war Britain. Instead Jamaica sets the unchanging, imagined context for a criticism of Britain, both past and present.

Alongside this is his story of survival and strength, rejecting a colonial passiveness, and an assertion of a British-Jamaican identity, constructed through an account of standing up to the violent racism of white 'teddy boys' in the 1960s. However, Dave also used this account as a means of distinguishing Jamaican (male) identity from the essentialised 'black' of white racism. Though reluctant to talk at first, Dave was passionate in his delivery of his story, pacing the room and talking loudly for much of the interview.

> Well, the teddy boys, them were worst because they had flick knives, all sorts … From the moment they see you that's it. If you can't get out of it, you's gonna be dead … We couldn't go to a dance … to a picture … We have to have a gun so they don't just jump on you any more. They's too scared of us … And that's what *we* … That's what get to me … *Jamaicans* get rid of teddy boy. Yeah, no all these black. No African, no Barbadan, no Trinians, *Jamaicans* get rid of teddy boys … 'Cause we're not scared of 'em. We live in a country where police carry guns so we're used … to all this violence so … we wasn't gonna have it … No! We start retaliate and they have to stop it.

His description of the trajectory of change is a reversal of the nostalgic narratives of belonging to the estate, suggesting instead a gradual improvement (see also Loader and Mulcahy 2003: Chapter 5). Describing the irrational malice of people on the estate in the past, he sees their leaving as a blessing and those that have come since as better, reflecting a limited but society-wide improvement. Using the example of trying to bring up his three children on the estate, he stressed their vulnerability to abuse and his conflicts with other (racist) parents over the behaviour of their children.

> It used to cause more trouble but it's quite all right now, it's not as bad because most of them, they went. It was different people came and they was better.

For Dave there is no reason to look back at the history of the estate as rosy since his earliest experiences were worse than now. Despite the improvement in his position implied by this suggestion of progress, his position is relative and he still feels vulnerable to malicious accusation from neighbours.[10]

It is amongst stories of exclusion and exiled identity that there is a real sense of people's frustration, anger and fear at being trapped in a place in which they do not feel safe. Those telling such stories expressed a determination not to give in to the pressure from other residents to move, and stress their survival and strength in staying on, as if it was their choice. Unable to choose where to live, they were also unable to seek solace in belonging. For these residents their house plays a central role as a refuge in their stories of survival.

Of these the most besieged was a young woman, Irene, whom I had deliberately sought out because she had been mentioned so many times as an outsider or 'troublemaker'. Of Irish Traveller origin,[11] she had been housed on the estate when she became pregnant six years earlier. She described having been involved during that time in arguments with people on the estate which included several fights, her windows smashed while she and her children hid under the bed, and threats to burn her house down while she was in prison. She too explains the hostility as irrational racism and draws on a language of strength and survival to justify staying on, though she admits she has little choice.

> 'Cause the reason I stayed is I wouldn't give them the satisfaction to say they got me off the estate. Do you understand what I mean? I'll stay and stick it out and put up with the torture. Till I find a nice house for myself and somewhere to go to … If I had the money I'd have gone long ago … And the housing does, should know all about them … One certain person called me the other day and said if the housing is getting built around here I won't be moving into them … 'cause peoples around here are saying they don't want me on the estate, who I had the arguments with. … But that's not right, is it? … That's racist.

Both Dave and Irene express a profound sense of isolation, not merely from the estate but also from a wider society that they feel has been, and still is, prejudiced against them. In the face of such hostility they stress their strength and capacity to defend themselves when it became violent.

The future offered by a radical change in this place is more hopeful and justifies their having stuck it out this long – so long as they do not find themselves excluded again in the selection process for rehousing. Ironically this gives them a commitment to living in the area in the future that made them more anxious about the implications of the changes taking place and their isolated position. There were also those who told similar stories of embattled isolation but who expressed no desire to stay. Rather they stressed how long they had been on the housing list, waiting to leave.[12] But they too were wedded to this understanding of 'sticking it out alone'.

Keeping a distance

Markedly different, these last accounts tend to distance the speaker from the estate. Instead these residents associate themselves with their profession, church or social network unrelated to place. They express little sense of being trapped or surrounded though one described experiences of racial harassment.[13] Rather they describe their life decisions as chosen, and their residence here equally so, even if their options were limited. They stress the location and houses as factors that attracted and kept them here.

One couple who expressed this most clearly was Carl and Sue, in their early forties, who had had to move when their previous landlord had sold their house. Having moved of necessity this was at first just a place like any other. They describe their growing attachment to the area not in terms of its neighbourliness (though they do say it had a good 'community spirit' at one time) but of the likelihood of their buying there.

CARL   I mean, it was just another place just at first but then we become quite attached and see the potential of the area … you know, it was just a matter of watching to see what happened. Well, we'd have loved to have had a four-bedroomed anyway.

SUE   Oh, yes.

CARL   Probably if we did have one …

SUE   … we would have bought it …

CARL   … we would have bought it already, yeah. But at the moment we do want, we definitely don't want to move from here now …

SUE   … No, we want to stay in the area now, not because of the, it's so convenient for so many things, into town, you don't have to drive to town, you can walk into town …

CARL   It's convenient, it's very very convenient.

This does not suggest that they could not live anywhere else but that they like living on the estate because of its convenience and its future potential. Though watching what happens and hoping for improvement, they keep an emotional distance from an area in which they have lived for ten years. Similarly they describe their willingness to live there because they are on the edge, away from the trouble in the centre of the estate. Though aware of problems they repeatedly assure me that it has never affected them. They maintain a distance from the immediate area, describing their networks in relation to the church they attend elsewhere, their work and friends and family in other cities. Although investing in a business nearby, involved in city-wide ethnic minority and community groups and in the past heavily involved in the campaign to save the local primary school, they imply that these investments have been rational rather than emotional, as choices rather than ties. Now cynical about the likely success of participation processes (in the light of the failure of the primary school campaign) they are sceptical about becoming involved in the regeneration process.

This narrative of distance is mirrored in the rather different account of a relative newcomer (only four years). Pete, in his early thirties, associated himself less with institutional ties and referred to his social network (through gambling) only as 'associates' not friends. Pete too describes the estate as a place like any other, with no more than, if not fewer, problems than other places he has lived. He stresses his desire to keep himself to himself[14] and maintain his independence relishing his anonymity and guarding his privacy from the gossip of this 'tight' community. When asked if he knew his neighbours, he replied:

Yeah I know the neighbours, I know a few others round here and things like that. I just say hello, do whatever I've gotta do and just mind me own business like ... Come home, watch the telly or video, whatever, and just go to bed. Just keep myself to myself ... That don't bother me like. I mean I just enjoy myself really, just me, that's it.

More limited in his financial ability to leave than Sue and Carl, Pete asserts an extreme independence, insisting that he has 'great fun' thinking only about himself, avoiding intimacy with other people,[15] despite the presence of his girlfriend and baby. Although this is an extreme version of keeping a distance, and superficially very different from identification with social institutions and professions, these residents share a common value of independence, in contrast to the stigmatised 'dependence' of those around them. They maintain a description of themselves as able to control their lives and make decisions, regardless of where they live.

These accounts distance the speaker from identification with the place they live, both viewing it with detachment and detaching themselves from it. They are able to distance themselves from the stigma attached to the place and the people living there. However, their insistence on their independence and their capacity to choose their own course adopts a language of individual agency that denies the limited scope of the choices available to them and ascribes their position to character (Sennett 1998). This leaves them potentially open to a sense of failure due to character, despite these assurances of individual strength. Less able to maintain a narrative of choice, Pete takes his to an extreme of a series of stories of events that happen to him and around him but that he survives alone and untouched. In Pete's case this narrative can thereby verge on fatalism (Linde 1993; Douglas 1986).

Imagining place: the uses of nostalgic narratives

What these nostalgic narratives of belonging, and those of exclusion or distance, begin to illustrate are some underlying differences amongst residents' accounts that spring from their experiences of their position both in the wider world and on the estate. They outline the importance many of these residents attach to their status in this locality (or sense of exclusion from it), with the exception of those who keep their distance from it, though even then their self-image is to a degree relative to those that live in the area. Nostalgic stories of the area's past can seem, to an outsider, evidence of a close-knit, supportive, organic community. There is a danger of accepting nostalgic narratives as indicative of a unified identity or community, rather than a desire for security.

Contrasting an ideal with a flawed reality, nostalgic narratives offer a forensic resource through which to identify threats and lines of belonging (Douglas 1992). The exclusionary effect of this nostalgic narrative lies in this forensic capacity and resort to an essentialism in the face of change (Young 2001). Even amongst those who appear united by this rosy image of the past there lie deep divisions between constitutions of belonging and blame for decline. Although this estate retained some of its original residents and many shared a narrative of continuity of 'community', its use also supported exclusionary discourses that made it a potentially threatening place for newcomers and identifiable 'others' to live. Those able to survive this outsider status seemingly unscathed distanced themselves from emotional attachment to the place, even if willing to invest in it. During the consultation process issues of providing an 'authentic', as much as representative, voice of this community made a process of establishing who was part of the community, or not, particularly urgent and important to claims for prominence in the consultation process.

Notes

1 One narrative of belonging to place is split here ('born and bred', 'surviving community' and 'learning to be local') to reflect the contested nature of 'belonging' and a generational difference in orientation to the future and commitment to place. I have implied these further differences and blurred lines on purpose to distance these narratives from a sense of determinism.

2 All names have been changed to preserve anonymity.

3 References to an idyllic childhood in life stories have been seen as a means of creating a 'defended self' (Hollway and Jefferson 1997) or a way of looking back to a time when they were valued and respected (Davis 1979). While they may reflect a search for security or claim to identity, the significance of these stories should not be over-stretched.

4 Equally so in presenting themselves to me as a person writing about Millton.

5 Unfortunately I had since mentioned my own background as daughter of a single parent and he filtered out these references substantially thereafter.

6 Referring to a brief move out to the suburbs when she was married.

7 I do not mean to suggest that a sense of isolation and the use of a narrative of nostalgia are mutually exclusive. One elderly man, for example, 'born and bred' in the area, looked back on a time when he had felt part of the area before his wife died. However, the abuse his disabled son had received and disputes with neighbours and children had left him feeling as isolated and excluded as those who do not look back with nostalgia. Like others, he uses that nostalgic narrative to reconcile his sense of belonging with his changed position and desire to leave.

8 Although most of those who used this narrative considered themselves part of an ethnic minority this is not a narrative unique to them, nor do those who consider themselves part of a minority ethnic group exclusively use this narrative.

9 In this he mirrors the 'juggling' of identities observed within immigrant life stories (Revill 1993), in part a process of 'identification' by which a sense of self is constantly redrawn but which can appear particularly contradictory in the way they bring together multiple discourses of identity, including colonial.

10 He was the only resident to refuse the tape recorder at first (but took pity on me after a short period of note-taking) and looked alarmed when I acknowledged him in public once. He seemed nervous of how others might react.

11 Irish Traveller refers to a minority group that, in Ireland, lays claims to distinct ethnicity (Helleiner and Szuchewyzc, 1997).

12 I will explore these further in Chapter 5.

13 Although all those who used these narratives were of ethnic minority origin their use of these narratives seemed unrelated to ethnic identification and so I have not stressed this. However, they did contrast themselves to those who 'belonged' to the estate. This distance may have been heightened by their perceived 'otherness' but also reflected their constitution of themselves as independent individuals.

14 This contrasts to others who use this language in reference to not 'grassing' but then, once relaxed, talk more freely within a nostalgic narrative of belonging.

15 He also described his life as being troubled by difficult relationships with family and partners, which I felt impacted greatly on his desire for independence.

Chapter 5

Relating to others

The ways in which residents used narratives of belonging echo some classic discourses of 'us and them', identifying and denigrating others while reinforcing a positive self-image (Riggins 1997). This plays down negative qualities of 'us' and heightens a focus on the negative qualities of 'them', identifying 'them' as a threat to the security or values of the community. As such it can mask disharmony amongst community relationships and exaggerate the threats and problems caused by 'others'. A narrative of decline of community also belied some clearly close relationships between residents, which, though often not visible because of a lack of public indoor spaces, continued to be sustained in visits to each other's houses.

Gaining an impression of relationships on the estate was made difficult by the privacy of such relationships. Nevertheless, the difficulties of 'snowballing' were a swift lesson in the tensions between residents. It was also possible to observe people mixing at public events and when my visits to residents happened to overlap with people dropping by to see them. Consultation events, wandering around the estate, bonfire night and 'clear-ups' of the estate gave me opportunities to participate in events at which residents came together and to hear and observe gossip and discussion. Not only did people tend to group in very separate pockets (to the extent of having five bonfires in close proximity) but these divisions figured large in the way people talked about problematic 'others'.

This chapter is concerned with the way people constitute local problems in relation to dangerous 'others', in particular through discourses of pollution, defilement and invasion (Douglas 1966; Hacking 2003; Sibley 1995). Importantly, how residents constituted others was contrasted with a positive sense of themselves, identified, as Chapter 4 suggested, in markedly different ways. They describe rather different groups of 'others' in different terms and highlight somewhat different problems for which they blame these 'others'. Firstly, a broad narrative of belonging to place constitutes newcomers, strangers and traitors in contrast to a notion of themselves as supportive, welcoming and loyal, though being 'born and bred' was a more exclusive belonging than that of 'surviving community' or of those 'learning to be local'. Secondly, those who used a narrative of lost 'family values' conceived of themselves as 'decent' in contrast to widespread immorality. A third narrative of 'sticking it out alone' expresses the strength in isolation of those on the receiving end of the violent irrationality of those who constitute them as 'other'. Finally, a narrative of keeping a distance is the least explicitly othering but talks in terms of independence, implicitly but silently contrasted with the stigma of dependence attached to council estates. I will begin with the narrative of 'decency', which is most clearly expressed through a language of defilement and cleanliness.

Decency and immorality

The polarisation between good and bad within these accounts explicitly hinges around notions of morality as a fixed set of rules or values. Respectable, 'decent' behaviour is contrasted with immorality, with striking references to cleanliness and dirt through which these moral differences are expressed. Contrasting themselves to others' dirt, those who use this narrative frequently refer to their own cleanliness, particularly in their house and its immediate surroundings. A value system that at first seemed to bear little relation to place is, through this discourse, rooted in a strongly spatial and personal dimension. Equally, those who use it refer to those who are not like them as 'over there' or 'that side' or in the next street, apparently easily identifiable by their dirt.

Dumping rubbish

Most strongly expressing this distinction, Barbara and Rick, an elderly couple[1] living in the centre of the estate, were very specific about the distinct parts of the estate that had gone downhill, separating their row from others and identifying the worst culprits close to them. 'It has gone down, though this part hasn't, this part is good. On that row, they are good, but it's over here [pointing to another row].' When I asked what Barbara did not like about them she talked about their neglect of their houses and gardens, expressing an interpretation of disorderly appearance as 'not caring' (Wilson and Kelling 1982).

> They just don't care what they do. You know, the houses, they– they've just left 'em. I mean, I've got a garden there ... but what you've got to look at is the grass, it's growing like that and weeds and all what not, and then they start throwing, we've got an island in the middle there and they're throwing rubbish on that so, erm, I just don't want to get next to 'em.

She tries to get on with them, she says, but her husband explains, 'They aren't very clean.' Their houses and gardens indicate the disorderly, undisciplined nature of these people. By contrast the couple nostalgically recall how nice and *clean* people were before things went downhill.

Rick argues that they need to put 'decent' people into the houses 'who would look after them'. This understanding of 'decent' people makes them very easy to spot by looking at the condition of their houses. The poor condition of the estate to Barbara and Pete says much about the people who surround them and who they blame for its decline.

> BARBARA   It's a dump. It is a dump. *Now* it is. Never used to be. I mean the people that had these houses before used to cut all the grass out there at their fronts, but not now, not these that's in 'em now, leave 'em ...

> RICK   I mean, how people round here, if the dustbin is not, they don't, they no empty 'em because they're, they're too lazy to get out ... They dump all their bags somewhere round here ... in empty houses.

For Barbara and Rick this rubbish, the key problem they identify in the area, is a sign of a decline in the respectability of those living around them. The dumping of rubbish is a problem (of defilement) in itself but is also an indication of the character of neighbours who are described in these terms as other. In contrast, Barbara frequently drew my attention to the state of her house and her maintenance

An example of a proud display of respectability in one corner of the estate

of her garden. Just as important in identifying indecency amongst others, this outward appearance of her house displayed her own respectability to the outside world.

Maintaining boundaries

Similarly, the space in and around the house could create a sense of separation from the disorder beyond it, as a sanctuary keeping the otherness out (Sibley 1995).[2] Doris, in her sixties and retired, also continually pointed out how much she needed to clean and redecorate her immaculate house. Like Barbara and Rick, she distinguished her part of the estate from the rest. 'See there is only that row belong to this estate, what we say is *our* estate.' Having maintained her house well she sees its possible demolition, because others have damaged the estate, as unjust. She does not want to move:

> I've not done anything to make this area a mess. I've tried to … I'm the only one that ever goes out and sweeps the front here. I am out here some nights at 10 o'clock, when you see the odd bobby passing in his van, and he goes like that to me [friendly waving and smiles]. And I think, bet they think 'that bloody woman is crackers out there, sweeping up the front.' But it's a thing that I've always done. And I go out where there's cameras out on the road, and I'm 66! And all the young 'uns'll walk past it, on the road and all that … and they say to me, 'You don't work for the bloody Corporation.'[3]

This story of young people teasing Doris for doing a job which they do not see as her responsibility is implicitly one of changing values. Even the policeman, symbolic of order, must think she is mad, but there is an implicit vindication in the reference to his waving at her. She maintains her corner of the world, in contrast to other people's neglect. Despite the danger out there, indicated by the presence of cameras, she, though vulnerable, is brave enough to sweep. It is a short story of defiance of an otherwise threatening presence. Her conflicts with 'young 'uns' feature heavily in talking about the space around her house. At the back she has put up a large fence to stop stones being thrown through 'so that they can't see me and I don't want to see them'. At the front she sweeps and keeps the area free of dirt. Her activity, she suggests, has also stopped young people hanging around and deters them from the empty house next door 'because they know how we have been here and kept it', demonstrating, she suggests, a willingness to report them (Merry 1981). Going out on to the road, mowing and planting flowers in the grassy area opposite is a way of creating a space that keeps others away. It gives out a message both of respectability and of separation and exclusivity.

Noise

Doris goes to considerable lengths to keep these influences away from her property and sees it as her place of retreat from the rest of the estate. However she never goes out alone, because she feels an easy target, which sounds more like being trapped. Despite her efforts to exclude the estate she cannot keep out noise and this forms another layer to her characterisation of disruptive others. The shop figures large in her account of decline. Responding to my asking if things have changed on the estate while she has lived here, she says that 'it has changed a lot since they pulled that shop down! We can go to bed and we can go to sleep!' The noise had been 'terrible':

DORIS   … and yet it was only lads from round here. I mean some of these people, it was their children, you know, what they don't seem to care about … I mean, now, they are all round [pub further away] … It's terrible round there of a night, terrible … We've not had very much trouble with the pub … It's been that shop.

JACQUI   And what was the problem? With them drinking?

DORIS   Well, it was drinking and it was the stolen cars and, you know. They used to be there until 2, 3 o'clock in the morning. Then it would break up, then the next you ... It was all the cars, screaming and shouting round, you know. Never got to sleep.

The noise worried and affected her, not only because she could not sleep but also because it invaded her otherwise protected space. She was made conscious of these people's dangerous proximity. Those she blames for ruining the estate are almost entirely from the next street ('the Drive') and it is their children she thinks make all the noise. She talks about the behaviour of adults from 'the Drive' in the same terms, of their 'shouting and screaming'. Again she points out the injustice that those same people go to consultation meetings and shout about the condition of the estate when it was their lack of control of their children's behaviour that caused it.

It has gone down, but it's gone down for the people that's *let* it go, the ones who do all the shouting [at meetings] ... but it's their kids that's done it. But their kids are growing up now. But they're still hanging around street corners. My kids have never hung around, you know ... [the] Drive is a lot to do with what's gone on round 'ere ... and when you go to meetings, they don't, er, you just sit away from 'em. I mean, it is just a different part ... to round, just here.

Their 'screaming and shouting', the cars and noise, and even stories of children walking around with hammers and axes or tying other children up in trees, form an unequivocal story of how threatened Doris feels by people from 'the Drive' and, by association, their noise. She does not want to know about it, or be near it, but cannot keep it out. Her extreme separation from the rest of the estate perhaps makes the invasion of noise across the boundaries that she has erected, and so assiduously maintained, the more anxiety-creating for her.

Rotten apples

These accounts associate 'decency' with good maintenance of homes and gardens, as visible signs by which people can be judged. However, their emphasis on cleanliness and defilement is overlain with different nuances in the ways in which men, in particular, talk about otherness and respectability.[4] So Jack, priding himself on his 'family values', describes the indecent, who have caused the decline of the estate, not only in relation to their unkempt houses but also in reference to their deviance from the sexual respectability of traditional family structure. In particular, prostitution symbolises this moral decay, their immorality affecting others and spreading the rot.

> You get one bad apple and it does ... you get prostitution and like, er, but we've thought about ... particular families that were living over there, and spoke to the council about it and said 'Why with us? We'd be all right if it weren't for them', and she said [housing officer], 'You'll bring them up to your level.' I said, 'They don't, they just drag the rest of the estate down.'... Their kids ... you talk to them, but they never did anything to 'em ... just let their kids carry on, their kids, their kids, that's what happened round here.

Again his focus is on lack of parental control of children, particularly by their mothers. He describes a decay in the behaviour and discipline of families and their potential to infect the rest of the estate, dragging it down to their level of immorality. Their presence has an impact on the reputation of the estate and he does not want to be 'tarred with the same brush'.

These residents' accounts of the area's decline distinguish themselves from the rest of the estate. Rick, in response to my repetition of his sigh about 'too many changes', began talking about another group of 'others', again described in terms of their dirt and disorder, whom he and his wife blamed for the decline of the area's reputation.

> RICK   And then you've got all the dark–loads of Irish people, haven't you?
>
> BARBARA Oh, yeah, donkeys running down the streets!
>
> JACQUI Donkeys?
>
> RICK   Yeah, oh aye, donkeys, machinery, machinery ...
>
> BARBARA You walk down t'lane you'd see all t'horses tied up, wouldn't you? ... Thought, what's it coming to, this estate? ... Used to be terrible down there till they pulled them houses down. Honest to God, people used to say, never taxis, they'd say ... 'No, I'm not taking you on

there ... they'd bloody rob me.' ... And we used to get that. I said, 'don't class everyone the same'.

Quickly diverting from talking about the 'dark ... [ies]', which he presumably thought unacceptable, Rick shifts to talking about the 'Irish' and the chaos caused by their animals and machinery.[5] Blaming the reluctance of taxis to come to the estate on their presence, and implicitly assuming they are thieves, the couple associate the decline (into criminality) and loss of reputation with their arrival. Again concerned not to be tarred with the same brush, they imply that the impact these people had on the appearance and reputation of the estate also affected how respectable people outside it saw them.

A connection made within descriptions between 'others' and dirty objects that surround them is particularly explicit here. Whether rubbish, scrap metal or animals, these are objects that defile or contaminate the estate in the same way that the immoral and undisciplined are described as 'rotten apples'. It is a discourse of disgust used here by those who are acutely aware of the stigma attached to the area and who do their best to distinguish themselves, both discursively and visibly, from these 'others'.

Coming from such isolated positions, these accounts compound the sense of isolation with this exclusiveness. Their emphasis is on residents' responsibility for maintaining their property and their values, and they identify problems *within* the estate. The resonance between this narrative and an understanding of responses to 'signs' of decline that inform a 'broken windows' theory is very apparent here. This reflects shared interpretations of visible disorder as indicative of a decline in moral responsibility. This is not an assumption shared by other residents using other causal explanations of decline, if they mentioned it at all. Their accounts contrast greatly with a second narrative, which instead stresses the impact of 'strangers' on the surviving community and the responsibility of the Council for the maintenance of the estate.

Belonging and strangers/newcomers

As I have already suggested in Chapter 4, the notion of whether a person is 'from here' or not could vary with definition of belonging, the fragility of that status a part of its power. This was often expressed as being 'known', by reputation or personally, an assertion of both belonging and safety (because I'm 'known'), despite contradictory stories of people also knowing those who had burgled them. Constituted in opposition to the 'good' people who live here 'outsiders' are, within these accounts, threatening and traitorous, both causing, and being in themselves, the problems on the estate. There is a much stronger emphasis on the problems caused by the Council having allocated houses to 'strangers' when residents died or moved away, a policy often interpreted as deliberately driving the existing community out.

Driving us out and moving them in

So Tom, a man in his late forties, trying to describe the changes on the estate brought it down to 'bringing strangers, like I call strangers, on to the estate, yeah, who has no sympathy, no loyalty.' When I asked where they were from he started to tell an often-repeated story of the council advertising elsewhere for tenants, again referring to the arrival of 'the Irish'.

> From what, from what I understand and I don't know how true it is, I've heard the Council advertised in Wales and in Ireland for tenants … So we got a few Irish families in. Now I mean … say [name], he's Irish, you've only got to get two more of 'em people and that's it. And that's what happened basically. Anyway it ended up with a shooting [Yeah?] Yeah, there was a lot of trouble, I mean. That was probably … that was probably the worst time.

Although it's not clear whether or not he is referring to travellers, Tom associates Irishness with violence, perhaps reflecting sectarian conflict in his childhood to which he refers,[6] or stereotypes formed through media coverage of the Northern Ireland conflict. It only needs two or three Irish people to come into the place to make things fall apart, he asserts, directly attributing blame to these outsiders for an escalation in violence that culminated in a shooting.

Importantly, Tom's story ties this influx of 'Irish' explicitly to what he believes to be the housing allocation policies of the Council. The rumour of advertising elsewhere for tenants lends credence to the fear that the Council is deliberately moving people from other places into the estate, in an attempt, Tom goes on to suggest, to drive out people like him. In his view this deliberate introduction of outsiders is proved by the contrasting difficulty experienced by relatives of existing residents in securing a house on the estate.

Tom's reference to the lack of 'loyalty and sympathy' of these 'strangers' is tied to a notion of protecting the area from officials and an unwillingness of loyal residents to give information about one another. So, for instance, when talking about the problems caused by one of these outsiders, 'Irish Irene', Kate describes her as 'grassing people up left, right and centre' and possibly even as 'planted by the Council' to get people out of the estate. She, like all who use this understanding of belonging, implies that she can speak for everyone:

> I don't know whether she's been planted here off the housing to scare people off, you know, because a lot o' people ... they'd be scared at the sound of her Irish accent, you know what I mean. Whereas we know she's full o' shit, you know what I mean ... You get to that stage, you think, 'fuck it, bring who the fuck you like' ... Three times I've battered her and not knocked no sense into her one bit ... What can I fucking do? It's not sinking in, you know.

Kate's story of justifying violence implies self/community-defence from the danger Irene poses, but also on the grounds of teaching her a lesson, to know her place. Also described as causing trouble *for herself* by being too 'in your face', Irene is blamed for having breached rules of more passive integration, though this again provides justification for racism (Helleiner and Szuchewycz 1997; Riggins 1997). Her foreignness is tied to not knowing whether she can be trusted not to 'grass'.

Tom, in particular, associates strangers' arrival with potential vulnerability to interference from officials. 'If you get a total stranger family on this estate they [the residents] are very, very suspicious, very suspicious.' If not related to existing residents, you are automatically suspected and seen as threatening, whether as an informer or, as with the last person to move on, as a paedophile. When asked why this person was suspected of being a paedophile, he explained:

> Everybody knows everybody. Someone strange comes in they all look, they all want to know who it is. They know strangers straight away ... And we had this guy came on, one guy and his kid, both of 'em from Blackpool, you know ... So the obvious thing is 'Why are they gonna leave Blackpool to come on the [*] Estate? There's something wrong with 'em.' And the obvious thing is, 'He's a paedophile' [*laughs*], right, and he got shunned ... And he might have been, we don't know ... and then apparently he left very suddenly, which prompts the question, he probably *was* under police protection ... If there's

somebody on the estate who they don't know they feel very, very vulnerable to them.

The leap to thinking that this stranger must have been a paedophile is justified in relation to not understanding why any outsider would want to live on the estate, that this is purely an allocation made by the Council. Tom laughs about these suspicions in retrospect, though continues to hint at reasons for suspecting this family of being under protection of some kind (implicitly perhaps a 'grass'). He paints a sympathetic picture of residents, stressing their vulnerability to the newcomer. They are vulnerable both to dangerous strangers in themselves and to their ability to expose residents to the gaze of officials, he explains, because people on the poverty line make ends meet by operating on the borders of illegality. Without knowing all about someone and being sure of their 'loyalty and sympathy', people feel exposed. However, it is the potential danger to children posed by strangers that he emphasises, spreading the blame to the Council for housing paedophiles and mitigating any blame that could be directed at residents for harbouring suspicions.

Defending the area

This description of the influx of 'foreigners' causes contradictions with nostalgic narratives of decline. Tracy, for example, when talking about the loss of the old Millton families, qualifies her story of lost community with an acknowledgement that people still know each other and so can spot strangers. She talks confidently about feeling safe because she knows everyone and they know her. Like Tom, she explains this sense of 'being known' in terms of 'territory ... Yeah, like everywhere, be suspicious ... They know who's ... If someone strange come into the area, 'what they up to?' This initiates a story to illustrate how much people defend the area from strangers. However, it is significant that this is a story about two 'black' strangers, the emphasis on their colour reflecting racialised assumptions of dangerousness. Tracy's friends, having watched these men for two weeks – 'not always the same two black fellas and in three different cars' – they 'pulled them and asked, 'what you doing round here?'

TRACY   Wouldn't tell them where they lived or anything like that, so he just said to her, 'Well, you won't see us again now'.

JACQUI So what do you think they were doing?

TRACY Don't know what they was doing, but when you've got kids and that you can't, you know … kids get took away now, you can't risk anyone like that being … hanging about, but that's what I'm trying to say to you about anyone strange. They watch you know, if they see you a bit too often.

Her story again justifies this watchful suspicion as protective of children against dangerous outsiders. These accounts are full of stories of dangerous 'others' coming in from outside, the ultimate dangerous strangers being black men or paedophiles. These stories stress threats (risks) posed to the most vulnerable, especially children and elderly, representing the innocence and vulnerability of people living on the estate, in need of defending.

Defending the vulnerable

Associated with the worst moments in the decline of the estate, like the shooting in Tom's account, these stories of invasion often link the presence of strangers with a climax of random violence. Such stories relate to events that pose a threat to the innocent, particularly in relation to dangers created by drug dealing on the estate. Kate, for example, talks about the horror of 'a black man' chasing a dealer through her house, and, on another occasion, cars being driven across the grass chasing other dealers, as dramatic exemplars of the scale of the problems on the estate.

It was rife, honest to God and you was scared of a night to walk out, you know, because there was always flying … You know, the green hills over there a bit. Was all stood there once with the kids. Well, my kids was only small toddlers playing about in the grass and you're stood watching 'em, talking, and the next thing there's a car full of coloured lads comes flying on the grass and it … it could'a killed any one of the kids, didn't give a fuck. But it was chasing these dealers, you know what I mean, and you're thinking, fucking hell, what's …

Again referring to the colour of the drivers implicitly heightens their dangerousness. As in the stories of violent Irish people, these stories often link black men with guns. So, continuing with her account of how frightening was this car chase, she links the danger they pose to stories of gun violence in Moss Side[7] and a shooting there at about that time. The problems associated with dealing are constituted as those of bringing on to the estate dangerous outsiders who are competing for the drug trade. Again it is the risk they pose to children, rather than to herself, that Kate emphasises as a way of bringing home the story of innocence in the face of danger. Displacing blame away from the local dealers, however, she tells this story to highlight how bad things had to get before the police did anything about it. Such stories of random shootings or other threats to innocent bystanders stress the justifiable fears of vulnerable residents in the face of such threats and emphasise the need for authorities to protect them.

There is, however, a dilemma posed by the protection of people who belong and are involved in illegal activity but who may also be bringing strangers into the area and so exposing residents to danger. The problems associated with drug dealing and the trouble at the local shop are constituted in these terms, as bringing in outsiders who cause the problems, thus displacing blame away from community members. This dilemma was one that Kate and her mother Doreen expressed in their attempt to explain the dangers posed by 'smackheads' (heroin addicts) in the area.

DOREEN   You get them squatting in the old houses, not the ... you see ... we used to have, just have drug dealers here.

KATE   Yeah, but he just ... Walking about, old people were getting robbed all the time ...

DOREEN   ... left, right and centre, yeah.

KATE   You know, because the dealer was, dealers was bringing 'em on, you know.

Unwilling to blame dealers who 'belong' but at the same time blaming them for bringing in addicts who then rob the vulnerable, they overcome a sense of divided loyalty by blaming 'others'. Kate blames the (Pakistani) shopkeeper for letting people deal nearby and sees the demolition of the shop as a decision made by local authorities to get rid of dealing. More importantly, she explains the growth of drug dealing and increased numbers of addicts on the estate as the result of the opening of a needle exchange nearby, again turning attention (and blame) on to the actions of official outsiders.

One woman related a telling account of a group of 'mothers' who negotiated a peace with local dealers, asking them to deal less openly in front of children. Though dealing persisted it was subsequently less blatant and in return, dealers contributed money for local events. Though this resident found this move morally ambiguous she described the situation as 'better to be with people that you know than [those] you don't know ... It worked both ways ... As long as they were keeping their part of the bargain so we kept ours, you know.' This story of reciprocity with local dealers lies in stark contrast to the treatment of outsiders.

Defending community

Having reached that peak of danger though, in Kate's eyes, the estate is now 'back to normal', close to a nostalgic ideal (if the old families were to come back). This contrasting peace is constituted around a lack of outsiders, even if the estate is almost empty. But achieving this ideal defence from an outside world would require some closely guarded boundaries. Ian, though with a very restrictive notion of who belongs (only 'old' families), is not alone in expressing a desire to build a wall around the estate to prevent strangers from coming in:

> If I had a choice, when they've built this estate, build a 12-foot wall round it to keep 'em out.

Some of the young boys (aged between 13 and 15) at the youth centre also expressed this image of an ideal 'gated community' capable of keeping out the dangers and harassment from both strangers and police, unless the latter were needed:

WILL   Well, I think there should be a big fence round one area, and have a pass to get in where you live.

JACQUI   Yeah?

WILL   Yeah.

JACQUI   Why would you like that?

WILL   So no one could come in. Like bad people.

CHRIS   Yeah ...

STEVE   Fences and things, you know, so people can't come in and with guns and all that.

WILL   And keep the police out.

CHRIS   Keep the police out.

STEVE   Want no police, yeah ...

WILL   Don't want no police.

STEVE   Just when you need 'em, like people robbing cars.

Amongst these young boys the distinctions between people who belong and do not are more blatantly[8] racist but can also include drug addicts as 'others' to be kept out or in their place. When I asked these boys what the problems were in the area they gave me a list of outsiders – 'pakis, paedophiles, smackheads' – and talked about getting them out, if they could, or going 'baghead[9] bashing' to punish and keep the addicts who robbed away from the area. Whether these addicts belonged or not was problematic and they seemed to occupy a position on the borders of belonging that depended on their behaviour. Like those who 'grass' they were seen as traitors and subject to internal control. The boys also prided themselves on an active maintenance of territorial borders through violence, to keep 'blacks with guns' out.

These accounts of the estate emphasise the impact of dangerous others in the past and the continued threat they pose to the vulnerable and innocent community, symbolised by children and the elderly. They constitute local problems in these terms as caused by outsiders or traitors. These strangers or traitors are described as a threat to the values of this community, to 'loyalty and sympathy', as well as a physical danger (risk); an understanding that attempts to foster a positive impression of those conscious of being seen as violent and to blame for, or at least complicit in, the decline of the area. Tom, for example, insists that though 'people think we're Millwall supporters', the violence is coming in from outside. Seen as violent, they stress the violence of others. Throughout these accounts decline and local problems are described as caused by outsiders. Though this position is difficult to sustain when some of the dealers live on the estate, as do some of the addicts and 'kids', this understanding of 'us and them' either denies belonging or mitigates against a poor group-image through a displacement of blame to authorities. Ironically, these accounts share an understanding of official negligence, to which I will return in more detail in Chapter 6, with those who experience being seen as outsiders on the estate, a narrative reflecting a similar sense of powerlessness in relation to authorities. Although denigrating outsiders, the accounts above emerge from a position of powerlessness relative to the outside world and though expressed through an experience of relative power on the estate, that position is both fragile and limited to the estate. Without that sense of bounded security and status, the third narrative evokes the experience of 'being other'.

Being other

This third perspective expresses isolation compounded by an acute awareness of prejudice against those who use it, an understanding which informs an interpretation of their vulnerable position on the estate and the problems this creates for them. Equally polarised, their description of their relationships with other residents is expressed through a language of *me* against them. In this they share some of the understandings of their position with those using a narrative of 'decency', particularly in their description of their home as a sanctuary. But their narrative expresses a more beleaguered sense of vulnerability to attack and a description of others, including authorities, as complicit in the attacks made on them. Acutely conscious of perceptions of them on the estate and in the rest of society, they describe themselves as other. They tend to characterise those who are prejudiced against them in the same terms through which they are denigrated, turning racist and derogatory discourses on their head.

Besieged

The most besieged of these accounts is that of Irene, the young (mid-20s) Irish woman commonly referred to as a 'troublemaker' by other residents. She describes the rest of the estate in terms of large families, united against her. 'If one comes to your door and the whole army, do you understand what I mean, you get all the families coming to your door.' This escalates to the whole estate when

The whole neighbourhood gangs up on me … Then it stops for a bit and then its back up again. Do you understand what I mean? And then the police come on the estate, somebody's house got busted in. They all come to me.

She echoes narratives of belonging in suggesting a united estate undermined by grassing and her belief that residents suspect her of informing. She describes herself as a scapegoat. They 'pick on' her because 'they know I'm on me own and I've got a nice house, the kids is always very smartly dressed', implying that they are jealous of her. Emphasising her cleanliness, she counters the depictions of her, or other Irish travellers, as dirty. Like some of the 'decent' women above she apologises for her (pristine) house and points out how much work she has done to it. Though she explains this scapegoating as racism because she is Irish, she argues that they 'pick on' her because they perceive her as an easy target. Isolated and vulnerable, she suggests they see her as weak in having no extended family to back her up.

If I had family living round here I wouldn't think they'd do half the things. They wouldn't even think of coming in the door. See I'm not moving. Every day you open your front door and you're wondering what's going to happen next. And you wonder what your day is going to turn out like and you wonder who went to the housing and told something to the housing about you. Do you understand what I mean?

Not only do people think she is a 'grass', Irene also thinks people are reporting her to the housing authority and trying to get her out, which, in fact, several people said that they were doing. She highlights their hypocrisy in their willingness to do to her what they accuse her of. Without the support of an extended family she feels exposed both to being attacked on her doorstep and to being reported to the housing authority for what she sees as 'petty' arguments over children's behaviour. Her stories of people coming to her door, surrounding the house in the middle of the night and threatening to burn it down accentuate her sense of being hemmed in by this hostility, and the haven she has created being constantly under attack. While others describe beating her,[10] Irene stresses the threats to her home, communicating her sense of being under siege. Countering this image of weakness she emphasises her strength in staying on, not only in surviving but also through studied behaviour that signals to others that she is strong (Merry 1981).

Isolated

This account of being under siege is at its most extreme in Irene's descriptions of attacks on her home, but threats of impending violence are a feature of other similar accounts. Any other problems in the area pale in comparison and hardly feature in their conversations with me. When he first moved to the estate Dave, the Jamaican pensioner introduced in Chapter 4, found people were 'like animals over here', a reference to the violence of people on the estate. Using the same language to describe them as he used in describing the way he was treated on first arriving in Britain, when his family were also treated 'like animals', he subverts the bestial discourse of racism, suggesting instead that racists are themselves inhuman in their violence.

Like Irene he describes large families uniting against him. In one such story, after being spat at by a boy through his window, he had gone out and hit the boy, bringing the whole family to his door later. Fearing for his own safety he had gone out and threatened them with a knife and they had run off and called the police. Their reaction was, he implies, unreasonable and, though such troubles have reduced since a lot of these families have left, people could still be unpredictable. When I asked him if he had ever tried to tell the council about the problems, he said that he had not but that they knew anyway. Like Irene, he believed that the authorities knew what happened on the estate and he accounted for the changes in occupancy as action taken by the council to get rid of those families.

> They knew what was going on. That's why they get rid of so much of them because some of them was ... tinkers ... And we wouldn't have it right because they was too bad. Right and they, they, they, they had to put them somewhere else ... They used to use this estate as a dumping ground ... Them what wrecked the estate and they threw them off.

His description of the decline of the estate begins here to sound a little like those who saw outsiders as the problem and he drops into talking about 'we' as he talks about the 'tinkers', whose behaviour would not be tolerated. Describing them in terms of a discourse of disgust, the council having using the estate as a 'dumping ground' (for 'rubbish'), he blames these others for the condition of the estate.

Though throughout the rest of his account he uses stories of isolation and defence, in this identification of a group lower in the pecking order than himself, he begins to adopt a language of belonging.

However, despite his continual assurances that he can fight his own corner, Dave's focus on the security of his house echoes the isolation and defended boundaries of Irene. Worried by children climbing through his garden, who might create trouble for him with their parents, wanting his fence put back up and his door made secure, his concern for his invaded boundaries and their vulnerability to breach again communicates a sense of being under threat, especially now that the estate stands half empty.

> The area, the only thing we need now is just, just to secure us until they fix it … I just want my home secure a little more, you know what I mean … I just don't like how they close them all, the houses, them on my own and do you know, man. The guys them ride around on the bicycles and look and look and they know what's going on.

Although he has never been burgled he talks about the danger these guys on bikes pose, as a watchful presence, able to catch him when he is out and burgle his house. This sense of being watched and surrounded in their homes, and that the council know what is going on but do nothing, is a feature of these accounts. This reflects a dual sense of powerlessness in relation to other residents and authorities. As such they feel an easy target.

Targeted

For Tim, a Vietnamese man living on the estate with his elderly mother, this isolation was expressed through a very disturbing sense of being watched and targeted. He tells a story of walking home when he had been targeted in this way by a driver:

> There was a day that I almost got hit by an Englishman[11] driving a car. The reason behind that, I think, is that he thought that I saw a murder. The driver drove on to the pavement, didn't actually hit me but hit the wall. Then that man reversed and just accelerated at high speed and went away.

His suggestion that he was singled out because he had been mistaken for a witness of a murder says much about his understanding of the

If you look closely you can see that this window is covered with mesh to stop it being smashed

nature of this place. Taking only a part-time job so that he did not leave his elderly mother vulnerable to burglars for too long, he made decisions about his life on the basis of being a target. He worried about being attacked by gangs of men if walking in the area and did not try to socialise locally. He had put makeshift bars on his windows and had not replaced most of the possessions that had been stolen when he was burgled (three times), resigning himself to the possibility of more.

The situation had worsened since his neighbours left 'because they used to ring the police for me when anything happened' and he now has no access to support from anywhere. No longer reporting, he is continually harassed by young people (Merry 1981). He attributes the difficulties he has had directly to his 'foreignness' and can see no solution other than to get out of the area. He has been waiting to be moved for eight years.

These people's accounts refer not only to prejudice and threats from people living around them but they also describe an equally prejudiced response from authorities, or at best a negligent one that is worse than useless. In this context of no help, no protection and a sense of being targeted, concentration on the safety of their house, and their ability (or not) to protect themselves and their borders, plays a large part in the way they talk about themselves and their experience of living in the area.

Keeping a distance

This last narrative uses less explicit references to otherness and those who use it do not tend to blame others for the problems on the estate. Distancing themselves so markedly from events on the estate, there is an overriding sense that problems do not affect them. Instead these people describe the estate as a good place to live because of its location, some good neighbours and their ability to live here, largely untroubled. Most importantly this is a narrative of avoiding conflict and maintaining independence.

Avoiding conflict

Pete, a man in his thirties and a newcomer to the estate, had had problems with getting secure housing, and had left his previous residence because of his connections with dealers who were arrested and where people associated him with the dealers' arrest or with their dealing. He is the most extreme example of this active avoidance of conflict, for obvious reasons. Just as those using a narrative of 'being other' described the area as having united families, so does Pete, and though unaffected by them, he is slightly dismissive of their parochialism. 'Its all like a family, a family reunion thing round here, but they don't bother me. They don't bother me and I don't bother them.' I asked him whether he felt people helped each other. The question prompted him to talk about helping to stop fights, partly referring to his work as a bouncer, but also in reference to fights between other residents.

> Know what I mean, you just mind your own business like, you know what I mean. If you see your next door neighbour kicking the head out of his Mrs or whatever you just keep ... just mind your own business ... If you get involved in something that don't concern you, you end up to be the villain. So what do you do? You just play the three eyed monkey, don't you. See no evil, hear no evil, speak no evil. Got no problems, have you.

Although a particular response to talking about domestic violence, this was an unusual response to this question and illustrates Pete's understanding of the dangers of involvement in other people's lives, assuming that it would bring about further conflict. He stresses the need to avoid involvement so that people do not turn to blaming you instead. Like Dave, throughout the interview he tried to impress on me his ability to look after himself and, particularly at the beginning, with his toughness and connections to those even tougher. But this concern with the potential for retaliation should he get too involved in other people's lives again hints at his sense of vulnerability. Despite this he describes the estate as no better or worse than any other. When asked why he has stayed, he begins to suggest he chose to:

PETE   Just, I wanted to stay. I don't like nothing about it, you know, but it don't bother me 'cause I don't get involved. I just come here, go, come and go, come and go. So it don't bother me, the area.

JACQUI   So it doesn't matter where you live?

PETE   Well, it don't bother me, no. So far as I've got a roof over me and I'm not on the streets.

But continuing, he puts this choice in the context of an alternative of homelessness. Not being bothered by it, in this context, begins to hint more at the survival of those 'being other'. But unlike those accounts, Pete describes the estate as very safe, that no one would rob or harm him. His girlfriend explains that they would be 'scared of him because ...' He interrupts:

PETE   I mean, they see a black guy and they say, oh, I'm not gonna touch that black guy's car.

JACQUI   Really?

PETE   Oh, aye, yeah.

CERI   Lad next door, someone nicked a motorbike one night a few weeks ago. When he realised it was a black guy he ran for it. He was trying to nick it and everything, wa'n't he.

'Stereotypes?' I suggest, and he nods, confessing that he does nothing to stop people thinking that way. Like others who use this narrative, he is much more unwilling to suggest racism than those who use one of 'being other'. Though these accounts all hint at stereotyped perceptions, they are unwilling to suggest antipathy. Pete uses their stereotypes to his own advantage, doing nothing to reduce people's fears of him and maintaining his distanced and, by that, secure relationships with other people. Nevertheless, his security, both in the past and currently, seemed quite fragile.

Keeping a distance

Pete's narrative is an extreme version of 'keeping a distance', however, and most of those with similar perspectives admit to some minimal connection to other residents. The couple, Sandra and Carl, who had been involved in trying to save the school, in fact described themselves as knowing a lot of people on the estate. However, they too emphasised the importance of not being seen as an easy target, unlike some Chinese friends who had been harassed until they left. They stressed that they themselves had never had any problems, implicitly blaming their friends for their own victimisation. However, their location at the edge of the estate was very important to them, distancing them from problems at the centre of the estate. They admit that they would feel more trapped if they lived in the midst of things.

CARL   I've always said that if I ever lived on an estate I wouldn't like to live in the middle of one. I would like to live on the outside or …

JACQUI Why's that?

CARL   I don't know [*laughs*], probably I would feel more isolated? I don't like to have to walk into the middle of a place to get to my house … 'cause probably all the things that happen, it's always been the middle and if somebody's gonna congregate they congregate in the middle.

Repeatedly reinforcing the impression that they have not always lived on 'an estate', they implicitly stress that they do not belong here, on a council estate. Although both Sandra and Carl had good relations with people through their children, who formerly attended the school on the estate, now that the school is closed and those people have left, they do not socialise there much, nor allow their children to mix with others on the estate. Instead of belonging to here they emphasise their connections with the rest of Manchester and the outside world.

The stress on being connected to outside of the area contrasts greatly with the other perspectives above. Placing Millton much more in the context of other places, these accounts also tend to view its problems in that wider context. Being somewhat distanced from the impact of such problems they tend to downplay 'drugs' and 'kids hanging around' as problems that you would find anywhere. The accounts differ in how they think these can be resolved, Pete being fatalistic, while Carl is frustrated with the lack of action from the Council, but they share a belief in the relative lack of power of authorities, to which I will turn in Chapter 6.

Toleration and independence

Though there is an implicit understanding in these accounts of the difference between themselves and 'dependent' people on the estate, these people's sense of connection to people in wider society does not suggest that those residents are 'other'. There are more grey areas in the ways they characterise people that they live around. Nor do their relationships with residents and the appearance of the estate impact on the way they see themselves, though they are keen to disassociate themselves from it. Theirs is a very individualised understanding of their lives and those of other people, expressed through values of independence and toleration. When describing a good neighbour, like themselves, it is their toleration and reasonableness that makes them respectable.

CARL   Never had any, any aggravation whatsoever, you know, they're respectable people.

SANDRA   They are.

CARL   And tolerant at the same time in the respect that, you know, we all, you know, have our time when we want to let our hair down and, you know, when we just try not to abuse, you know, that.

Although this conception of respectability taps into a mainstream discourse of individual freedom and toleration (Sennett 1998; Van Dijk 1997), their understandings reflect an emphasis on knowing the limits of freedom, being reasonable, accommodating and accepting. Although Pete has a more exaggerated version of this, his desire to be left alone has fuelled his move here and is one of his reasons for liking living here. Although these people differentiate themselves from other residents they do not tend to associate the problems of the estate with residents' character but believe they are instead caused by factors beyond residents' control: by design, by closure of schools, by people leaving, by lack of policing. In this they share with those who claim to belong a tendency to ascribe to local government responsibility for dealing with and causing problems, but not the sense that neglect has been malicious. Their more flexible sense of belonging, and their connections to outside areas, distinguish them from the other three accounts.

Constitution of problems: otherness, boundaries and responsibility

What these causal narratives illustrate is the impact that notions of otherness and, in effect, the identification of themselves as a group or individual, can have on the constitution of local problems. With the exception of the narrative of 'keeping a distance' these various accounts blame the decline of the estate, its peaks of disorder and, most importantly, the problems that have affected them, on 'others'. Discourses of disgust – of defilement, invasion and dirt – provide a repertoire for describing dangerousness (Douglas 1992) and the negative qualities of others (Riggins 1997). They all contrast their positive self-identification to that of others, distancing themselves from blame. Those 'keeping a distance' may not use this language of disgust but are equally suggestive of their own positive qualities, contrasted, though often silently, with intolerance, insularity and dependence. There is a resonance throughout these accounts between residents' self-identification, descriptions of others and their constitution of local problems.

This does not suggest that their experiences, fears and concerns are not real to them. Nor do I suggest that their understandings of what they fear and blame are purely a 'defence' against a deeper sense of insecurity (Hollway and Jefferson 1997). Rather, my emphasis on the personal import of these accounts, of their relation with people's sense of who they are, is suggestive of the way in which anxieties about change and position in the world can be expressed through this negative portrayal of others; anxieties not restricted to subordinate positions (Van Dijk 1997). However, conscious of stigmatisation, both of themselves and the place where they live, all of these residents distanced themselves from blame for the decline of the estate, the stigma of association with its current condition and the problems around them.

The exception perhaps points to the rule. Two young men (both aged 23) who had been involved in drug dealing since their early teens and claimed the estate as their 'manor', locate themselves at the centre of the reasons for decline. They thereby retained a sense of control over and, most importantly, status within the estate, though they expressed regret for having caused the decline:

JIM   No, we're – we used to sell the drugs on there, you know what I mean, both fucking …

PAUL   [*interrupting*] I don't sell drugs!

JIM   [*Laughing*] I don't give a fuck, man, we did! We've done it all on there, init. But it's done now, it's gone, you know what I mean. Half the houses are trashed. Where the school used to be, it's been knocked down, as you can see there, you know what I mean, everything's gone bad on there.

They do not distance themselves from the estate's decline and frankly blame themselves for it. The potential to be judged by the appearance and reputation of the area, as unclean or immoral, welfare-dependent, violent or criminal, underscores most other accounts. These narratives inhabit positions of conscious vulnerability to stigmatisation and prejudice of others and distance themselves from blame by attributing it to 'others' (Kasinitz and Hillyard 1995).

In addition there are some underlying strands within these descriptions of narratives of decline and change that importantly relate closely to a sense of having no control over these problems. These 'problems' are constituted as just beyond or on the boundaries of people's capacity to control or keep otherness away. They are by definition problems that are the responsibility of someone else to deal with. Operating at both a spatial and a psychological level, the more anxious you are about your capacity to defend your boundaries of control, the more immediate may be the 'problems' that cross them (Sibley 1995). Those isolated on the estate in this way tended to be concerned about other peoples' children, noise, rubbish, or violence breaching their immediate boundaries ('decency and immorality' and 'being other'). Those with a wider sense of territory ('belonging and strangers/newcomers'), unconcerned about the space around their homes, described the threats posed by 'outsiders' coming into the territory of the estate and of 'grassing' betraying the boundaries of belonging. Although over-simplified, this distinguishes between the ways in which people identified and prioritised 'local problems'.

These problems represent things beyond control. For those isolated, what they are able to control may seem much smaller and more urgent, and they might perhaps come across as more anxious than those with more social capital. However, those least anxious to defend boundaries, with a narrative of 'keeping a distance', had least investment and social capital within the estate. With more investment in, and access to, wider networks they did not base their sense of position and security on where they lived. Within all these narratives it is at the borders of this sense of control that threats/ risks/'problems' are identified.

Throughout these accounts people told stories of successful resolution of problems dealt with through an assertion of authority (e.g. 'teaching Irene a lesson' or 'baghead bashing') or problems they had not been able to deal with for a lack of it (such as over other people's children). Many of these responses are centred around putting these 'others' in their place, reflecting power dynamics within the estate and disputes over borders and behaviour of children. Where these problems lay beyond the bounds of their authority their frustrations at the denial of their authority, or being unable to call on an outside authority, feature heavily.

Not only is this influenced by a sense of where authority lies but of what personal claims to authority they possess. Of course there are variations in people's sense of vulnerability to other people and organisations, to not being taken seriously and having no status to exert influence. Their sense of their own position (and identification of themselves) is reflected in their constitution of problems and their identification of the limits of their own authority and responsibility. In this sense understandings of relations with authorities, beyond those bounds, begins to access the 'dispositions' of these residents 'habituated' within those relative positions. It is to these underlying understandings around relations with authorities that Chapter 6 will turn.

Notes

1 All of those who expressed this distinction strongly were over 60 or in their late fifties, but this is not mirrored in all accounts from elderly people.

2 This is not to suggest that the space around a house can indicate how a person thinks but that this thinking is the product of this interpretation of appearance when surrounded by poorly maintained houses.

3 A word used by older residents instead of 'the Council', a vestige of the City Corporation.

4 There is a gendered distinction in the way in which these men talk about cleanliness, referring less to their own cleanliness but still identifying it in the behaviour of other families. This perhaps says something important about the involvement of the elderly women in this cleaning activity. Men talk about their gardening role or buying of lino rather than carpet because it is easier for their wife to keep clean, rather than themselves doing the cleaning.

5 This is a reference to Irish Travellers, hence the reference to scrap metal, a trade in which many travellers engage (Helleiner and Szuchewycz 1997).

6 Tom makes some passing references to the division of Protestant and Catholic as a feature of his upbringing in the area and in people's choice of school.

7 Moss Side is an area of Manchester, some distance from the estate, with a large Afro-Caribbean population which had for some time been notorious in the press for shootings.

8 These interviews and focus groups were also undertaken during the war on Afghanistan, and people seemed less guarded about expressing anti-Muslim, usually expressed as anti-'Paki', sentiments.

9 Heroin addicts.

10 See Kate's description of 'knocking sense into her', above.

11 This is translated from Cantonese.

Chapter 6

Relating to authorities

In this chapter I turn to the ways in which residents attributed responsibility for *dealing* with local problems, particularly to government agencies. More than attributing blame for failure (Pitch 1995), this looks at assumptions of where power lies for resolving problems and their own in relation to it. I have suggested that some of these problems lie just beyond or at the borderlines of people's sense of capacity to deal with them. In addition, they are, by their association with difference, problems that people may also feel that they do not wish to get involved with. Put simply, if people constitute problems as those that are beyond them, ones that they wish to distance themselves from, and have no authority to deal with, these problems are perhaps constituted by where power to deal with them actually lies or perceptions of where it should lie. In the context of calls for greater responsibility or capacity for resolving problems to be promoted within communities this conception of authority is crucial to understanding the potential problems with such a notion.

Rarely needing to prompt conversations about the role of authorities in the decline of the estate, the concentration on state agencies implicit throughout this chapter, rather than private or voluntary institutions of governance, is one created by a tendency amongst residents to attribute power and legal responsibility to local government.[1] Although the participation process involved encounters with wider partners in local governance, few residents attributed responsibility to private and voluntary organisations, though suspecting influence over, or by, state organisations. This focus on the local state drew on a legal discourse of formal justice by which their rights were protected by the state as citizens (Merry 1986), thereby constituting dealing with these problems in terms of rights to be protected and upheld (Merry 2003).[2] This discourse is widely used as an ideal of legitimate governance from which it often falls short.

The focus on state bodies within residents' accounts also reflects a sense of exposure to state surveillance through welfare regulations, policing and their housing, and of being identified as a 'problem' themselves. Conceptions of their own position in relation to agencies, particularly how agencies think about them and their ability to influence agencies or be treated fairly has, I want to suggest, an enormous impact on their sense of vulnerability and abandonment. In this way I am trying to bring an understanding of relationships with government to the centre of people's narratives of fear, insecurity and change.

An assumption of state responsibility is coupled, throughout residents' accounts, with assumptions about the capacity and extent of state power and resources, relative to their own and that of others. Assumptions about the relative power of state organisations and their own capacity to enlist their support is important, I want to suggest, to residents' sense of security and was echoed in their orientations to participation. What these residents all share is a justice ideal of equal treatment. Where they differ is in how they explain the gap between this ideal and the reality. Their explanations for failure and neglect are rooted in entrenched causal explanations of inequality of provision and differential treatment.

For the majority of residents, contact (or lack of contact) with authorities focused around attempts to move, repairs to houses, rent arrears, benefit claims or council tax payments, reporting damage and rubbish to operational services and the housing authority and contact with the police as both victims and offenders. There is a universal appeal for more policing amongst these residents. However, what I want to stress is the way that residents' expectations of the provision of security echo their understandings of legitimate governance and their concerns about the potential for inequality of treatment. This desire for security is coupled with a desire for justice. Along with the constitution of local problems in relation to 'others', the four narratives I have already outlined are also differentiated by their causal explanations for failure of the local state and explanations for inequality. Such explanations are implicitly habituated within positions relative to these power dynamics and perhaps most indicative of 'habitus' (Bourdieu 2002a). I have named these differing perspectives 'wilful neglect', 'doubly isolated', 'the deserving' and 'fatalistic acceptance'. Standing in contrast to the other three and closest to a conception of community capacity for self-governance, is the narrative of wilful neglect, which places government failure at the centre of an explanation for decline.

Wilful neglect

What differentiates these accounts from others is an understanding of purposeful or negligent running down of the estate by government agencies. Those using this narrative attempt to second-guess the actions of the Council[3] and interpret events as indicative of hidden plans and interests. Underlying this is an assumption of the strength of Council power, relative to their own, and an emphasis on their legal obligation to protect their rights. The assumption of an all-powerful and particularly all-*knowing* authority (Them), threatening, callous and neglectful, and opposed to Us, underscores this explanation for decline as government failure to deal with, or contributing to, the invasion of 'problems' brought in from outside.

Hidden agendas and interests

Tom most clearly expressed this narrative and was strikingly consistent in his interpretation of events as driven by a 'hidden agenda'. His explanation for the gradual emptying of the estate reflected this search for hidden interests. He suggested that the land was worth more than the Council could make in rent, and the estate's decline a product of deliberate Council neglect to get rid of residents and justify regeneration for financial gain. Though some residents had moved or died, Tom believed that the Council had a deliberate no-lettings policy:

> We all thought there was an 'idden agenda, no lettings policy anyway. People come off houses which were OK, they refused 'em. They were not letting that estate, although it was not official.

While turning down those he saw as belonging who wanted to move in, the Council brought newcomers in, a seemingly illogical allocation policy explained as an attempt to empty the estate. A no-lettings policy had been unofficially in force for a long time for the same reason. The estate became 'the land that time forgot', losing the school, the shop,

A now boarded-up house with leaking roof and gutter long left unrepaired and deteriorating

the pubs and the sheltered accommodation for the elderly. Although not sure that the Council could have stopped this decline, Tom argues that they should at least have *looked* as if they cared:

> I think the council should, could have been *seen* to be doing something … If you think no one cares about you, you think, you tend to lose that self-respect anyway and lose respect for the estate. The way … 'we're all Millwall fans [*laughs*], nobody cares about us' [*laughs*]. But I think we do get that.

He emphasises the capacity of Council neglect to compound the psychological effects of economic marginalisation. Residents interpret neglect as a reflection of how little government (or society) cares about them and lose self-respect and respect for the estate. People feel that 'no one cares' [meaning society/government] *about them*, a rather different understanding of a discourse of 'no one cares' than Wilson and Kelling's (1982) assumption of a reference to disorderly neighbours.

This neglect, he implies, is a product of prejudice, of being seen as 'Millwall fans', hooligans undeserving of help. But, he goes on, 'They have got a duty of care and they've neglected that.' He contrasts an ideal of how government should be (fulfilling a legal obligation to care) with how things are, reflected in particular through this use of a legal discourse of negligence (Ewick and Silbey 1999; Merry 2003).

It is this reality of inequality of resources and treatment that Tom seeks to expose (Ewick and Silbey 1999). He attempts to uncover how the neglect of the area could act in the interests of more powerful groups. Convinced of the power of government agencies to change and control, his conspiracy theory reflects this overriding sense of powerlessness to influence local government because of these 'hidden interests' and prejudice (Skinner 2001). He treated the consultation process, like other encounters with institutions, as a high-stakes game which he, an amateur, was attempting to play against seasoned players (Ewick and Silbey 1999). Often very stressed by this constant attempt to find the reality beneath the veneer, Tom repeatedly suggested that residents enlist the help of a lawyer or politicians (who would know the game).

Men, in particular, used this narrative of financial interests to interpret change. Ian, though claiming generations of family in Millton, for this reason saw little point in the involvement of residents in consultation:

> I know for a fact, they're not gonna take notice of these people. It's a multi-million-pound thing. Millions and millions, what you could ever *dream* of. They're not gonna listen to what a few people … The priority is … what it'll be here is for private houses.

He explained that 'they don't want us here any more. It is simply a matter of money. Business, right … So move us out and move the rich people in.' Money represents power, not least because it opens doors to influence, gives you bargaining power and enables you to live where you want to live. That the poor can be moved out, with no means to prevent it, reflects a fatalistic dismissal of the chances of resisting the impending disintegration of what little is left of Millton.

Playing with our lives

There is, however, a significant difference between men's and women's accounts in this regard. Though women express a similar sense of powerlessness in the face of official decisions, there tends to be a less explicit emphasis on *financial* interests. Instead the power of the Council is described in terms of arbitrary and capricious control. Kate, describing the hatred which residents feel towards authorities, emphasises experiences of mistreatment.

> The people now, the residents, they hate the local authority. They hate 'em, honest to God. They hate the police ... They hate 'em all, because of the way they've been treated off 'em in the past.

Having had considerable contact with various agencies herself, her frustration with their treatment of her springs, in particular, from the response she has had as a consequence of a violent relationship. Her husband's violence forced her to put her children into care and social services persuaded her to have her youngest child adopted at birth. She had been prosecuted by her husband when she fought back and, finally, having left him and battled to get her children back into her care, was now attempting to get a house nearby, away from the overcrowding at her mother's. However, the housing officer, after leaving her 'dangling for two weeks', had offered the house to someone else. Kate is typical in describing officials as 'playing with our lives'. She shouted:

> You know, and games like that! And I mean I'll never forget that now ... I'm fuming, you know, because I really had me heart set on it, you know, and for it to be just taken away as quick as it's come. They really play with people's lives and they've played with a lot of people's lives on here, as far as they're all concerned.

Her frustration over the housing authority's failure to give her a house, or at least to give her a clear answer so that she could prepare herself and her still traumatised children, can only be understood in the context of this background. The police's response had favoured her husband, often dismissing her as 'the gobby cow'. Only when she showed them the boot-shaped bruise on her pregnant stomach did they take her seriously. Their lack of sympathy and her sense of being still suspected by authorities with regard to her care of her children heightened her sense of being both unsupported and under scrutiny. She retained a strong sense of the injustice of her treatment, indicative of wider inequality in the authorities' treatment of people like her (Ewick and Silbey 1999). Though an extreme, this tension between *need for* and *threat from* agencies is found throughout these accounts. Not viewed as innocent victims in the eyes of authorities, they experience a contradiction between a discourse of equal rights under the law and muted or threatening responses to their assertion of these rights.

Both men and women tried to second-guess the likely actions of the Council, but women tended to draw on stories of past behaviour, rather than a discourse of interests, to suggest the possibility of deception and arbitrary decisions. So Kate, amongst other women, warned that the current regeneration might simply signal a repeat of past demolition and movement of residents from flats nearby which were to have been refurbished.

> They've had all this jargon before with the flats and then they got shoved here. Been here 20 years and it's all happening all over again, you know.

It is a history that suggests that if they move they may not get back. These women share with men an understanding of decisions being imposed. They emphasise the callous disregard with which local views and people were treated in the past and still are. As Kate explains, the decline of the area could have been prevented if the authorities had just:

KATE   Paid a bit of interest for a start, you know, instead of just plonking us here, and leaving us to it, you know what I mean, and then …

JACQUI What do you mean, paid you a bit of interest?

KATE   Listened to us when it first started getting that bad, you know what I mean.

Though mirroring men's understandings of unequal provision and lack of credibility, importantly, their credibility is not so explicitly tied to money. These women tended to be much more willing to participate in consultation events. Though no less wary than the men, they voice a determination 'not to let them [The Council] do whatever they want this time'. This difference between men's and women's narratives perhaps reflects gendered experiences of contact with officials, both in the responses of officials to them and the reasons for contact (Merry 2003).

The relative position of these residents to authorities is also constituted through conceptions of gender. While men suggest that they are seen as violent hooligans, the reason why they suggest they are not taken seriously does not challenge a conception of masculinity as strength but is instead due to financial capital. Men describe their contact with institutions and officials in terms of a game (though without the resources to win). Their lack of financial capital, rather than personal attributes, undermines their credibility. However, their local status could be undermined within public meetings, which men would often dismiss as pointless; all right for women, not for them. Women, however, focused on the dismissal with which they are treated. This perhaps follows as much for relations with men on the estate[4] as for relations with authorities, and reflects their double marginality. Though they share the same suspicions of official promises, the sense of the futility of involvement with agencies that is evident within men's narratives is modified amongst those of women.

Us against them

What these men and women also share is an understanding of us and them, constituted around their accounts of belonging to place. They assert their safety in 'being known' within the boundaries of the estate and stress the danger from outsiders and strangers, including threats of interference from government agencies (and informers). Knowing each other ensures that they can be trusted not to 'grass'. 'The more people know each other the less likely they are to inform on one another,' Tom explains. But, as a result, 'people get an attitude it's us against them.' When asked who 'them' are, he explains:

> The establishment ... police, Council, any kind of official body. It's us against them and everyone's ... got that ingrained mentality that they've got to ... do for ourselves ... It comes from unemployment... because ... they go and do something that they *can* do that's obviously gonna be illegal ... whether it's contraband ... someone selling a packet of fags, yeah, that is still obviously illegal but then you got the cri ... you got the drugs and in between that you've got a spectrum of crime ... I mean you can get a family of false claimants, their attitude is ... it's the only way we can manage.

Tom links the committing of minor offences, or falsely claiming benefits in order to cope, with unemployment and plays down the criminality of offences (with the exception of drugs), even though they are illegal, implying that it is wrong to enforce the law against minor offences and pleading sympathy for those committing them. People believe that they have to look after or protect each other because their activities do not bear scrutiny from official bodies. They are put in a position, he argues, of unwanted autonomy and self-preservation, of 'not grassing', in order to minimise the intervention of outside authorities that could be damaging to people who are not necessarily considered criminal, though at the same time they are inadvertently protecting those he does see as criminal (see also Walklate and Evans 1999). With little control over what follows from reporting, such a step is seen as a betrayal (though, as with a belief that no one steals, not 'grassing' may reflect the ideal rather than reality). Not 'grassing' needs to be understood in the context of these relations with authorities, not just as a protection of crime. The taboo reflects a myth of omnipresent law enforcement without reporting (Ewick and Silbey 1999) as much as a protection of crime, and residents could both look down on grassing and call for more police protection. Reporting clashed with loyalty to community.[5]

Young people seemed particularly concerned about this rule of 'not grassing'. One boy (13 years old) complained that the police do not protect them from 'blacks' coming on to the estate with guns but also claimed he would not report it. 'I'm not going to tell the police 'cause you'd be labelled a grass and be thrown out of the area.' Though repeating this rule, his friend of the same age later illustrated the behaviour of the police through a story of attempting to report these men with guns. Disbelieved and dismissed with a wish that they 'would get shot', they were outraged at not being taken seriously. Some of the girls, complaining of police harassment, argued that the police should instead be enlisting their help in catching 'real criminals'.

LISA (aged 17)   What's the point of chasing us?

JANE (aged 15)   Should be chasing murderers.

LISA   'Cause they're just making themselves on top
and they're not gonna catch no one by
chasing everyone from the streets, are they!
They want people to stay on the streets
where we can see who's doing what but if
they're chasing everyone off the streets ...

Like older women, these girls interpret the behaviour of police as simply an exertion of arbitrary power to make the police feel 'on top', in contrast to what they should be doing, which is protecting residents.

The depiction of authorities as threatening is a particular feature of these accounts. They do not question the legal responsibility of authorities to help and protect them but they do question the inequality of practice, with those who have had most contact with agencies tending to be most critical (Ewick and Silbey 1999; Merry 1986). Faced with the power of the Council and the lack of respect with which they are treated, all of their stories hint at the difficulties posed in expressing themselves to officials in a way that will be taken seriously. They feel they are not being believed, and this communication gap becomes particularly important when trying to enlist the help of agencies with disputes with neighbours/newcomers. Kate, for example, reads the Council's inaction in an ongoing dispute with Irish Irene as proof of partial treatment, with the authorities believing her opponent instead.

> It's like the trouble with [Irene]. There's a neighbour there, causes murders with everybody, now you try and report her, you've got no chance. They won't listen to you. As far as they're concerned it's us harassing her.

With Kate and Irene mutually complaining about each other to the Council, Kate reads their inaction as preferential towards Irene, because Irene is a 'grass'. Her 'grassing' justified violent retribution (see Chapter 5) and being reported in return. Irene and at least two other women had become embroiled in this dispute, reporting one another, and there had even been suggestions of a petition to remove her, but they seemed to reach stalemate as all felt vulnerable to accusation and eviction.

Abandonment and exposure

These are stories both of abandonment by, and exposure to, state agencies. However, it is in references to public police that a sense of powerlessness and isolation is most acute. Stories of police neglect not only criticise their unequal treatment of residents but also inequality of protection. Similarly attributing power, and especially knowledge, to the police, these accounts also used an understanding that their neglect was planned. Partly informed by experiences of local illegal-drugs law enforcement (of long-term surveillance and crackdown), their accounts again draw on a notion that law is automatically enforced rather than instigated by complainants (Merry 1986). The lack of regular policing is read as deliberate neglect. Tom, for example, interprets the lack of a police presence as proof of a 'no-go policy', allowing a certain amount of lawlessness in the area. 'The police *must* have known about it [drug dealing] because it [was] so fucking blatant.' Their policy only encouraged open dealing and contributed to a sense that 'nobody cares' if they deal on the estate.

> If you think that nobody cares anyway, right, we can do what we want, right, the police don't come on the estate anyway so they won't get us right.

Though the dealers were arrested in the end, it does not allay his criticisms of the length of time it took the police to do anything.

However, his perception of the police is twofold, criticising both their lack of intervention and their heavy-handedness. 'They run this area, it's as simple as that, you know, they've definitely got that attitude.' Like some of the young people he suggests that their exertion of authority only serves to boost their sense of power, 'over-policing and under-protecting' them (Loader 1996). He suggests that residents' safety is sacrificed for more powerful groups in other areas, while enforcing a heavy-handed 'disciplinary policing' (Choongh 1998), arresting people for trivial insubordination.

> We don't see ... plus, when you do see 'em ... They got some bloke arrested for swearing right ... for swearing! ... I mean, if you wanna build up a rapport with people you don't do that. You swear back at 'em.

This dual approach is attributed to higher-level policy and face-to-face contact respectively. Tom argues that the police should instead be fostering good relations with people, be sympathetic to their circumstances and protect the area like any other.

Neighbourhood defence

The injustice of police neglect is illustrated, in particular, through stories of abandonment in the face of dangers from outsiders. These stories were often used to impress upon me 'just how bad things got' before anyone did anything about them. They are sometimes used as precursors to stories of neighbourhood defence. These stories of neighbourhood defence have some quite clear narrative patterns, unsurprisingly reflecting discourses of exclusion (Helleiner and Szuchewycz 1997; Riggins 1997), justifying violence in the absence of control by public police. They focus on the threat from 'strangers/ traitors' – drug addicts, black, Asian or Irish/gypsy others, informers and paedophiles – to children and the elderly, justifying violence as the defence of the innocent.

One of these stories, told by Kate, describes the powerless position she was in when caught in the middle of territorial conflict between dealers, heightened by the lack of support from police. To summarise, the chase ran through her house and the one chasing had threatened Kate with a gun and searched the house. Her friend ran for help from police in a car on the other side of the estate, but the police drove off. Though they returned ten minutes later with backup, by that time the dealers had left.

> It was really bad, that's how bad it got ... and we had no cooperation at all off the police whatsoever and for 'em to drive off, you know what I mean! I'm thinking, fuck ... I'll never set foot in me house again.

As in her story (in Chapter 5) of cars driven through the estate endangering children, she suggests that only if a child was shot would the police realise the seriousness of the situation. But in the meantime they were willing to sacrifice the safety of innocent residents, ignoring their pleas for action to 'put an end to all these drug dealers, stop the smackheads coming on'. This abandonment had got to such a stage, she continued, that local gangs of lads, rather than the police, now kept the addicts out of the area. She implicitly justified 'baghead bashing', as young boys called it, as neighbourhood defence in the absence of police protection.

> It got to the stage ... now where, if any smackheads used to come on ... all the gangs, all the lads used to leather 'em. So now they don't, they won't come on here now because they've either got the stuff took off them, what they're trying to sell ... or they're just getting leathered for being on the estate ... We don't have like the dealing here now.

Rather than condemning the destructive male dominance of public space (Campbell 1993), both men and women implicitly condoned young men's defence of the estate from outsiders (Suttles 1972) and encouraged their surveillance (Bursik and Gramsmick 1993). Another male resident told a similar story justifying the burning out of flats occupied by 'smackheads', and denied their 'rights to respect under the law'. Both men and women argue the legitimacy of territorial violence and punishment as a response to these dangers posed by outsiders. Not all residents who use this narrative of wilful neglect mention or endorse neighbourhood defence but such accounts are an important extension of an understanding of unequal provision of security and state abdication of their responsibility to protect. As such these accounts are unique in suggesting that residents are at all capable of dealing with problems as a 'community'.

That these accounts at times legitimise a form of territorial or punitive violence is disturbing and I have included these stories here partly as a warning against potentially naïve notions of community capacity. They also represent a contradiction to notions of the toleration of crime that a culture of 'not grassing' is often assumed to indicate (Walklate and Evans 1999). Although this violence is by no means endorsed by all using this narrative, these stories reflect a particular understanding of collective authority and legitimacy, as an alternative to the legal authority of state agencies. However, what is fascinating about these accounts of local action is their deep entrenchment in understandings of governmental failure as much as of communal strength.

Central to these accounts is the sense of 'us and them'. However, unlike their discourse around outsiders, these accounts recognise that authorities can be both threatening and needed. Despite stories of 'neighbourhood defence' it is these residents' overriding belief in the 'duty of care' and responsibility that authorities have to protect them and provide them with adequate and equal services to other areas that makes their accounts particularly interesting. Empty houses, withdrawal of services, lack of police presence and so on are explained as indicative of wilful neglect, as signs of *authorities'* abandonment of them and, more widely, of social inequality. This is a fundamental contrast to 'broken windows' theories. Authorities are constituted as heavy-handed or capricious, a conception of power over residents' lives that assumes a degree of knowledge of but disregard for them that necessitates minimising contact, despite need.

Doubly isolated

These accounts correspond to that of 'being other', describing their own isolation in the face of the threatening behaviour of other residents. They share with those using a narrative of 'wilful neglect' a tendency to second-guess the reasons for their abandonment by authorities. They do not use a causal narrative of financial interests but, experiencing a double marginality they, like the women above, also attempt to explain why they are ignored or not taken seriously. They explain bias in credibility as a product of societal racist prejudice against them, exhibited both amongst authorities *and* people living around them. This leaves them doubly isolated and unprotected. Though also using a legal discourse of state failure to protect their rights it is the sense of being left unprotected in a hostile environment that differentiates their accounts from those of 'wilful neglect'. Unable to call on the support of anyone else, they emphasise their self-reliance and defiance, defending *themselves* rather than the community.

Unequal rights and protection

These accounts use a narrative of injustice, built around a causal explanation of racism. Dave, for example, a Jamaican man in his sixties, told several stories of the prejudice of authorities when he had needed them and of unjust accusations made against him. He describes the hypocrisy of the Council and police in terms of their being capable of 'telling lies', whether about redevelopment, promises to repair his house or in court. The condition of the estate compared to other areas is unjust and as a tenant paying the same rent as he would anywhere, he argues, he should have the same standards as others. 'They should give us a little extra stuff what other people have. ... We not living like this for another three years!' He does not interpret the lack of expenditure as indicative of hidden financial interests or a desire to drive him out but as the product of a lack of care.

Much more critical of the police, his explanation for differential treatment is more apparent in multiple stories of encounters with racist police. These stories are focused around their stop and search powers and he again talks about their 'lies'. They lied in court, for instance, and got away with it because it was his word against theirs, when they planted drugs on him. He tells several stories of wrongful and brutal arrest, referring to his experiences in the 1960s and 1970s of openly racist policing.

> They don't care. Once you're black you have no rights, yeah. And that's the way it was for a long ... even now. If you don't watch it you still have – It's not like before, it's a bit better, but even now you've got loads o' them. Try to do things, they plant you ...

The police have got better, he says, but his stories of the way they have dealt with more recent problems are still overlaid with an understanding of negligence due to racism. They do not take complaints made by people from minority ethnic groups seriously and respond as if these complainants do not have rights that they are willing to uphold. So, for example, he illustrates the police's racism in their failure to protect the Asian shopkeeper from 'the kids'.

> They used to just tease that guy down there and when he call the police, they don't even come. I used to hear a man what was down there telling they used to do all sorts with him. [JK: Yeah?] Yeah, the police don't bother, man. But you, you make anybody call them on *you*, right – Jesus, you see how quick, how many vans come.

Not only do the police appear to take no notice, to be unconcerned at the problems the shopkeeper experienced, the injustice of their enforcement is clear in their overreaction to complaints made against anyone who is 'black'. Dave describes similar unequal treatment when relating stories of disputes with his neighbours, caused by racist abuse and violence. He became angry, walking up and down the room, at times shouting and waving his arms about in rage at the way he was treated by the police. They did not take him seriously, believed his neighbours over him and failed to protect him. One of these stories was of his attempts to defend his daughter who had been repeatedly beaten up by a girl living a few doors away. These attacks had been openly racist, which his daughter was better at expressing than he. Having seen her several times, 'her face all smashed up', he had in the end gone round and hit the girl back and as a result was given an injunction not to go within 100 yards of her house till the case began. The girl had thereafter goaded them by coming near them and then reported him.

> No matter what you tell them [the police] they don't want to hear it right and when that girl come next door here we phone them … She's next door, come and take her away from here because she's teasing us, right. Nobody comes so they only for one side sometimes … and they won't believe me right … And then *she* phone, the one say I was at her house, try to do the same thing again and they all come down and they banged loads o' them, three, four vans out there, yeah. So that's the way they are.

Again he interprets the failure of the police to react as racism. Whatever he says, they seem to misinterpret him. He has called them many times, and is not an innocent victim, both facts potentially undermining his likelihood of receiving a sympathetic response from the police (Merry 2003).

Self-defence

Dave's stories of racist violence or abuse all justify self- and family-defence because the police neither protect him nor take his side. In the story he told of hitting the boy who had spat through his kitchen window at his children (see Chapter 5), after chasing off the boy's family with a knife, he did not, he continued, hide from the police that he had a knife to defend himself.

> I show them it and they have to give me it back. I say I'm not hiding it, I have it to protect my life. *You* not protecting it, right. I said ... man comes to kill me, what you want me to do?

This story was the only time that he described the police as on his side. In the context of his increasing sense of physical vulnerability, his anxiety about his security belies his assertion of his ability to defend himself. Like those telling stories of 'neighbourhood defence' he warns of an impending threat from which he should be protected but it is a much more immediate threat to his person and house, being surrounded by hostility. He dismisses the police as 'useless' in protecting him because they are never there and do *not* know what happens, especially when compared to the surveillance of the 'lads' on bikes. This is in marked contrast to the assumption throughout accounts of 'wilful neglect' that the police do know what goes on.

> Them is useless. ... They supposed to have the area policed, right, and in too much months now I never see one walk past here. So them is useless. They wait until when you get done, that's the time they coming ... No, we want a regular police on here or they fix one of these house up, man, and put a caretaker into it ... and let him walk around and check the few people them that live, let we feel a bit better.

He wants a permanent presence on the estate, even if that were a caretaker; someone who can watch and deter the men on bikes and make him feel more secure. That a caretaker is equivalent to the police equates their presence with permanent guardianship and deterrence. There is, however, an implicit assumption that this person will differ from the police and be a neutral, unprejudiced witness to what is going on who might take his side.

Neutral witnesses

This desire for a neutral witness is echoed in the account of Irene, the Irish woman described in Chapter 5 who felt so besieged in her house. Again she expresses frustration with housing and police who she feels do not take her side in disputes with other residents. Rather than a caretaker, she talks about wanting a CCTV camera outside her house so that she can produce proof of the threats and beatings and the housing authority will believe her.

> The housing should put up cameras and let them see from the cameras theirselves, do you understand what I mean, let them see for theirselves … I've got 'em if they're on camera, haven't I, do you know what I mean?

Although Irene sees the attacks on her as racist and as using her as a scapegoat, she does not have such a strong sense that the authorities are racist. Rather she sees the authorities as not believing her because it is merely her word alone against many others. Not only isolated, she is also very frightened by the threats of eviction with which she is now faced because of reports against her. Like Dave, she feels she needs a witness to prove to 'The Housing' that she is the one to be believed and enable them to 'find out theirselves who's causing all the trouble around the estate'. Having been asked if she felt she was being blamed, she replied:

> That's what I mean, all the time. I got reported to the housing the other day about the kids … and it wasn't my kids at all … and I had witness for they didn't. It was a different story then. And then the housing called round and says that we can get evicted … over kids!

The housing office and police, she suggests, have become the tool of her neighbours' threats and she is being dragged in over 'petty little things' for which, however, she can be evicted. It is a game in which she has little credibility and she looks for other witnesses, as on the occasion above, to support her story.

This desire for surveillance as a permanent presence is an unsurprising response to a sense of constant threat and continuous harassment. Whether cameras, caretakers, or more police, any form of surveillance is acceptable to these residents to whom the present response offers little protection against threats from locals, and little likelihood of justice. Tim, a Vietnamese man living with his increasingly senile mother, described how, when he was burgled and his mother threatened, the police had merely asked if he had insurance and an alarm. He could only throw his hands up, shake his head and sigh, 'Useless. They don't do anything.' In fact the only other time that he had come into contact with the police was when they had arrested him for non-payment of council tax, which he had paid. This only made him more despairing of their lack of protection and of how little they took his situation seriously or sympathetically. Even in trying to move away he felt let down by the housing authority who had offered him only houses in the local area where he would still be surrounded by the groups of young men that at the moment terrified him. They had clearly not understood why he wanted to move, nor saw the urgency of it.

These residents' relationship with authorities is central to their doubly isolated position. They all talk about 'sticking it out' or having to put up with their situation while the housing authority and police seem to see no urgency in their situation. For them the lack of action is as clearly manifest of racism and prejudice against them as the actions of residents. Authorities are not assumed to know what is going on, nor is their neglect seen as intentional, but their inadequate response is instead explained by their unconscious (and sometimes conscious) racism. In the absence of protection each of these residents resorted to ways of defending themselves and their property, resigning themselves to the burglaries or anticipating violence and defending themselves physically. Since the threat surrounds them constantly, they each talk about the need for continuous surveillance rather than face-to-face authority with local knowledge and sympathy. As much as protection, this is about having proof of the level of harassment with which they could enlist the help of authorities because they have few allies locally. Disappointed by the biased response they receive, they see this as confirming their belief that their rights are not upheld nor taken seriously. Again the gap between their vision of unbiased legal authority and the reality has suggested to them that this uneven response is because of how they are perceived. They look to a symbolic figure of neutrality and protection to replace a flawed present; if not public police then

CCTV and caretakers without their dubious history. This stands in sharp contrast to accounts depicting relatively good relations with authorities that now follow.

The deserving

The first of these has a fairly positive view of authorities and assumes professional competence is hampered by a limited ability to control the area, blaming this difficulty on the sort of people living around them.[6] In contrast they present themselves as the voice of 'decent' citizens, their main concern being that they not be 'tarred with the same brush'. They argue that they 'deserve', rather than share equal rights to, good local services and protection, not least from other local people. They are disposed to trust the professionalism of those working in local services and assume that they would help them if they could.

Inefficiency and waste

Apportioning so much responsibility for decline to other residents, these accounts do not blame state authorities for decline. If there is inequality in provision it is the product of the behaviour of residents not staff. Doris, retired, paying her rent from small savings and proud of her self-reliance, is typical in dismissing other residents' complaints about local services. She had always received good services because she, unlike them, is reasonable and polite.

> They all moan about if you phone the housing and nobody comes to 'em. I only have to phone the housing and they come to me. But I don't give them a load of abuse.

She explains failings on the part of local authorities as inefficiency rather than policy, particularly when talking about the police, whose poor response time she finds difficult to account for except in such terms.

> I think the police should come a lot quicker. Oh, yeah, I mean they come and when they do come they come in three or four vans, like, you know, all them. And it is well after the event has happened, everybody's gone ... But I think they waste a lot of money on other things, I do.

Though she suggests that the police overreact and waste resources, as does the Council more generally, she tends to blame this waste on those causing them to be called out. She compares police responses to the fire service, 'who always come in minutes, even though the fires were probably started by the same kids who called them.' She would rather account for police failures through this understanding of local youth wasting their time and resources, again blaming the behaviour of others for failings in state provision.

Tarred with the same brush

These are essentially accounts of police ineffectiveness in the face of criminal deviousness. Though Doris felt the police could come more quickly, they are also hampered by 'the lads'' ability to pre-empt them:

> Well, I think if the police had o' been there quicker ... but you see, they all have these scanners, the lads ... so they hear when there's messages and they know where it's coming from.

Explaining police ineffectiveness in the face of this illicit surveillance she also expresses frustration that they do not understand the danger of reprisals, of 'having your windows smashed', if criminals found out that she had called the police. She was anxious about maintaining her anonymity and did not want the police to come to her house. She interprets their requirement for specific information when reporting as unwillingness to trust her and their slow response as 'tarring her with the same brush' as those who make hoax calls and waste their time.

> I just think they think it's a no-go area ... I don't think they want to be bothered really, the police now, round here. Because we always say to them, you know, 'We are not all the same that's around here'. But when you get on the phone ... 'It's not a hoax or anything, we want you to help us, but we don't want them coming to our front doors. Because round about here, they know exac' ... They call it 'grass'.

She explains police neglect as a reaction to the way they perceive people on the estate. But the injustice is not in the differential treatment but in their lack of recognition of her as respectable and deserving, even if others are not. Like those who felt 'doubly isolated' she argues for a constant guardianship of the estate to counter that of other hostile 'lads' around her.

Loss of (moral) guardians

However, authorities are a rather distant presence in these accounts, a passing reference if I do not initiate a question about them. There would be no need for them if the people who were causing the problems were absent, nor can local services deal with the wider societal changes in moral values that these people's behaviour signifies. So these accounts bemoan the lack of parental control of children and are keen to have a much stricter vetting system for allocation of housing. The police represent a symbolic authority able to exert control over other people's children that they cannot. Their presence forms part of a nostalgic narrative harking back to a time of 'values' and safety, now lost, and symbolised by the 'bobby on the beat', rather than police officers arriving on masse or not at all (as in the quote above) (Loader and Mulcahy 2003; Loader 1997). In this way the loss of the 'bobby' is also related to a loss of traditional (patriarchal) authority over family and children. The introduction of neighbourhood wardens might fulfil this role, Doris argues, removing the necessity to report by restoring that lost (imagined) order to the area.

Jack, in his fifties, also stresses the need for a youth centre to be run by professional people – police, if possible, to exert control over young people, rather than 'volunteers' (i.e. locals). His is a very paternalistic vision of authority, whether his own over his family or that of state agencies over other (dysfunctional) families. Like Doris, he is defiant in his willingness to report (even his own son when young), which he sees as part of a sort of moral citizenship. When I asked him about a time when he had been accused of being 'a grass' when walking through the estate, he assured me that:

> They know I would report them to the police, they know that. If I get into a situation where I am afraid to walk around this area, then I would say that's it, I'm getting a camera. Too many people close their doors.

Despite his defiance, at the time he was worried by the accusation and his immediate reference to the possibility that he could become more frightened in the future suggests he still is a little. His intended acquisition of CCTV in that instance represents a surrogate police presence, able to protect him and setting him apart from those who ignore criminality and implicitly condone it.

The failure to provide this level of guardianship and the gradual loss of other services, particularly in not employing caretakers who would have prevented vandalism and 'forced people to keep 'em [houses] up to standard', exposes the Council to criticism for false economies and cutbacks. Likewise, these accounts suggest that introducing the wrong kind of people into the area meant that young people had had no alternative authority figures, resulting in a vicious circle. Nevertheless, Jack's is typical of these accounts in sympathising with what they describe as an uphill struggle to counter the culture of crime and disorder that has developed on the estate. Having descended to this level, Jack argues, it will take generations to repair the damage, young people now having no 'respect'. He implies that teenagers and older are beyond redemption.

> It would take a long haul, trying to re-educate the ones who are, like – not the eight year olds now, but the ones who are 15 and 16. … They're so used to – for the last five, ten years or whatever – of standing on street corners watching kids rob cars and that is their excitement, … The local authority's trying to get back to where it is … but that's what we're gonna try to fight against now.

He here relates himself with the local authority's effort to get back to the way things were. Involved in meetings with regeneration staff,[7] he suggests that they have a common goal, or battle, linking regeneration to a wider restoration of moral values and discipline.

Reasserting discipline

This understanding of a moral decline is expressed through a nostalgic narrative of a loss of discipline amongst both children and adults. This draws on a sense of belonging to a wider, implicitly national, 'moral community', rather than place, symbolised by particular figures of moral authority (Loader 1997). Doris, for example, harks back to days when rent officers would enforce the cleaning of front steps and suggests that this should be part of the work of wardens or caretakers, forcing people to maintain their houses. Some of the sympathy expressed for the uphill job of authorities is for their loss of disciplinary power to maintain standards of behaviour, mirroring their own loss of influence over local children. Jack bemoans the banning of corporal discipline, which he blames for the loss of control. This lack of discipline, he suggests, is the result of an emphasis on rights, crippling people's ability to control children, and by implication, the disreputable and criminal that he sees about him. His wife, Sarah, agrees:

That is the top and bottom of it really. Now it's all civil rights and what have you. It has gone much too far. There is no chastising whatsoever. You don't mean to tell me that you get a child to behave itself without a little bit of discipline.

Touching on a legal language of 'reasonable chastisement', they go on to clarify that they do not endorse beating children but that people now feel unable to punish them at all. Picking up on a public discourse of 'rights and responsibilities', they emphasise this failure of parents to fulfil their responsibilities in disciplining their children, and the over-emphasis on the rights of the undeserving.

Though these accounts suggest disappointment with local authorities, they argue the need for their presence as moral guardians to maintain both standards of behaviour and the appearance of the area. The improved appearance could also signal to the outside world that this is a respectable area, attracting other 'decent' people, and prevent themselves from being 'tarred with the same brush' as those currently around them. They assume that they have common values and goals with agencies trying to improve the area. Their criticisms focus, in particular, on the lack of a police presence as the authorities that could deal with other people's children, the problem just beyond the boundaries of their own authority. Surrounded by disreputable or threatening others they stress the need for this presence as a source of moral discipline, of which the 'bobby' or rent officer is symbolic and the warden or caretaker a potential surrogate.

Those using this narrative present themselves as the 'moral voice' of the area. As such they imply that they 'deserve' to be heard above the voices of those who 'shout', both in the provision of services and in the current regeneration process. Being surrounded by people who cause the problems, especially their children, they see the solutions as those of 'cleaning up' and vetting those who want to move back in on the basis of their behaviour. Authorities should maintain these moral standards. This emphasis on control and exclusion differs substantially from the last of these narratives. Those using this last narrative, though equally confident of receiving a good response from local authorities, do not tend to blame residents for local problems.

Fatalistic acceptance

What differentiates these accounts from those preceding is their criticism of services in general, rather than suggesting inequality of provision. They are pragmatic and resigned to poor services everywhere. Any difference in provision is explained as situational, particularly because of poor design and the difficulties of policing the estate. These accounts use a causal narrative of flawed reality, which could be better but they do not see themselves as in a position to influence changes made by agencies. In this they express some familiar visions of imposed decisions made behind the scenes which may be affected by financial interests, but they do not describe their effects as exclusionary or unjust.

Resignation

Pete, for example, when he talks about the changes afoot in the area, sees little point in going to meetings. Rather he emphasises that these are *Their* decisions and that They will make them regardless of him. Instead he has resigned himself to moving and hopes that he can come back.

> Basically it's *their*, it's *their* decision, whatever *we* say, they don't listen. They don't take much notice of what the *public* says. They only want to do what *they* think is good and whatever ... So, basically, we're just, leave them to it, because what say have you got?

Cynical of the realities of his position in a negotiation with authorities, he resigns himself to waiting 'until the demolition man is outside'. In contrast to his assertions of self-reliance he stresses his lack of control over 'changes made' to the estate, deliberately emphasising the passive voice. His independence works within the parameters of their decisions. He describes his conflict with the housing authority over rent arrears, incurred while in prison, in similar terms his resignation not restricted to the subject of consultation. He again merely resigns himself to paying it, though he does not think he is liable:

> Nothing you can do. ... I say, 'Well that's impossible for me to have all these kind of arrears.' They said, 'Well, you owe it to us,' and I say, 'Well, how can I owe it to you when I was in jail. I can't live at two places at the same time.' But I just, know

what, sick and tired of arguing with them but you don't get anywhere.

He ends his story with his usual sighing response of, 'Well, yeah. So that's it really. Something you've gotta live with. Part of life.' His inability to influence or argue his case is something to which he is resigned.

Even Carl and Sandra, who had been heavily involved in trying to influence decision-makers to keep the school open, had been left cynical by the protest and its failure to prevent the school's demolition. Carl was now sceptical about their ability to affect decisions once made. In fact, Carl explains with heavy irony, he had been using a similar argument to the one that developers are using now: that a good school could attract new people. His experience has made him see any participation in the current process as fruitless. Though he and Sandra continue to be active in other developments in the city, Carl still sees such meetings as a political 'talking shop', unlikely to bestow any real power on lay participants.

> They say that you have a say but they don't really do nothing. All they'll say is they have gone round and spoke to everybody.

Although their argument is founded in the experience of going to a lot of meetings, and they were more hopeful prior to the failure to save the primary school, they are now as cynical of their likely success as Pete. They never attended any of the meetings about the estate. They too seemed to have become more sceptical with greater contact.

Inept management

Though never explicitly suggestive of inequality or prejudice, these accounts do hint at similar sentiments to those of 'the deserving' when complaining about the poor housing repairs service. The service, they say, is not flexible enough to arrange a time around working commitments, assuming instead that people do not work. Consequently, Carl and Sandra have not been able to get their repairs done. This assumption of the repairs service does not suggest injustice but inefficiency and inept management based perhaps on assumptions about Council tenants being unemployed. The couple are, however, much more sympathetic to the difficulties in policing the area because of its design, and put the decline of the area and the crime down to this problem of layout, for which the police cannot be held responsible. 'It's like the crescents in Hulme. It's the design, it's designed for criminals, it's definitely designed for criminals.' For that reason, Carl explains, 'it cannot be policed, there's no way, it's just impossible for it to be. With so many alleyways there were too many hiding places.'

However, his comparison with Hulme is a positive one, seeing the latter area of Manchester's successful redevelopment as indicative of the potential for this estate if redesigned. Carl suggests that the estate has been deliberately wound down ready for demolition, but he does not see this process as threatening nor prejudicial, though it has made the situation worse in the meantime. The difficulties of policing the estate justify its demolition, an argument creating an impression of objective distance and rationality, removed from the implications of the demolition for himself and his family.

Fallible policing

Despite this sympathy for the day-to-day problems of policing the estate Carl suggests that the police have no 'strategic deterrent', by which he means that they do not target their policing, such as concentrating on the wall near the retail park which people climb over with impunity.

> Well, I mean, for example, if I knew that the police were on a covert operation to catch me then I'd be disinclined to want to go and climb that wall or ... I wouldn't be so, so presumptuous as to just go blatantly and just jump over the wall, do my business and come back, feeling, you know, a sense of security about it.

Though he suggests that the police are failing to do their job properly, he does not explain this as intentional. However, he too argues the need for a policing presence as a deterrent and it is not coincidental that this wall is near where he lives.

Pete too expresses a sympathetic vision of the police, describing them as simply 'doing their duty' and needed. However, his is a more cautious acceptance of their behaviour, having had more negative contact with them. He explains that, like anyone, they need careful handling to avoid becoming a target for harassment *by* them.

> I mean, I've had my ups and downs with the Old Bill before but ... if you were all right with them and don't give them the, the need to harass you, they won't harass you. If you start

being loud with them and that, be rude or whatever, sometimes they like the action. 'Fucking let's go look for such and such a person 'cause he'll give us ... a good time'.

Despite police harassment of him or people he has known, he is again reluctant to suggest prejudice but attempts to understand their behaviour through a process of imagining himself in their position. Only human, he implies, they will react better if you talk to them in a friendly way than if you address them aggressively. Some will 'go over the top' in responding aggressively, but, as in everything, there are 'good and bad' in the police too. He and the couple above go to great lengths to try to comprehend other people's behaviour in this way, as the product of human fallibility. Again it is this acceptance that there are 'good and bad' people and places everywhere, and no issue that is black and white, that differentiates these from other accounts.

This narrative is characterised by an attempt to distance the person from the situation, compare this place to others and put themselves in other people's positions in order to present themselves as responding rationally to it, without judgement or emotion. They exhibit acceptance and resignation, reluctant to suggest injustice or prejudice, though there are allusions to the illogical responses or misconceptions of others. They do not see policies as intending to drive them out, nor newcomers as threatening. They do, however, share with the first two narratives (of 'wilful neglect' and 'double isolation') a distinct pessimism about their ability to influence those in powerful positions. But they do not express the frustration with authorities that characterise those accounts, instead resigning themselves to limited influence. Their emphasis on individual choice and freedom, even if limited, does not leave much room for explanations of injustice, though these are always hinted at. Distanced from the estate, its residents and with an objective distance and rationality that gives them credibility when in contact with state agencies, they rarely suggest stigmatisation and explain poor services through generally fallible systems.

Disposition and experiences of inequality

Amongst these widely different visions of relationships with authorities there are some startling similarities. Above all there is a widespread sense of the inequality of the services provided by authorities. Though this in itself is not surprising, the assumption of prejudiced or intentional neglect amongst three of these narratives is striking. Even in the last there were hints at misconceptions guiding mismanagement of Council estates generally. Within these accounts the assumption of neglect leaves an overriding sense of abandonment and being left to their own devices. This provides the basis for a justification of self-defence/neighbourhood defence and either an assertion of credibility with authorities (distancing themselves from blame) or a despondent pessimism about the possibilities of influencing them. All these accounts share a common assumption that state authorities are those responsible for maintaining order and dealing with problems beyond their borderlines of responsibility and authority. But equally their assumption is that residents may be ignored when they request help. There was amongst all these residents a tendency to expect to be excluded, ignored, passed over or conned into co-option.

All suggest that there is a danger that they will not be believed or listened to and their potential vulnerability to being seen as the problem makes reliance on authorities for support problematic. Amongst narratives of 'wilful neglect' and 'double isolation' this is compounded by a sense of vulnerability to the actions of authorities whose law enforcement or unwillingness to believe them could land them in greater difficulties. There was an awareness that this caution with regard to authorities could also be interpreted as protection of criminality by association with 'not grassing'. The tension between need and exposure to authorities' intervention is central to understanding residents' sense of social exclusion (Sennett 2005) and their anxieties about regeneration. Echoed amongst those more inclined to 'fatalistic acceptance', this despondency about the possibility of influencing more powerful government bodies seems only exacerbated by contact with agency staff. This is a pattern noted in people's experiences of the criminal justice system (Ewick and Silbey 1999; Merry 1986, 2003) whereby people's treatment and experiences fall short of their expectations of a neutral defence of their rights embodied within a discourse of formal justice. Those with least cause to rely on agencies for help, though most willing to call the police, were distinct for their belief in their capacity to work with and influence local governance if they distinguished themselves from disreputable others. Those most disposed to participation were thereby also those least disposed to sympathise with their neighbours, and with least social capital. Only amongst the still wary women who used understandings of 'wilful neglect' was there any similar willingness to see a faint possibility that their voice may be heard, despite past experiences.

Residents' explanatory narratives expose understandings of powerlessness, particularly relative to state authorities, a position which has differing implications depending on how that position is understood to have been caused and what repercussions it can have. Explanations for social inequality inform these accounts of inequality of provision and injustice. They reflect 'habituated' (Bourdieu 2000a) explanatory narratives. They are used to interpret the actions and inaction of authorities of all varieties.

Though inequality of security is also used to justify self-defence or neighbourhood defence, these residents all express a desire for protection in the form of a representative of legitimate authority. This representative is variously constituted as sympathetic, neutral, disciplinary or deterrent, but these residents all argue a need for a constant presence, potentially provided by a caretaker/warden (though this role and purpose might be differently conceived). Importantly, this does not imply a demand for more punitive or exclusionary enforcement. Visions of policing or caretaking differed in their understandings of legitimate authority which in turn echoed their explanations for inequality more widely. Their explanations for social inequality underpin their narratives of decline and neglect.

The two narratives of 'wilful neglect' and 'double isolation' both read the decline in the estate's appearance, and the actions of officials as indicators of how residents are viewed by society and state agencies. Decline is explained in terms of this stigmatising inequality. For those isolated and surrounded by prejudiced neighbours and authorities (doubly isolated), professional 'broken windows'-style explanations of decline as indicative of social breakdown are well nigh irrelevant, while such a suggestion is hotly contested by those who describe the community as close knit and supportive (wilful neglect). In fact it is only amongst those 'deserving', who regard authorities as on their side, with whom a reading of the appearance of the area as indicative of social (moral) breakdown strikes any chord.

Using a legal discourse of rights the first two narratives (wilful neglect and double isolation) are driven by a deep sense of injustice. Though the foundations on which they base their rights differ markedly – belonging or equality – in accordance with their position of inclusion and exclusion within the estate, they share a similar disposition towards a justice ideal. Similarly those who voice a narrative of 'fatalistic acceptance' expressed their adherence to values of tolerance, equality and individual freedom associated with this justice ideal though marred by a flawed reality. Less disposed to suggest injustice, however, they lean towards fatalism with respect to their position. Those least disposed to draw on this legal discourse (the deserving) see themselves as the upholders of moral values and find in this another discourse of entitlement embedded in law and also capable of questioning it. 'Deserving' protection they vigorously call for exclusionary enforcement to control those around them.

In this concentration on relations with authorities I have tried to highlight the importance of these explanations for the area's neglect, and what they reveal about explanations for social inequality, within these narratives of decline and change. All these accounts assume that state bodies should solve the problems in their area and protect them, and most describe the long-standing neglect and failure to invest in the area as contributing to, if not causing, its decline. They all share a common understanding of where the responsibility for dealing with problems lies – with authorities.

However, this assumption of the need for authority protection is in tension with the potential to be identified as problems themselves. The concern for credibility is thereby particularly acute during regeneration. In a stigmatised place residents may be keen to distance themselves from blame by blaming others (as in Chapter 5) while claiming to belong to a credible community (Kasinitz and Hillyard 1995). Those who feel doubly stigmatised by authorities and/or their neighbours are left beleaguered and defensive, equally pre-emptive of the prejudice that they assume they will face. Where these dispositions resonate, or fail to, with those of officials has important implications for understanding processes of consultation. Part III will now turn to these official dispositions.

Notes

1 A tendency to talk about 'the council' as a generic term for all government bodies was only, occassionally, distinguished as 'police' and 'the housing' and some mention of social workers, youth workers, as individuals. This focus was prompted by my enquiries as to what residents thought of the work of these agencies but was largely in response to their comments. On the whole I did not prompt people to talk widely about private security, voluntary bodies or wider state organisations unless they referred to them first.

2 Some residents also drew on the Etzionian communitarian discourse of 'rights' and 'responsibilities', particularly of parents, when it cohered with their own understandings.

3 'The Council' is used largely as a broad reference to state agencies. I have borrowed this terminology to avoid a distortion of this meaning.

4 Several men, particularly using this narrative, described women as illogical, 'screaming', 'nagging' and 'petty'.

5 Merry (2003) makes this observation in relation to a clash encountered by women in cases of domestic violence that can contribute to repeated withdrawal of charges. These same notions of betrayal, loyalty and loss of control are apparent in these wider stories of encounters with agencies.

6 There is some overlap between this narrative and 'wilful neglect' amongst those who use a more exclusive narrative of 'belonging'. More critical of newcomers living on the estate they also use a narrative of a need for discipline of people on the estate.

7 Like most residents he does not tend to distinguish between agencies.

Part III

Working There

Chapter 7

Imagining and managing change

I have separated professionals' and lay narratives in part to highlight the difference in cultural capital that residents and professionals command on entering a dialogue, a difference echoed in the change in tone and style of language used. These interviews hint at a gulf between positions.[1] Where these professional scripts differ, of course, is in their more explicit use of specialist discourses and knowledge. I want in this chapter to explore the causal explanations embedded in their accounts of the area's decline. These are presented as professional theories and delivered in such a way as to stress the rationality of the speakers, presenting themselves as credible and knowledgeable about the area and its problems.

Most striking amongst these professional understandings was the use of a narrative of 'spirals of decline' which, like nostalgic narratives amongst residents, has a 'forensic capacity' to identify causes, triggers or conditions of decline (Douglas 1992). What is significant is the way in which these stories are used to justify solutions (Stone 1988). The widespread use of this account creates an impression of coherence and broad agreement between professionals.

Despite this similarity between professional accounts of the estate's decline there are some significant differences in the causes/triggers/conditions that they identify and the solutions that they espouse. So, for example, architects or planners tend to argue that problems are rooted in architecture and faulty planning to which they have the architecture and planning solutions. Though some present similar solutions, such as mixed communities, to be implemented in accordance with the Urban White Paper, these are justified in ways that reflect professional fields.

However, differences in emphasis also reflect differing roles in regeneration and the governance of security. I have divided this chapter into two sections to draw out the resonance between professional fields that echo these roles. The first of these presents the accounts of those involved in the planning, marketing and development of city strategy. The second section presents a similarity in the accounts of officials involved in neighbourhood management and policing. I have named these two sections 'driving change: providing vision' and 'managing change: providing respite' respectively. These first are expressed by public and private sector partners involved in imag(in)ing the future and steering change[2] while those involved with direct management reflect an emphasis on implementing change. Within both sections I will explore the similarities and differences in identification of problems and solutions in detail.

Driving change: providing vision

The two professional scripts outlined in this section are voiced by those who are among the most powerful in the inception of the regeneration of the area. The first of these is used amongst private developers, planners and architects.[3] I have named this a 'vision of utopia' to reflect an emphasis on the future as a break with, and free of, the problems of the present. The second is used by housing strategy (not to be confused with local housing managers) and regeneration professionals involved in the development and promotion of city strategy. Both scripts hinge around a notion of a failed market, which no longer attracts newcomers, investors and, spiralling further into decline, has lost population and potential consumers or tenants/taxpayers. This provides resonance between them, though an emphasis on social exclusion distinguishes public sector discourses. I have called the second of these scripts one of 'strategic governance' to reflect this strategic vision of policies to promote the city's competitiveness.

Both of these understandings adhere closely to renaissance policies. What distinguishes them is their differing identification of the problems causing market failure and the way in which the (similar) solutions they offer hope to produce attractive, prosperous and safe areas. These scripts share mutually reinforcing goals of growth and security, particularly explicit in the way 'visions of utopia' value activities around consumption while drawing on nostalgic images of a safe 'community' (see also Massey 1994).

Visions of Utopia: imagining and marketing the future[4]

This planning/marketing script is led by a utopian image of the future and those using it tended to present themselves as the drivers and visionaries of regeneration, rather than implementers of policy (MacLeod and Ward 2002). Bill, for example, one of the private developer's team,[5] describes their role as 'providing an incredibly strong vision that's giving people an immense amount of passion and enthusiasm to deliver' and drive change. Theirs is a story of the estate's inevitable decline due to fundamental flaws and consequent market failure, spiralling into further decline, which now necessitates radical change and justifies rebuilding. The following will outline two core ways in which they use a story of 'spiralling decline' to identify problems (and justify associated solutions); firstly, created by low density and design, and secondly, created by the poor image and management of council housing. These accounts are driven by intended utopian outcomes, which I outline as density and natural surveillance and breaking down social divides.

Density and natural surveillance

Bill's elaboration of the main problems in the area is typical of the private development team in his focus on the poor design and, in particular, the low *density* of population of the estate. Decline was inevitable he argues because the small population limited the viability of the local market for shops and services, while poor layout encouraged crime, made policing difficult and prevented passing trade, all contributing to further decline.

> Physically, I think that there's a problem fundamentally with the design of the area, that ... we've all said it isn't dense enough to support all the elements that we'd normally expect within a community: shops, a greengrocer's and newsagent's and stuff. I think, in terms of the design of the estate, it has facilitated crime because of the cul-de-sacs. ... It's created no-go areas.

This understanding of a flawed market stresses the necessity of rebuilding both to increase population density, in order to sustain commercial activity, and to reduce crime. Bill's association of consuming activity with a community is typical of this script, which tends to associate a loss of community with the loss of such activity. This also links a gentrifying agenda, bringing in people with more disposable income, to one of creating safe public spaces in which there are enough people for a 'natural surveillance'. The benefits of consuming activity are deemed twofold, in creating community and deterring crime.

This discourse around density is rooted in claims to a natural orderliness of a properly functioning place. Bill even suggests that higher densities will dissipate people's fears about crime as more people are out on the street.

> The way to address it [fear] is simply to get more people living in the area, looking out round the streets. So if something does happen on the street then there's the chance that a significant proportion of people will actually ... well, it becomes self-policing basically.

Fears will be allayed by new circumstances capable of 'self-policing'. He argues for the deterrent effects of a form of natural but panoptic surveillance, whereby people will control their own behaviour, 'knowing that you're actually being watched by somebody'. In contrast to security technology and public policing, he associates this 'natural surveillance' with an equally natural 'community', able to self-police. His colleague Jack stressed that this concept of 'natural surveillance' was a guiding principle of the master-plan,[6] ensuring that there are no places to hide and plenty of people around.

So when they get off the metro at night, for instance, they'll be walking past high street shops and restaurants and things like that. So there's life, there's people outside, there's people coming and going, so therefore it's safer.

This image of naturally policed public space is again tied to consumption and leisure activity. Density is presented as a solution to market failure and crime, offering a recipe for an attractive, prosperous and safe area. However, it is tied to another solution of creating 'mixed communities'. Despite the implication that this will bring in people with higher incomes these developers tended instead to refer to this as an attempt to break down social divides.

Breaking down social divides

Creating 'mixed communities' is justified in relation to the problems created by poor management and 'dumping the unwanted in the area', as Jack puts it. They emphasise the poor image that council housing has acquired as a result. However, the need to mix is understood as a wider social project of breaking down 'inherited class divides', as Bill refers to them, and integrates different forms of tenure within different groups, implying mixed tenure offers a solution to class divisions. Again this reflects a utopian vision of a change that will shake off the burdens of the past.

Despite the emphasis on mixing, this vision of utopia is one that aspires to sameness. This is typified in an analogy used by all those in the private development team, of buying a car from the appearance of which no one can tell how it has been paid for:

In that if you go out on the road and you look at the number of Ford Fiestas around they're all exactly the same ... There isn't any sort of social class ... associated with how you come to be driving that car and you're not looked down on if you're paying for it by hire purchase.

The same principle, they argue, could be applied to the development. The analogy suggests that onlookers cannot make judgements about the person in the car or home. It illustrates an understanding of equality as sameness. However, it is a difficult analogy to sustain without a degree of denial about the ways in which objects such as cars and buildings are imbued with cultural signifiers. This is particularly apparent when extended to a future 'mixed community' where Bill describes:

143

> ... a pub where the locals go and ... a good percentage of
> the new population go and there's an integration and not an
> exclusion between the two ... And I'd like to think that there
> is a genuine inability to being able to distinguish whether that
> person living in that flat is shared ownership, social rented or
> an owner occupier, whether they're a solicitor ... unemployed
> or ... in a lowly paid work ... But I suppose the class thing still
> hangs heavy in UK society; where you're from and what you do
> and what you earn and what kind of car you drive is still too
> important in a lot of senses.

His ideal community is one where income and social divisions are
not apparent but his utopia is hampered by those same divisions
embodied in people's judgements about earnings, status and,
ironically, what car you drive.

This combination of mixed tenure, good design and density of
population is presented as the 'panacea' for almost all problems in
any area (Lees 2003). Both density and mixed tenure are stressed
in their capacity to create successful communities. This vision
of community focuses primarily on the benefits of consumption
activity and secondly on attracting a mixed population to sustain
a local economy. However, it maintains a studied distance from a
gentrification agenda, Gerald, for example, suggesting 'the desire
to move in more middle-income people' comes from government.
Instead his is an image of creating a harmonious community with
a 'rich social mix' of young and old, rich and poor, able to provide
passive surveillance and mutual support.

> You get the old ladies talking to each other and passively looking
> at what's going on and looking after their grandchildren, and,
> you know, if you get people with, with families they tend to also
> have a community spirit and use the space during the day.

Though this nostalgic vision of a sustainable community is seemingly
contradicted by an emphasis on conspicuous consumption (MacLeod
and Ward 2002), bars and cafés along the canal front are also described
as the means to attract and build this community (Imrie and Raco
2003; Massey 1994).

This script provides a utopian vision as a solution to the problems
of the present. What differentiates these accounts from those of local
authority professionals is their focus on residents as consumers and
the creation of self-regulating areas capable of sustaining local markets.

Like the nostalgic narratives of some of the residents this vision of utopia acts as a way of imagining a situation without problems. The assumption of the possibility of a balanced functioning market informs a causal explanation of market failure and the solutions are offered as a means to restore conditions for successful competition. Ironically this emphasis on market rejuvenation is one they share with local authority officers equally keen to create sustainable housing markets able to attract and retain residents. Where they differ is in the threats they identify to the sustainability of an area and a less utopian vision of self-/market-regulation.

Strategic governance: limited capacity and reasserting control

This second professional viewpoint is distinguished from these utopian visions by a stronger emphasis on the need to revive the local housing market *and* reassert control. It is expressed by housing and regeneration officials at a strategic level in the local authority. They too use a story of 'spiralling decline' to explain a failed market but there is less sense of inevitability. Rather than fatal flaws, there is an understanding of 'triggers' to decline that are amenable to proper management. Nevertheless, in the context of low demand and economic/geographic polarisation between council housing and other housing tenures (due to increased home ownership, lack of resources, allocation policies and stigma) (Lee and Murie 1999; Lund 1996) their emphasis, in line with city-nationwide strategy, is on 'restructuring' the housing market which they have limited financial capacity to deliver.

Although these officials also describe decline as housing market failure their explanation for it stresses their limited capacity to manage the problems engendered by the change in demand for council housing due to financial restrictions and central government policies. Their limited capacity justifies (and necessitates) partnership with private sector partners and the need to restore healthy and sustainable market conditions that will require minimal intervention in future. Their role is in 'steering' or 'enabling' (Atkinson 1999; Johnston and Shearing 2003; Rydin, 1998) the creation of 'sustainable communities' capable of attracting and retaining population and services, diluting geographic/economic polarisation through 'social mixing'.

I want here to highlight the way these scripts resonate with an explanation of market failure and present similar solutions, though justified through different understandings of local problems. I will explore this difference in explanation of decline as 'low demand and descent into disorder' and in their understanding of social mixing as a solution capable of 'creating sustainable communities'. There is another emphasis within this script on intensive management, which further differentiates it from private sector narratives, but as this mirrors that of local managers, this is explored in the next section.

Low demand and descent into disorder

With less emphasis on a fundamental flaw in design these officers' accounts of spiralling decline focus on crime and disorder as a trigger to the decline in appearance and loss of control of the estate, creating a poor image and reputation and resulting in low demand for the area. One of these officials, Chris, briefly summarised its history in these terms.

> Not long after its inception ... it soon showed signs of decline ... the initial signs were anti-social behaviour, crime and disorder issues, which led to it becoming stigmatised and having low demand. That became a dangerous cycle of, a downward cycle. It soon started to become one of the most notorious areas around the city and most difficult to let.

'Void' properties on this 'difficult-to-let' estate – a sign of low demand?

Having tried 'hotch-potch attempts to turn [it] around', a more radical approach was now needed. Although Chris justifies rebuild, this account also stresses the 'trigger' effect of crime and disorder, plunging the estate into a decline in popularity. The emphasis is on the collapse of the market, the low demand, rather than density.

Though these officials admit to poor management, their accounts identify tenants' problematic behaviour as the real triggers to crime and decline. Anne's description exemplifies this denial of inevitability:

> I think [the estate] is fairly typical of any area where basically the … housing market has collapsed and you know … the whole neighbourhood just isn't working and it's … sort of in this spiral of crime basically … It was poorly designed to start with. Potentially in another area it could have probably worked quite well but because of sort of where it's situated, plus the fact that you have a lot of, shall I say, relatively poor people placed in there, you know, it just degenerated into chaos before you knew it.

Design may have contributed to decline but the combination of putting a lot of 'poor people' in an estate situated next to the city centre was tempting crime and caused a descent into chaos. Though distinct the estate is also typical of areas where the housing market has collapsed because the neighbourhood does not work and has descended into crime. Anne assumes neighbourhoods can 'work', in a very Durkheimian sense, but that behaviour needs to be managed in such areas, both to retain population and more especially to create change. This emphasis on intervention in disorderly behaviour to support regeneration was especially striking when officers explained the Council's enthusiasm for Anti-Social Behaviour Orders (ASBOs) in terms of their importance in changing the city's reputation for crime acquired in the 1990s, and promoting its image and competitiveness. Anne typifies the way these officials associate the use of ASBOs with the protection of regeneration and investment.

> We actively use them because, you know, in terms of, like, where there's considerable investments going into an area … you don't want that investment, you know, destroyed again and people's lives ruined and areas just to degenerate completely, you know, because of some toerag who just has nothing better to do.

This admission that the drive to address 'anti-social behaviour' relates so strongly to protecting the investment in and image of regenerated areas is astonishingly unembarrassed. It is reminiscent of an emphasis on increasing competitiveness through image-making within the planning/marketing perspective. Where the two differ is in these officials' understanding of a need for 'intensive management' of open spaces and behaviour to restore the conditions for a successful housing market, as opposed to design solutions. Though both imagine a future released from the problems of the present, this emphasis on reasserting control and restructuring the housing market legitimises state intervention to effect their removal. It was particularly associated with the introduction of new powers, the City Council being especially enthusiastic in its implementation of eviction powers and Anti-Social Behaviour Orders compared to other authorities.[7] Though seemingly contradicted by an understanding of limited capacity this control thrust reflects a dual emphasis on short-term intervention, to reverse the spiral, and long-term measures to create sustainable local housing markets where management need only be minimal. It is suggested that creating 'mixed communities' offers this long-term, sustainable solution to the problems of market failure experienced in council housing estates in the north.

Creating sustainable communities

The assertion of the limited capacity of state agencies mitigates responsibility for a loss of control (through poor management) while more openly legitimising a state-steered gentrification (Imrie and Raco 2003) in partnership with the private sector. The need for 'market restructuring' in the face of polarisation justifies this policy of 'social mixing', which these officials, importantly, refer to as 'mixed tenure'. Although they associated this solution with a need to combat the problems causing and created by market failure, they emphasise the failure of past central government policies that have exacerbated stigmatisation of council housing while encouraging home ownership. Tending to associate poverty with one and wealth with the other, they argue this history necessitates mixing tenures, rather than increasing disposable income, though that outcome is implied. Referring to the regeneration of the wider area, Anne explains:

> You're creating more of a multi-tenure area. This is very much single tenure at the moment, right across the board, and it does need a greater mix and for the area to work economically. ...
> And the whole thing really is about, you know, creating new

developments which are going to be sustainable long term and everyone can benefit from.

This associates deprivation and decline with single tenure (council) estates and the solution to this problem so constituted is thereby hoped to be in mixing tenures. However, these officials also emphasise a commitment to tenants and dealing with social exclusion that differentiates their vision from the more utopian ones of developers. What 'mixing' hopes to achieve is to make communities more economically sustainable. In this instance, though it is a promotion of dramatic population change, these officials express a commitment to the people who are living there, that 'if they wish to stay we will find a way of enabling that to happen'. Mixed communities in this way again offer a 'panacea' to both market failure and social exclusion (Kearns 2003).

Building 'sustainable communities' also, however, involved an implicit dispersal of 'problem families' concentrated on the estate. While support and intervention in their behaviour was stressed as necessary, the need to protect 'the community' created a tension with the duty to house those 'in need'. The compromise notion of a 'rebalanced' community was of one able to cope with the presence of one or two 'problem families'. In such circumstances, Chris argues, problems can be managed and kept within reasonable limits:

> Some people's view is that ... if you keep those people there those problems will never go away, whereas (and that may or may not be true to some extent), but whereas, you know, we were looking at building an area which could cope with those sorts of issues and problems ... The idea is to have a successful area whereby you can manage those issues.

There is an assumption of a continued management role rather than self-regulation and, in the short term, of intervention and exclusion.

The two professional scripts, of utopia and strategic governance, are voiced by professionals offering a vision for the future and strategy for implementation. The second of these, however, creates coherence between a dual understanding of limited capacity of the state to create a sustainable future alone and one justifying intervention to restructure the housing market and regulate behaviour to secure that future. This coherence is achieved through an understanding of intervention as market-supporting. The two scripts share a strategic vision of successful markets and endorse gentrification through shared goals of building a sustainable, secure community. This vision justifies 'intensive management' to promote that renaissance and protect that future. Partnership with the 'community' to achieve this is emphasised more by those *implementing* policies to manage this regeneration process, to which I will now turn.

Managing change: providing respite

This second section turns to the explanation for decline of those involved directly in local management, in particular those involved in the local Crime and Disorder partnership, termed Local Action Partnership (LAP).[8] This included local authority officers previously involved in housing management, regeneration[9] and police. What was striking about these officers' accounts was that, despite their different roles, police and local managers had very similar understandings of the way in which change could be achieved.

This similarity in outlook is focused, in particular, around a need to provide the community with a period of 'respite' from the disruption of crime and disorder if regeneration was to be successful (Hancock 2003; Walklate and Evans 1999). As with public sector strategic managers above, their script was rooted in an understanding of the limited capacity of state agencies to restore order alone. They stress the need for community participation and collaboration in local governance as well as effective partnership between professional bodies. A chief concern is to restore confidence in local agencies.

In order to draw out the similarities between local managers and police perspectives I will explore them together. The first part of this section will again look at the similarities and differences in the way local police and managers use a story of 'spiralling decline' to explain a loss of control and the withdrawal of community. The rest will then be devoted to two strands within their understandings of the means of effecting change: 'building trust through enforcement' and 'providing respite'. They emphasise problem-solving in partnership and it is only in some differences in their explanations of decline that there is any hint of past discord.

Loss of control and withdrawal of community

Conditions for crime
Police and local authority officers use a story of 'spiralling decline' in differing ways. Most importantly while police officers tend to stress

the *conditions* that caused decline, local managers stressed, like their housing strategy counterparts, the *triggers* to decline. Specifically, police stress the factors that made the area difficult to police while local authority officers stress their past incapacity to manage problem behaviour and its effects on surrounding neighbours. So, to look at police perspectives first, Ted, involved in local policing for many years, is typical in describing problems of design that made it 'difficult to actually police' and a 'drug culture' created by:

> A lot of unemployment in the area, a lot of drug use in the area, and the natural design of that particular estate, a needle exchange ... All led to really that lovely little estate, with a drug dealers' you know, known for street dealers.

These conditions made policing difficult but were not within police powers to tackle. This implicitly blames other government agencies for creating conditions conducive to crime. In addition to suggesting the growth of a deviant culture, these officers argue that housing allocation policies concentrated 'problem families' on the estate, again mitigating blame of public policing for the failure to control them. Ted explained:

> You reap what you sow, quite honestly. But certainly when it was quite a bad area a lot of it was because the villains actually lived within that estate and, really, what the hell were they doing, you know, being housed there?

Things were improving now, Ted's colleague Kath argued, as efforts to demolish, open access routes, and remove the 'social dross' were acting to 'just completely cut that spiral off and send it going the opposite way'. She saw the area as on the up.

However, many of these changes were not considered 'police work', but instead a sign that housing and other agencies were at last working to change those 'criminogenic' conditions. There is a tendency for these police officers, in contrast to local managers, to see this area as a problem solved. Terry, another officer who had worked in the area a long time, stressed that the area was now 'a non-event in regards policing is concerned, there's no great problem with [the estate]'. Officers variously attributed this recent quiet to the removal of the shop, the eviction and imprisonment of some of the 'problem families' and the 'swoop on open drug dealing' some years before. Though dealing has not stopped there is now 'a semblance of peace' as it is less open. The displacement or removal of problematic people had been the successful means of achieving this recent calm.

Fear and lack of faith

Though the estate does not present a policing problem any longer, these officers suggest that the effect of this period of drug activity had been to cause a withdrawal of the community. During that time, Ted explained, a lot of the residents had been 'frightened out of their wits, you know, they just wanted to shut their door and hope it would go away'.

Officers lamented the impact of intimidation on reporting and on people's willingness to provide witness statements, often relating this problem to the 'grass culture'. Common to most council estates, Ted suggests, fears of retaliation may be unfounded but are difficult to overcome:

> Sometimes wrongly, you know, wrongly intimidated. 'Cause the intimidation is up there [pointing to his head] rather than physically but, er, there is a reluctance sometimes of, er, you know, 'It's him, but I'm not going to tell you it's him' sort of thing … Would you give us a statement? 'Cause you're all we've got, quite honestly' … 'Sorry, no' … That still exists, you know, a lot of bridges to build.

Emphasising intimidation rather than criminality, he implies room for change if residents could be assured of protection and successful prosecution.

The problems presented by a culture of 'not grassing' are echoed amongst local authority officers, who tended to refer to them as a 'tolerance' of crime. Sheila expressed frustration with this tolerance which, she argues, intentional or otherwise, protects criminals:

> It's like there's a kind of tolerance of a certain kind of behaviour that exists … If people who do that kind of thing aren't shown that there's a consequence to their behaviour then what's to stop them behaving like that?

The reluctance to report limits the ability of agencies to address crime and disorder, to prosecute and show that there are consequences to this type of behaviour.

It is this emphasis on the need to reassure, rebuild relations and encourage reporting that provides a point of coherence between police and local authority perspectives. Both stress the damaging effect that fear has on people's 'quality of life' and on perceptions of the police and local government. Not only does this contribute to the withdrawal of community, it reduces reporting and participation in local governance. Frank (local authority) explains:

> If you're scared to go along to the public meeting at the end of the road about something you're very interested in because a) what might happen to you on your way there and back, and b) what will happen to your home while you're not in it, then it's social exclusion, it pins them into their homes.

This typifies a local authority association of withdrawal of community with social exclusion, suggesting that fear hinders participation, reconstituting the 'socially excluded' as the fearful. They imply that active enforcement to counter fears thereby also offers a means to tackle exclusion (from relations with governing agencies).

Tackling triggers of decline

Both local authority and police use a description of 'spiralling decline' to explain this withdrawal of community and loss of control. However, local authority officials particularly stressed the effects of environmental decay and disorder on residents' perceptions and behaviour, triggering decline. Their understandings were most clearly informed by 'zero-tolerance' notions of policing, what Frank called 'the sort of New York broken windows theory of crime' whereby:

> ... you need to jump on everything because of, you know ... a broken window turns into ten broken windows, a smashed building turns into a burned down building, turns into people leaving.

He explains that poor environment can create downward spirals in behaviour because people read environmental decline as signs that 'no one cares' (Kelling 2001; Wilson and Kelling 1982), or as he puts it:

> If everywhere's a mess why should I ... do my garden up because people only wreck it and everywhere else is a tip anyway.

As well as managing disruptive behaviour there is a significant emphasis throughout local managers' accounts on managing residents' perceptions. Improving the physical environment and encouraging residents to maintain their properties sends out, he argues, a contrary message to one that 'no one cares', reversing the decline.

This appeal to a broken windows theory gives credence to the story of spiralling decline, beginning with small problems that escalate. It justifies intensive management of low-level disorder to reduce fears and risks of a future spiral into decline. Though police officers tended not to see policing of disorder as 'police work', Ted, for example, stressed the importance of responding to complaints about disorder in order to encourage further reporting and increase faith in local agencies. 'It takes a lot', he argued, 'for people in the area to … phone the police, 'cause they don't like to involve us.' Although both local managers and police tended to blame one another in part for the failures of the past (to manage estates or police low-level disorder), they both now claim that they are bringing the other 'round to our way of thinking'. The most important shared perspective on addressing these problems of fear and lack of faith was that of building trust through enforcement.

Building trust through enforcement

Understanding this loss of faith as one of disappointed expectations of enforcement, these officials all assume that trust can only be rebuilt by demonstrating a capacity to actively enforce.[10] However, the combined effect of a consequent unwillingness to report or give evidence has diminished the capacity of local agencies to prosecute. Without information on which to base this enforcement the emphasis was on improving relationships, encouraging reporting and acquiring information.

Building bridges

The need to 'build bridges' with the community (see quote from Ted above) in order to gain information had some important implications for conceptions of community policing. Although police officers emphasised the need to understand local people, only one officer, who had been brought up in the area, stressed this in the context of overcoming stigmatisation. Their emphasis was instead on the importance of and current success in forging links with 'four or five good residents in order to keep abreast of what's happening on the estate', and responding to their complaints in order to encourage others to report.

The attraction of Anti-Social Behaviour Orders was precisely their capacity to bypass laws of evidence in criminal proceedings and offer anonymity to witnesses through the use of hearsay evidence, overcoming residents' reluctance to give evidence. These orders present an opportunity to demonstrate a willingness to address community concerns, particularly about young people's behaviour, that police had hitherto had few powers to address. Though people were still reluctant to report, Ted attributed this to slow prosecution and 'They've perhaps not got the full faith, if you like, in the fact that the system's still fairly young.'

Police officers describe the closure of the local shop, where youths gathered, in similar terms, as having had a positive effect on community–police relations. Mike was the most involved in trying to respond to complaints about the shop and, when it closed, expressed doubts about whether he had been right to oppose the renewal of its licence to sell alcohol. The 'off-licence', as he calls it, had really been 'the last lifeline of that estate' and the shopkeeper a victim himself. However, his concerns were outweighed by the improvement in community–police relationships.

> It was pretty obvious that I'd had some involvement, I went to court ... it was quite well advertised and I was responsible for that. Some people weren't happy about it but the majority were thrilled to bits. But I think it was the best thing that I ever did.

Though problems were only displaced, the goal of improving faith in the police was achieved.

Building confidence

Local authority officers also stressed the need to foster confidence in agencies by delivering on community demands and narrowing the gap between expectation and enforcement. 'We've got to bridge this credibility gap,' Frank urged. As confidence grew, he hoped, more residents would be willing to 'stick their neck above the parapet' and take a more active role in local governance. He implies that the provision of information to agencies is a way of standing together in defiance of intimidation.

> So then we need to encourage people to all step forward together with this, 'if you pass us information, we will treat it confidentially, we will generally do something with it, there will be generally consequences, we will protect you'.

Rebuilding faith in their capacity to protect and enforce will in this way repair relations with the community and restore a free exchange of information. However, in the meantime the dilemma remains, that without information they cannot enforce, but without enforcement they cannot build trust. There is therefore a need, they argue, to access other sources of information and surveillance. Both police and local authority officers justify the introduction of neighbourhood wardens and CCTV (overseen by a private security firm) as a means of gathering this information on behalf of the community. Frank, for example, describes wardens as '12 new sets of eyes and ears patrolling the streets as, potentially, are the post office, milk delivery and street cleaning.' These form part of what police officers, not uniquely, term a 'policing family' (Crawford 2003b). They can provide the information on which to base enforcement and environmental management.

A united front

Nevertheless, local authority and police officers tend, in particular, to stress the partnership between housing management and police as the means of widening their access to information and powers to intervene, especially to control disorder. Once they had overcome data protection legislation and improved communication the LAP had been able to use police information to implement housing powers which, Frank pointed out, 'were in many ways greater and more effective than the police powers on anti-social behaviour agendas'.[11] Police also described the benefits of partnership in terms of this increased combined capacity when police were aware of tenancy regulations. Information could be passed on to housing about the offences of tenants, then used to secure or threaten an injunction to evict. Frank described this early collaboration:

> The partnership had early on identified families who'd been causing nuisance for years, looked at their criminal records, 'Bloody hell, you know, 79 offences, you know … So then we started getting the housing consequences to kick in.'

It was particularly in the joint policing of youth nuisance that these officers described the tangible benefits of this partnership. Police officers stressed the way powers of eviction could be used as threats to force parents to exert control over their children, resonant of a form of disciplinary policing of behaviour. Kath was particularly enthusiastic about this collaboration. Legs spread on her desk, swivelling in her chair and handcuffs dangling, she presented an aggressive front throughout the interview and her tone is the most evangelical of these officers. Whereas in the past, 'youths causing a noise' had meant 'challenging 40 kids who by then have started running, which never worked', they could now 'pen them in and take names to pass on to housing'. Although she admits that 'there is no offence of standing on a street corner. However,' she goes on, 'it all becomes then under the people's tenancy agreement because the majority of people in this area are council tenants but they must limit the behaviour of their children. Parents can then be warned and hopefully … go back, chastise the child and that's the end of the problem.' The threat of eviction acts as an effective deterrent, she argues. 'It frightens people into behaving. It is working!' It is perhaps already beginning to have a net-widening effect (Cohen 1985; James and James 2001). Sheila (local authority) admitted that they were now so overwhelmed with cases of youth nuisance that they had had 'to concentrate on the top dozen'. They hoped this would have a deterrent effect and demonstrate to the community the seriousness with which they were treating anti-social behaviour.

With collaboration able to provide information about tenants applying for tenancy or in their first year of a probationary tenancy agreement, a precautionary exclusion was also possible, as people's past convictions could identify them as a 'risk' to the area. It could also alert police, Ted suggested, to the presence of 'a bad 'un living on the patch' who they could then 'keep tabs on. People say its harassment,' he continues. 'Yes it is, very much so.'

Frank describes this joined-up approach not so much in terms of 'problem-solving' but more as 'a united front' against anti-social behaviour. Describing the faults of past management, he contrasts these to what they are now working towards.

> They certainly haven't gone in in a joined-up way, which says if you harm one section of this partnership you're messing with all of us, basically. And we still haven't got there yet, we've still got work to do to make your behaviour have consequences when you try and get into the youth club and swimming pool and the library, or when you try to access housing services and what have you.

This 'joining-up' process is described as a way to ensure that once broken, the contract between agencies and citizens has consequences of exclusion from access to all sorts of other facilities. This joint capacity to confront anti-social behaviour and disorder is justified not only in terms of responding to community demands and fears, but as a means of providing 'the community' with a period of 'respite' from intimidation and disruption.

Providing respite

Providing 'respite' encompasses two important approaches to effecting change in the area. Essentially these officers and managers talked of the need to tackle crime and disorder to create a period of calm that would enable the community to recover. On the one hand this involves effective enforcement and, on the other, the fostering of a less fearful community less likely to spiral into decline. This can, however, motivate exclusionary approaches to providing 'respite' in the short term, at the expense of long-term approaches to changing behaviour. There is an implicit justification, not just of exclusion and control but also of banishment (Burney 1999) as a tool to effect change. Disruptive, problematic people are simply removed from the area.

Banishment

This exclusion to protect community is justified in terms of improving people's 'quality of life', a concern which has overtaken past aims of (Single Regeneration Budget) regeneration to include the most excluded through a community development approach. Sheila explained that experience had made her resigned to the necessity of removing a destructive minority if the local authority are to retain people and effect lasting change. 'You've just got to take people out of communities otherwise you can't arrest this downward spiral', she argued.

> In the end you have to make a choice and that's whether or not you're gonna work at the pace of the slowest person and have the whole community leaving the area because they won't live next to that kind of crap any longer.

This emphasis on retaining the community, rather than holding back the pace of change, legitimises the removal of this minority to create conditions for change and protect its future prospects. She could not help those 'who would not help themselves'. The rights of those few who cannot or will not change have to be sacrificed for the good of the future of the community. This protection of the future legitimises a precautionary governance (Haggerty 2003) described in terms of protecting people from the behaviour of a minority triggering another descent into disorder and decline.

Although warnings, injunctions and Anti-Social Behaviour Orders may encourage discipline and responsibility amongst some parents, these officers tended to assume that such a change in behaviour was unlikely. These 'problem families' and young people were likely to breach injunctions and either up-tariff to a custodial sentence or be evicted. Frank (local authority), for example, directly relates the utility of Anti-Social Behaviour Orders to the *removal*, not just control of criminal families.

> Some of the most notorious criminal families in this area are now starting to find themselves at various points down the legal road to possession proceedings and we've, we've had a couple of Anti-Social Behaviour Orders now where people have been, you know, 'thou shalt not do the following', and then they've done it, and then they've been charged with both the offence of what they've done and the charge of breaching their Anti-Social Behaviour Order and we've got two people in custody at the moment for breach of those things.

The combination of breach of the order and the new offence was, he stressed, enough for custodial sentences in these cases, removing the offender from the area, just as eviction orders (possession proceedings) were removing whole families on breach of tenancy agreements.

Though regrettable, such evictions were 'a necessary evil', Terry (police) argues, 'moving the problem to elsewhere.' A regard for the 'quality of life' of residents justified incapacitation or eviction, identifying 'the community' as the victim of their behaviour. (Feeley and Simon 1996; Burney 2000). Aiming resources at helping the offender change their behaviour while the community continued to be victimised, he argues, is not only ineffective, it is unjust.

Creating a period of 'respite' from the impact of crime and disorder is described as essential to the lasting regeneration of the area. Frank explains the need for a forward-looking precautionary governance of risky and disorderly behaviour explicitly in terms not only of preventing another spiral into decline but of protecting the investment in the area.

> The figure that's been spoke about being spent in this area in the next few years varies between you know £250 and £400 million ... And whilst we've got some of the levels of crime that we've got at the moment, you know, that undermines anything we try and do, you know ... It's an issue for retaining people,

attracting people, retaining businesses, attracting businesses. It's got to be a priority agenda for me.

Tackling crime and disorder is a prerequisite to regeneration. Otherwise this disruptive minority is considered not only a threat to people's 'quality of life' but also to the sustainability of the area, to the housing market and business investment. Their presence could cause another spiral into decline and exodus from the area, wasting this enormous investment. Powers of eviction offer a means of permanently reducing the concentration of 'problem families' in the area.

Taking back control
The other side of this promotion of change is an understanding of the need to encourage 'the community' to 'take back control'. If change is to be lasting, residents cannot simply rely on agencies to create it. They have a limited capacity to do so alone. It is also up to the community to change their behaviour. Frank again explains this most clearly:

> It's the whole rights and responsibilities thing. You have got rights to receive the services you paid for, you've also got responsibilities within that … It's only a minority of households in which crime and disorder emanates but it needs saying, the responsibility starts with yourself and your behaviour and the behaviour of your children and your visitors.

Though not necessarily involved in crime, he argues, residents contribute to disorder and decline if they do not at least 'take responsibility' for themselves and those for whom they are responsible (and thereby comply with their tenancy agreements).

These officers all argue the need to foster responsible, *self-disciplined* communities whose behaviour challenges the intimidatory effect of a disruptive minority. This renewal of community is described in terms of mobilising the community behind an agenda for change. Frank continues:

> We, in terms of engaging the community, an idea we had there was that you've got a vast majority of people, even in an area of high crime and a poor reputation … don't welcome that and want to see it change. And the single biggest task is to try and harness that good-will into action behind the agenda.

He repeatedly refers to this latent law-abiding majority within high crime areas as 'hidden' or 'silent', fearful and intimidated (see also Crawford 2003a on this understanding). Officers described various ways of increasing the *visibility* of this majority by, for example, encouraging residents to put stickers in windows to show that they had signed up to a neighbourhood agreement, or organising public events 'to give the silent majority some sense that … there's actually more of us than there is of them.' They were a means of trying to reduce fear and unashamedly rebuild the community to confront crime.

Increasing the visibility of this law-abiding community also inspires Frank's enthusiasm for residents' involvement in improving their environment. Environmental management is about making change visible.

> We've mobilised a few hundred people actually to be out on the streets planting up the greens outside their houses and we've started to create that upward spiral, you know.

This transformation is as much about changing peoples' behaviour as it is of changing the environment, associating responsible behaviour with maintenance of homes and gardens, and assuming a consequent physical and psychological transformation in the process of creating, what Frank calls, 'responsible communities'. It is indicative of a community 'taking back control', and sends a message of moral renewal.

Amongst police officers this encouragement of 'active citizenship' was more muted, and participation was largely restricted to provision of information and evidence. However, they too applauded a moral renewal of community and signs that residents are 'taking pride' in the area. Kath, for example, described the 'clean-up' day on the estate as a sign of residents' growing self-respect and self-discipline, a willingness to 'take responsibility'. It was changing the area physically and her opinion of its residents. She too uses examples of houses painted and events organised as evidence of a latent community, previously too despondent or fearful to take control. This is an account, shared with local authority and regeneration officers, of transformation and emergence from the moral pit of its past into clean streets and summer fêtes, drawing on a reversed causal narrative of the effect on residents of visible signs. It is a change facilitated by the provision of a period of respite from crime and disorder.

This is a very paternalistic and punitive understanding of regeneration and the local governance of security, both at a distance and intrusive. Used to justify intervention in the lives of those in council housing in particular, and perhaps in private rented accommodation in future, this script presents banishment or containment as a legitimate response to the demands of 'the community', the 'innocent victims' of disorder. Officers justify the precautionary exclusion of 'problem families' or their children, as well as a joint disciplinary role in getting parents to 'take responsibility' for their children. That this 'problem-solving' approach fits so neatly into a drive towards gentrification reflects the coherence of both strategies with 'zero-tolerance' approaches to disorder (Herbert 2001; Johnston and Shearing 2003). However, the use of sanctions under housing law mitigates against accusations of heavy-handed 'zero-tolerance' public policing, which would contradict an adherence to 'community policing'. Accountability is handed to housing management, and thereby couched in terms of the contractual nature of governance, made tangible in tenancy and neighbourhood agreements (Crawford 2003a). It is a style of governance which encourages compliance amongst a majority while justifying a precautionary approach to managing a risky minority (Garland 2001; Feeley and Simon 1996).

Relieving the present of problems for the future: vision and provision of renaissance

Professionals involved in the governance of this area used remarkably similar causal accounts of 'spiralling decline' to explain both decline and loss of control. This story had a forensic capacity to identify triggers or conditions causing decline, and legitimise interventions to address them. Though justifying different solutions to slightly differing problems these professional scripts all emphasise the need to regain control prior to the recreation of an area capable of self-governance and minimal management. This story of spiralling decline justified a dual conception of the governance of security as contractual and precautionary in excluding or managing a minority of people threatening the creation of 'responsible communities' and with the potential to trigger decline in future. It stressed the necessity of intervention to halt the spiral and remove threats to residents' present quality of life and future security and market sustainability. This explanation also legitimises restructuring the conditions, housing market and population of the area, in effect a renaissance through gentrification and banishment. Though private sector accounts differed in their vision of a future divorced from current problems, they shared with local government officials a conception of an orderly 'community' of the future released from the disruption of the 'unwanted'. Their contrast between an unproblematic community and a disorderly minority, now removed, typifies a shared understanding of governance to protect the majority. Chapter 8 will look more closely at this constitution of 'community' and of a minority of 'others'.

Notes

1 This is less marked amongst less senior officials working locally, who command a cultural capital that enables them to cross 'fields'. In some cases they were brought up in this or similarly deprived areas of the city.

2 Though local authority housing strategy officers share understandings of decline with local managers, I have explored strategic level officials' understandings separately in order to stress resonance with private sector narratives.

3 There is also a particular similarity in the account of a public sector official within the regeneration company. This may suggest a marrying of 'resonant' discourses due to a marketing role. Hastings (1999) has suggested that public sector officials have been more likely to alter their approaches in partnership with the private sector. In the context of debates about 'entrepreneurial' governance, the similar constitution of problems between public and private sector professionals is fascinating but beyond the scope of this study.

4 Thanks to the developer for permission to use this picture, though confidentiality prevents naming them.

5 To preserve the anonymity of the small number of officials working in this area I have not gone into detail about their roles and backgrounds. Though, as a consequence, these accounts feel somewhat stripped of personal detail, it is the professional identities and knowledges apparent here that I want to explore as that is the substantial difference between their accounts and those of residents.

6 The overall plan of the area and infrastructure.

7 The city's corporate strategy boasts the securing of more than 1,400 legal actions to deal with anti-social behaviour, more than half the national total and 13 anti-social behaviour orders (Manchester City Council 2001: 31). By 2004 this total number of ASBOs was 300 (Aitkenhead 2004).

8 This LAP is unusual for its small size (both within Manchester and nationally), covering only half the ward to distinguish this section of the ward from that of the city centre within which it is normally incorporated.

9 LAP officers had been closely involved in running Single Regeneration Budget projects in the area and shared offices with the urban regeneration company. Their activities were linked by proximity and working relationships as well as city strategy.

10 Flint (2002) also observed this understanding in Edinburgh and Glasgow partnerships.

11 This was the reason given as to why the partnership needed to be reduced to a concentration on improving communication between housing and police. This effectively sidelined other agencies from the partnership until just before these interviews and delayed further consultation with community groups until they could 'deliver'.

Chapter 8

Constituting community: the good, the bad and the ungovernable

Throughout these professional accounts there were some implicit assumptions about community and the nature of disorder and the disorderly that contributed to their conceptions of how to go about changing the area. What I want to explore in this chapter is the ways in which these professionals constitute 'community' and contrast it with a problematic minority constituted as 'other'. Their various constitutions of problematic people, and problems, reflect professional knowledges about order and disorderly people.

The chapter is divided into three sections looking at understandings of police, housing and regeneration professionals, and finally those of private-sector developers. Throughout these I draw out the ways in which these professionals constitute 'community' as *good* and draw the boundaries of community in contrast to 'others', constituted as *bad*, or at the borderlines of community. In particular I have highlighted the ways in which problematic people at the borderlines of belonging to community are constituted as disorderly, uncooperative or irrational in ways that constitute them, in contrast to an orderly community, as *ungovernable*. Each section draws out some of these similarities and distinct legitimating understandings of the disorderly, reflecting very different, in particular coercive, roles in governance. This distinguishes between the contractual/managed approach of housing/regeneration and police and an emphasis on market balance and natural surveillance amongst private developers. However, orderly behaviour tends by all to be constituted as constructive and supportive of the aims of governance while problematic people undermine those efforts. I will also touch on assumptions about residents' views, which have important implications for community participation. Throughout these accounts there is an attempt to reconcile understandings of a 'problem estate' and its residual population with a notion of a strong 'community' with whom regeneration is negotiated.

In particular I want to explore the constitution of a moral community within housing/regeneration and police understandings, as both means of control and aspiration for governance. There is a tendency to search for innocent victims in whose interests they work, and to describe the community in these terms. This constitutes disorderly 'others', in contrast, through understandings of moral boundaries of orderly behaviour and culpability (Haggerty 2003; Hunt 2003; Sibley 1995). They too use discourses of disgust, identifying these disorderly 'others' as dangerous and to blame for the area's decline, and legitimising their control for the sake of the 'community' from which they are excluded (Douglas 1992). This conceptualises problematic behaviour through mutually compatible and reinforcing notions of risk and moral deficiency (Hacking 2003). This is expressed by these officials within a narrative of transformation, both in their perceptions and in the make-up of the community, from an ungovernable place dominated by bad and/or ungovernable people, to a realisation and empowerment of a latent community (Crawford 2003a).

Local police

This change in perception is most marked amongst police officers who suggest a transformation from an ungovernable place to a now peaceful 'non-event' in terms of policing. This past tends to be described in terms of the 'bad' who had lived in or dominated the area, while its current relative peace is a result of police having successfully broken the 'culture' of crime and complicity they created. While there remain those 'difficult to police' they are distinguished from the bad and from the good community that was previously intimidated by them.

The bad/complicit

A culture of crime
The 'bad' tend to be characterised as 'out and out baddies', as one officer, Ted, put it, who have 'a culture of crime', particularly associated with drug dealing. This culture also extends to those complicit in crime, constituting some residents' reluctance to report

as protecting criminality rather than as fearful. So Ted's description of the past culture of the estate is blurred with his current suspicion that the locals have 'a code of the baddies':

> You know, anyone can walk through the estate in uniform and they'll shoo away, you know, the wolf whistles go up ... to alert everybody else who may not want the police around to stop what they're doing or vanish and then the whistle will go up again when they can come back again. But walkway estates are horrendous once that sort of activity takes place cause there's that many ratruns and escape routes, you can soon, you can lose whoever you're chasing.

What he describes is a level of organisation to protect criminal activity and a hidden yet widespread complicity in criminality. He uses a language of animal behaviour, intimating otherness, to describe the way people react to the presence of police, 'shooing' away into the alleyways and 'rat runs', letting out 'wolf whistles' to warn one another.

The estate was a 'hotbed' of open dealing in the past and this culture of protecting crime made the establishment of police–community relations difficult even after their arrest. Mike, a community beat officer, explained that residents' distrust, unwillingness to talk to police and tendency to scatter at the sight of him, made it impossible for him to deal face-to-face with people gathering round the shop in such a way that could 'avoid a policing based on arrests' and find compromise solutions. Although these officers distinguish between 'baddies', those complicit with and involved in crime, and 'good' residents, they were ambivalent about those who do not help the police. They explain their lack of cooperation as a deviant cultural development, of 'not grassing', that is getting worse as new generations are brought up with distorted values, defending criminality. 'It is a culture that is hard to break,' Ted suggests, one that in Millton 'is a tradition, it's an upbringing'. This understanding of a culture protecting crime links a conception of 'bad' activities to bad upbringing and values, particularly within 'criminal families', reproducing crime and deviant values in each generation.

Intimidation and insularity
These 'bad' families are also described in terms of their intimidation of others and violent family feuds. Officers implicitly associate them, through references to nepotism, in-fighting and the power they had

in the area, with organised, Mafia-like criminal families. Rather than being a source of stability, large families formed strong units difficult to police.

> You get a very, very strong family unit living there, difficult to – some are, you know, out and out bad families who are very, very – you know, they cause a lot of problems and their offspring are causing problems. But it's that sort of area. There's quite a big clan culture.

There is a suggestion that this insular behaviour, amounting to 'inbreeding', has contributed to what he sees as the strangeness of the people in the area, to their being 'a funny lot'. However, the violent reputations and sizes of some of these families intimidate others and provide the families with status and power in the area, at the expense of that of the police. Big, Irish families, in particular, are again associated with violence and retribution. Mike's description typifies this view:

> There's lots of Irish. They're big families, big families and they've all settled in this small area and ... these people have had reputations, whether it's, you know, they're a big family and they'll beat you up if you do anything wrong. But it's always a fall back ... and it does happen ... It's not just an idle threat.

The power of these families, these officers argue, has dissipated, as they have either left, been incarcerated or are now less threatening though still in residence. There has, since their dominance, been a reassertion of control, largely through a police crackdown on dealing some years ago. Nevertheless, this culture has had an impact on young people, Mike admitted, who try to associate themselves with and admire these criminals. 'It's sad really but it's the fact that they're somebody because they know somebody ... but I think more often than not it's just part of an image.' This culture persists amongst young people.

The ungovernable/difficult to police

Though the drug dealing culture has been broken these officers argue there remains the task of reassurance and changing the residual culture of 'not grassing'. Those not bad but disruptive hinder this process in continuing to intimidate and disturb the peace. These disorderly residents are referred to as 'problem families', officers adopting a term more usually used by housing professionals. The term refers in particular to the behaviour of these families' children and to their disputes with their neighbours. These families are not attributed the same threatening overtones as the 'bad' families and were described as the responsibility of other agencies to deal with, unless their behaviour begins to affect the wider community. The behaviour of young people and argumentative neighbours was thereby constituted as disorderly and, with limited powers to address such problems, to a degree ungovernable. These families are distinguishable from the 'good' by their inability to 'take responsibility' for their behaviour or that of their children but they are not criminally bad.

Disruption and corruption

The disruptive behaviour of these people, however, may still necessitate their removal on behalf of the community. The problem of the local shop, for example, is constituted in terms of behaviours particularly associated with a disruptive youthfulness that, though not necessarily serious, intimidates others. Another officer, Kath, explains that they:

> ... congregate, try and buy alcohol from somewhere and just to sit around in big groups, idle hands, so they got up to all sorts of mischief.

Noise, shouting, swearing, hanging around, doing nothing, racing cars, being drunk or on drugs are also linked to potential violence, escalating to dealing and other criminal offences, particularly when coupled with the presence of slightly older young men, who may also be influencing young people. Officers emphasise the age of young people when referring to the damage being done, the possible corruption, physically (drugs and alcohol) and morally, of innocent children by older youths. References either to children or older youths are suggestive of their moral capacity, the limits to their ability to be responsible for their actions (Sibley 1995). So, when diminishing the seriousness of the threat or need for police involvement, officers refer to children. When stressing the effect the behaviour has on residents, the presence of older youths around the shop is emphasised as a more threatening, culpable, disruptive presence to confront. However, the wildness of young children is also emphasised to shock and warn of the future if their behaviour goes unchecked (James 2000; James and James 2001). These children are ungovernable in terms of policing powers and distinguished from these more culpable older youths. Nevertheless, they present a problem to be addressed in order to reduce what one officer calls 'the intimidation factor'.

Lack of cooperation

In addition to the difficulty of policing young people, these officers associate the problems of policing the area with people's ambivalent or uncooperative reactions to the police. Though it is a quiet beat, incidents are not straightforward, implies Terry, because there are few innocent victims. Often deeply rooted in ongoing disputes, incidents can be complicated by people's past records and unwillingness to cooperate.

> Nothing is ever as it seems, nothing ever tends to be straight … If you get an assault the person who tends to have been assaulted may have previous convictions against the person that's been assaulting and may not like the police and may not want to help you. And it just makes it all very, very difficult and very hard.

The complexity caused by relationships between people on the estate and with police, makes this area difficult to police. This blurred distinction between innocent victims and offenders implies a difficulty in attributing blame. Kath describes (below) problems presented by 'domestic or family-related disputes' that spill out on to the streets in similar terms. She implies that these people demonstrate irrational violence and that they should be able to sort out disputes privately and reasonably, rather than needing police to step in. Again such incidents are difficult to police because of people's reluctance to cooperate or go to court, and investigating them could therefore, she implies, be a waste of time. She implicitly widens the boundary of the private to include in this category of 'domestic' neighbour disputes, a justification for derogation of rights to justice (Hudson 2001) and police protection.

> If you were a panda car driver you'd get sent to these jobs first, domestic with neighbours, you go along and people with noses squashed and blood pouring everywhere. 'Right'. 'I'll take a statement from you and get the people arrested.' 'OK.' So they give a statement, then two weeks later, 'I've decided I don't want to go through with it.'

There is an implication of increasing scepticism about the innocence of the victims, as well as frustration, within these officers' stories.[1] They also tend to associate withdrawal of statements with 'not grassing', suggestive of deviant values and culpability by association with protection of crime. They suggest that if a victim reports an incident but refuses, or subsequently withdraws, an identification of the perpetrator, they may want to claim criminal injuries compensation, the implication being that the claim is thereby fraudulent. They imply that these were not innocent victims and are undeserving of compensation or sympathy. None of the officers describe these events as frequent and they thereby sustain a dual and seemingly contradictory description of violence and complexity as well as of a peaceful non-eventfulness. The disorderly behaviour or ambiguous culpability of these ungovernable people, like that of young people, distinguishes them from the true innocent victims, the 'community', who support the police.

The community

There are two important ways in which police refer to the 'community'. The first is as a visible, if isolated, embodiment of the values with which they associate community. These have the appearance and behaviour of a moral community. They have previously supported and continue to support, the police and to report offences. However, police also refer to a less visible community who do not report because they are fearful and intimidated, rather than complicit or antagonistic. They rarely have contact with the police and so police have been less aware of them but they are talked about as the 'majority' of people. This fearful majority is indicative of a latent 'community' that continues to live in the area despite the disruption and intimidation of a minority of 'bad' and ungovernable people.

Supportive but reluctant to report

Though these officers tended to relate 'not grassing' to a negative cultural development, Terry gave another explanation that played down the protection of criminality. 'The vast under-reporting in the area', he argues, is due to people's fatalism or acceptance of petty incidents. Having grown up in the area, he remembers people's unwillingness to report in a more sympathetic light.

When I grew up you didn't make a complaint, you just got on with it. You either sorted it out yourself, if you were that way inclined and you had that ability, or you just accepted that that's what happens in life. That's more the case, that people are just accepting.

This makes Millton a tolerant place, making people less likely to call the police over the behaviour of children, for example, than in other places. Though it is the product of 'mixed up loyalties and beliefs', unwillingness to report does not always imply criminality. Nevertheless reluctance to report 'causes deterioration' when that reluctance includes not reporting activities around drug dealing. Reluctance to report is the innocent by-product of a positive trait, rather than an active protection of crime. However, like other officers, Terry suggests fear has caused people to close their doors and withdraw, a reaction to local drug dealing and a reflection of a societal change towards individualised lives. He nostalgically recalls past days of congregating in the pub on Sundays and street parties that exhibited for him the open 'community spirit' he thinks lost. People now 'just keep themselves to themselves and the area has become hostile' with a bit of a siege mentality.

Though tending to attribute 'not grassing' directly to a protection of crime, other officers all shared this understanding of a fearful, intimidated community. Despite their poor impression of the area in the past, they suggest that there have always been good residents too frightened to report or be seen to be too friendly with the police. Though in the past officers had seen residents as wilfully uncooperative, they hinted at a shift in their perception towards seeing a majority as supportive of the police, even if this support is hidden.

The forgotten population

Kath describes this supportive majority as 'the forgotten population of [Millton], who have grown up and lived a respectable life', in contrast to those who give the area a bad name.

When anyone says, 'oh, [Millton], it's a shit hole', they forget there are some very nice people live in [Millton] that keep themselves to themselves and keep a beautiful house and are always very welcoming ... I like to think that by being out there I'm representing that nice population of [Millton] that never

ever see a policeman until they're a victim or there's something going on down the street.

This 'nice population' are distinguished from the criminal, unwelcoming or unkempt, and are a law-abiding and self-disciplined community, unsullied by the corrupting influence of those who make it look like 'a shit hole'. They are the innocent victims of the area's decline, whom Kath feels she is working to protect.

This implicitly moral community tends to be described in terms of visible attributes that denote inner values. Though currently a visible minority, they represent a model for orderly community. Kath, for example, describes 'a little pocket of respectable residents, who have brought up their children well, work and look after their houses, and are now working hard to try and pull everybody else up with them and they don't want to be pulled down by them.' Though a minority, they represent a visibly moral portion from whom she hopes others will learn. Relating her policing to their protection she implies that they represent society's norms and values, in contrast to a deviant culture that had developed on the estate.

Restoring pride and values
Mike, like Kath, tends to associate these people's respectability with their attempt to maintain appearances and order in the face of surrounding chaos. They 'take pride' in themselves and their homes and form a small oasis of order on the estate. He talks nostalgically of a time when people's home was 'their pride and joy, while now, it's just somewhere you sleep.' He extends a loss of pride to a loss of 'family values', demonstrable in the way people maintain their home and bring up their children. Describing his own upbringing in these terms, he contrasts it to the disorderly and grubby upbringing of others.

> If you have a nice house and you send your children out … button your coat up, polish your shoes, keeping you clean, washing your face before you go out, it all starts like that and I think basic skills, parenting skills, will all stem … If you've got pride in your home it reflects – my mum wouldn't let me go out with a dirty face because it reflects on her home and her family. And I think family values seem to have been lost round there.

This associates external appearance of cleanliness and orderliness with internal values. Mike suggests a way of changing people's behaviour

A corner of the estate, frequently used as an example of this visible transformation, where residents had tended the space near their houses to mark the Queen's Jubilee.

and, by extension, the area, by teaching basic skills, including parenting skills, which, he implies, may also restore 'pride' and halt the moral decline. This process also represents a transformation of behaviour and psychology amongst those on the borderlines of ungovernability by encouraging them to 'take responsibility' for themselves. This has the potential to make a moral community more visible and restore those lost to its fold, a process of moral cleansing.

Throughout this account of the changes taking place in the area, these officers contrast those who have contributed to decline in the past, the destructive, 'bad' families, those uncooperative or unwilling to take responsibility, and the 'good' families, who have always supported the police and maintained their houses, though sometimes fearful and despondent. These emblematic characters typify categories of the good, the bad and the ungovernable that police also share with housing and regeneration officials. However, police officers use a distinct causal narrative of the cultural deviancy of a too close-knit community that causes a contradiction with a shared understanding of a latent majority intimidated by the few. They describe a reassertion of control by breaking a culture of insularity through the enforcement of sanctions against disorder to encourage reporting.

This re-establishment of moral responsibility amongst residents and a moral governance to support it, justifies both the removal of the bad and the support of the good – implicitly undeserving and deserving, guilty and innocent – identifiable by their support for the police. If residents are a hindrance and wilfully uncooperative or unresponsive to opportunities to reform, they are distinguished as ungovernable, explicitly irresponsible. As such they are constituted as to some degree to blame (Haggerty 2003) for their inability to discipline or control themselves or their children. They are excluded from officers' notion of the innocent community and constituted as risky 'others'.

This reconstitution of the 'undeserving' as irresponsible illustrates a shift away from a concern for need, rehabilitation or welfare, re-emphasising blame and agency for the sake of protecting the community, the responsible, supportive, respectable majority. This legitimises the otherwise morally and legally ambiguous coercion, dispersal and banishment of those not bad but potentially ungovernable. Unwilling or unable to 'take responsibility' for themselves, they may need to be excluded to protect the real innocent victims, the community, of whom the police had literally lost sight.

Housing and regeneration officials

Local government housing and regeneration officers used a remarkably similar constitution of community and of problematic people to that used by police officers. Again the community tends to be described as the innocent victim of the disruption caused by a minority. These housing and regeneration officials share a professional conception of the estate as one housing a concentration of problematic people and struggle to reconcile this with a conception of a community now 'taking back control'. They too describe a latent community that has been the victim of poor management of 'anti-social behaviour' but is now changing as 'problem' tenants are removed and good tenants encouraged to 'take responsibility' for the area.

Although this view justifies coercive exclusion in a similar way to that of the police, regeneration and particularly housing officials' understandings also reflect a parallel duty of care for those in need and vulnerable. This difference in role is echoed in a slightly different emphasis in their constitution of the 'ungovernable' which distinguishes between those who cannot cope and those who are wilfully disruptive. However, this distinction is again one that attributes culpability or incapacity to change that may nevertheless necessitate exclusion for the sake of 'the community'. Faced with criticism for past failure to manage the estate and potential criticism for excluding the vulnerable, they emphasise residents' demands to remove these 'problem families' and their efforts to respond to them. The community is again constituted as victim and vulnerable to the effects of this minority, even if that minority could also be described as vulnerable, and their exclusionary demands legitimate.

The community

The community is constituted by these officials in two ways that mirror the tension between its problematic past and its current involvement in regeneration. They describe a surviving community that has remained committed to the area despite its decline. These include 'good' tenants who maintain their homes and cause few problems in terms of management of the area. The majority are fearful, have withdrawn from community life and may be vulnerable themselves. However, officials stress that the area, or their perception of it, has changed and that current community involvement in regeneration programmes has pointed to the existence of a latent 'community' of which they were previously unaware.

Commitment and values

Frank, involved in the area's management for many years, admits that he has only recently become aware of a surviving community, having thought of it as a fragmented area when he worked there 10 years earlier.

> Back then I felt it was every person for themselves. I didn't think there was anything joining this community together. And all it was, I was wrong because I wasn't under the skin of the place enough, or something's changed, but we now have a thriving network of tenants' associations coming together.

Though unsure whether this demonstrates a change or his ignorance, he suggests an important change in his view of the existence of a community, evident in the growth of tenants' associations. This equation of tenants' organisation with community echoes his emphasis on 'responsible communities' participating in local governance, in contrast to competitive individualism, which had seemed to indicate a loss of community.

Although people have left the area and the residual population might be expected to be 'stuck', Frank stresses the remaining residents' commitment to Millton. These are people who, 'despite everything ... [have] a good form of affinity for the area and their neighbours.' His task is to 'capture that and prise it and encourage it' by appealing to two important aspects of 'community', to this commitment to the area and to basic values and 'standards' that all share. Frank's example of a 'community declaration' used in another area outlines the sort of standards of behaviour agreed upon.

> We worked with a group of residents to – for them to set down their own, not rules as such, just sort of ... a set of standards that they expected from people ... 'We do not expect people in this community to deal drugs. We expect people to keep their properties in decent condition. We expect them to be a responsible dog owner' ... And that was a very positive declaration for that community to make.

His emphasis on the word 'standards' rather than rules suggests the universal nature of these standards of conduct, contradicting his claims to local specificity. Such declarations are intended to bring people together around common values and moral boundaries of behaviour universal to any community. Linked as this is to a notion of commitment to place, breach of these standards implies a lack of commitment to the area's improvement. It constitutes 'community' along lines of moral conduct and commitment to place, again constituting the community as a moral majority.

A moral and vulnerable majority

The association between 'values' and standards of behaviour again suggests that morally responsible people are identifiable by outward appearance. They share common values and goals with local government and are good tenants, exemplified by keeping their homes in a 'decent' condition. In the light of the poor condition of the estate in general, these officials tend to emphasise hidden internal upkeep. This is exemplified in Anne's relatively recent first impressions of the estate. At first, with the estate in such poor condition and she herself 'ambushed' by residents with questions when walking around, she had found it threatening. This appearance, however, masked what people were really like, demonstrable, if not by the external appearance, then by their internal decoration of their homes.

I'm not saying that every house was in a terrible state. It wasn't.
I mean it was very obvious that there was immense poverty.
It was very obvious that a lot of people had a lot of health
problems. But there were some houses you went into and they
were just little palaces … beautifully laid out inside. And then
they'd come out to this chaos outside, you know, so … in a way
– in a way, it feels quite sad actually.

Despite the apparent chaos, the insides of some houses revealed signs
of survival and commitment that made Anne reassess the reasons for
residents' distrust and admit a failure of Council maintenance. Those
living in these houses, she implies, are blameless for the condition
of the estate. They are good tenants, let down by the Council and
undermined by the chaos around them. Anne also mitigates blame
for the poor condition of other homes in her reference to poverty
and ill health. These officials particularly referred to the vulnerability
of the elderly on the estate, 'in permanent fear of being mugged or
attacked and with a very poor quality of life'. Their presence adds
poignancy to her story of the impact of decline on residents. They
were the last vestiges of, and were symbolic of the fragility and
fearful withdrawal of, the 'authentic' community.

Demand for exclusion
This constitution of community as moral and vulnerable suggests
that this majority have the same 'standards' as anyone but that they
need protection from the effects of a disruptive minority. They are the
innocent victims on whose behalf the officials work. The minority are
implicitly excluded from this community and constituted as wilfully
(consciously) destructive rather than vulnerable or finding it difficult
to cope. Anne justifies the pursuit of evictions in terms of this relative
culpability:

I think the general population really, most people are quite
supportive of initiatives like that, you know. Most people don't
sort of consciously go out to sort of destruct properties, destruct
neighbourhoods etc. It's a small minority who do.

Residents, she went on, have been 'very clear that they want, you
know, tenancies whereby, you know, there's sort of a zero-tolerance
policy on anti-social behaviour, on neighbour nuisance.' These
exclusionary demands were, as Anne's colleague Chris puts it,

'coming from local people, not just the authorities'. This assertion of shared goals and demands for enforcement of tenancy regulations is always used in reference to the exclusion of a minority, justifying dispersal, eviction and restricted access to housing as a response to legitimate public demands. This excludes this minority both from the 'community' and from a voicing of demands. Implicitly, this suggests any opposition would put the critics' commitment to change, or their 'decency' in question.

The ungovernable

This disruptive minority is constituted as the polar opposite to supportive, responsible, law-abiding tenants who maintain their properties. As such this minority is constituted as problematic by virtue of their uncooperative or disruptive behaviour, criminal or 'anti-social'. In contrast to the standards to which communities adhere, these people – such as would-be dealers, irresponsible dog owners, tenants who do not maintain their properties and criminal families – do not keep themselves or those for whom they are responsible, under control. They are described as not only risky but 'irresponsible' and ungovernable because they do not respond to warnings. This irresponsible behaviour, however, is particularly associated with disorderly children, young people and their families. Often described as having been 'brought in' to the area, 'problem families' are implied not to belong. In this way they are also constituted as 'outsiders' as well as 'other' than community.

Risky and 'at risk' young people

Disorderly young people are constituted in contrast to good or redeemable young people. Younger children of these 'problem families' may be 'at risk' and still salvageable if their parents can be made to take responsibility for them. They are attributed a qualified culpability due to age, impressionability and faulty upbringing. Those a little older, though not entirely to blame without services, if they fail to take up opportunities to help themselves are then reconstituted as blameworthy and uncooperative (Hunt 2003). This intractable minority is implied to be irredeemable and needs to be removed in the interests of the majority. Their behaviour is described in terms of this lack of discipline. Frank, for example, described some young people as having 'gone naturally' (by which I took him to mean wild), drawing on a conception of children as dangerous if untamed (James 2000; Valentine 1996).

They had total, you know, they're totally detached in many ways and the crime, the crime that some of them commit and the nuisance they cause isn't, it isn't even conscious almost, it's gone naturally. It's the same as if I put that cup of tea there [bangs cup down twice], they'll smash a car window on their way past.

Though early intervention at eight years old, he argues, may prevent these children becoming involved in crime, by their teens they have become involved in more serious offences. This divides the salvageable by age, justifying early intervention and incapacitation for younger and older respectively.

Though small children can be described as vulnerable and at risk, the behaviour of young people is in general described as a danger to the community, excluding disorderly teenagers from a concept of community. Anne, for example, described the removal of the shop in terms of reducing the risks presented by young people from other areas gathering there. Unlike police officers she does not see the shopkeeper as victim and attributes responsibility for escalating problems to his sale of alcohol, and (at least toleration) of drugs, to children.

If ... you sell a load of cheap booze to the local youths and that who are bored, ... you sell more to underage youths, then ... before you'd know it ... they'd have a drinking party and then a car would be set on fire, a house would be plundered. ... When you have kids high on drugs and alcohol its a bit of a risk.

Although she describes these youths as out of control and destructive, she attributes their destructiveness to their intoxication, mitigating the responsibility of those under age. She lays moral responsibility for their behaviour at the door of the shopkeeper, legitimising the consequent closure of the shop as the reduction of risks to children and the community.

'Problem families' and 'itinerants'

This exclusion from community is likewise inferred for other problematic people on the basis of their behaviour, particularly apparent in officers' descriptions of 'problem families' and 'itinerants'. Anne, for example, draws on the past presence of 'itinerants' as exemplars of people whose behaviour and in-fighting had heightened fear and triggered decline. Not only are they considered outsiders, but their otherness is constituted in relation to their wilfully disruptive behaviour. She describes their arrival as 'the last straw for the community'. They are the antithesis of a settled, harmonious community looking after their properties.

> I don't know if you know a lot about travellers or not. They don't tend to live to the same rules as the rest of us. Some may describe them as anarchists really ... There were a whole range of issues around the travelling community, such as illiteracy, domestic violence is rife, and there's a lot of, I mean, its recognised there's a lot of incest as well ... and, you know, they are quite a vulnerable group. But when you move a couple of travelling families into an area which is already very vulnerable, it doesn't really help the area either ... So they caused chaos on [the estate] for quite a while ... A lot of the time they bring ... their relatives with them, so before you know it you have a fleet of caravans ... and they're not, again with living in a caravan there isn't sort of provision for picking up litter and washing facilities and stuff like that, so that can ... cause big problems.

These travellers are constituted as 'other' in several significant ways. Primarily 'anarchists' who do not share the same 'rules' (values) as the rest of society, they are described as the opposite of normal law-abiding citizens and their way of life constituted instead as dangerous, raising doubts about their innocence. The danger they represent is particularly clearly expressed in terms of defilement and pollution (Douglas 1992; Hacking 2003). Associating them with ignorance, violence, dirt and incest, they are described as disturbed, as well as disturbing, pariahs (Helleiner and Szuchewycz 1997). Despite their vulnerability to these problems, they are dangerous to a similarly vulnerable 'community' and bring disorder and potentially disease. Not only literally polluting, they may also bring relatives, invading the area.

Such descriptions of spiralling decline often outline problematic behaviours defined by the bounds of respectable and responsible behaviour, inherently immoral *and* risky in definition (Hacking 2003; Hunt 2003; Rose 2000). Problems caused by such 'problem families', and their escalation, are contrasted to cleanliness, order, self-restraint, lawfulness and useful work. Their riskiness and otherness is constituted along moral boundaries denoted by behaviour and appearance (Sibley 1995). This justifies their enforcement on behalf of the community, the truly vulnerable/innocent victim.

Wilful destruction and capacity to change
This legitimation of coercion in terms of a breach of moral boundaries of behaviour is most apparent when justifying the use of Anti-Social Behaviour Orders. A senior Council official, Christine, extends such problems to a national epidemic of incivility and destruction and describes a sort of compassion fatigue with regard to behaviour.

> People are just tired, well, you know, some people just seem to behave like animals, you know, they have just no regard for society, no regard for other people trying to live in the area, no regard for the law ...

Again such people are described as inhuman and, like their children, untamed. As adults, however, she holds them responsible, describing their thoughtlessness as a wilful and selfish individualism. They are constituted as irresponsible because they have not responded to help or threats. This reflects an understanding of a minority who are capable of changing their behaviour but refuse to do so. They are thereby undeserving of sympathy and forfeit rights to live in the area. They would play no part in the building of collective order and are again excluded from a conception of a future community.

Other colleagues describe a 'carrot and stick' approach to control (of providing facilities and exclusion from them) in similar terms, distinguishing between those who take responsibility for themselves or their children and those who refuse to. However, they also imply that there are those who are unable to change. Their problems are too entrenched or ingrained to be amenable to change in the short term. Though perhaps less blameworthy, they still threaten the 'quality of life' of those around them. They can be given support once moved.

A residual population
If 'problem families' are not moved people leave the area, Anne explains:

> Well basically if you get some problem families in there ... then the people who look after their homes ... and want to look after the neighbourhood, they think, 'Well, sorry, I've had enough', and they leave ... And what you're left with is, you know, the ones who don't really care or have no sort of ties with the area and it just all degenerates even further.

In those circumstances the people you would rather keep leave and you are left with a residual and uncommitted population stuck there.

The contradiction between this understanding of a residual population and a hidden 'community' of a vulnerable but otherwise responsible majority is glaring. This is in part because there are two understandings of 'community' operating here: firstly, of a community struggling to survive against all odds despite the effects of a minority of 'problem families'; and secondly, of a concentration of 'problem families' driving good residents out. In the latter the description is of people who are the opposite of a community, people who have no commitment and who do not care. The first offers the hope of developing a 'responsible community', bringing them out of their houses and participating in a reassertion of control. Constituting 'problem families' and their children as 'other' than, and threatening to the process of creating community, their removal is legitimised by reconstituting them as irresponsible or incapable of taking responsibility for themselves. They are thereby to a degree blameworthy, at least in contrast to the innocent victims of their behaviour. A 'carrot and stick' approach to management of the anti-social might distinguish the wilfully destructive or psychologically unable to cope from those who can change but guarantees neither a place in this community. This has importance for a style of local governance but also for how community 'demands' are interpreted and whose voice is accepted as a part of that community to whom there is a need to respond. I will return to this in Chapter 9.

Private sector professionals

Although there was some blurring of lines in the way that the private sector professionals talked about decline and the problems the area had faced in the past, their constitution of the community and its demands was markedly different in emphasis from their public sector counterparts. Unsurprisingly this reflected their relatively recent involvement in the area and their intensive work to involve the community in the planning process. Without coercive powers or a duty of care, they did not seek to legitimise exclusion. Not implicated in past failures they also did not tend to stress the need for a reassertion of control in the present. However, interviewing them towards the end of the consultation process for the master plan, their responses were coloured by a consciousness of criticism that they had failed to listen to residents' views and they were keen to demonstrate their awareness of and responsiveness to residents' views.

The community

A surviving community

These professionals were noticeably more convinced of an extant 'community spirit' on the estate, relating it to a nostalgic history of the area, and were less inclined to point to divisions and conflicts. They described a community that implicitly 'belonged' to the area, as opposed to those 'dumped' there through housing mismanagement. The effect of the latter was disruptive and corrupting of this community. One of the development team, Jack, for example, described the effect of this allocation policy through a language of 'bad apples'.

> It's been a victim of housing policy in terms of dumping the unwanted in the area. It only takes one bad apple to start to have an effect on the bunch and I think that a lot of bad apples have been cleared out now and what we're left with is quite a strong community ... In their own testaments they say, you know, it was great until ... the City Council started to use this as a sink estate.

He distinguishes between the 'unwanted' and the 'strong community', no longer undermined by their presence. Initially this appears strikingly similar to his public sector counterparts in its inference of the impact of a minority of 'bad apples' on the majority. Again these have been 'cleared out' to leave a (wanted) community, what he goes on to refer to as a 'hardcore', committed to the area. He too refers to residents' 'testaments' (testimonies) to the impact these 'bad apples' had. Their removal has, however, made them largely irrelevant to the present and the remaining residents are instead characterised as wanted and want*ing* to live here.

Though they tended to associate the existence of good residents, who were both committed and blameless for the decline, with their upkeep of their homes, they emphasised the poor management of public spaces, rather than anti-social behaviour, in exacerbating people's fear of crime. However, rather than finding the community fearful, he and his colleagues stress its resilience, exemplified in an oft-repeated story of an elderly woman who had confronted drug dealers every time she went to the shop.

> We've got [Mrs Jones] goes down and challenges the drug dealers. I mean she does a job that even the police won't do and she's getting on for 90, you know. All this fear of crime,

there's also an ability to, in some senses, confront it without antagonising the position and that quite surprised me.

This story of an elderly woman's vulnerability and bravery in the face of crime is used as an example of the failure of public policing. Despite this failure of housing and policing, residents have held out and Jack and his colleague, Bill, are both full of praise for their ability to cope. Bill's overwhelming impression of the estate was of a threatening place and he explained residents' ability to cope as a gradual adaptation.

> They don't, some of them don't feel safe there, do they. But they're fantastic at coping with it and I think probably if your area gradually becomes like that you become gradually able to cope with it.

Though existing residents are fearful, they cope well, though frail 'they've got fantastic spirit.'

Community spirit

Despite first impressions, they stress, this is a place with a 'community spirit'. All relate stories of this growing realisation since they started the project. Jack describes his impressions of the place as so fundamentally changed since his first drive around that he now sees richness where he had seen poverty.

> Obviously, when you don't know the people personally in the area, you look at it and you think that they are very deprived ... But in actual fact when you get to know the people you realise they're actually incredibly rich in a lot of senses. I mean, they have, they don't have a lot of things but on the other hand they do have a lot of things ... the family ties and the community spirit that exists.

He presents the place in this sense as a desirable place to live because of this community spirit. It is a romantic image of a community with family ties and neighbours looking out for each other. Although materially poor, these people and the place have a 'richness' in their lives that, Jack repeatedly argues, people like him, who have money but no time, crave. Though these sentiments are genuine, the descriptions also typify a general attempt by professionals to approach the project in a positive way. This linking of their professionalism with optimism (Quilley 1999) also reflects an emphasis on image making and the promotion of the development of the area. It forms a part of their professional salesmanship.

Outsiders

This community of close relationships, harmony, security and community spirit is also one where people belong and problems tend to be associated with the incursions of outsiders. Though keen to show they were aware of problems, with drug dealers for example, about which residents had complained, these professionals suggest that these people could only be outsiders or, at least, not the people they have met at public meetings. Dealers are constituted as 'other', as people who are not part of a community.

> Well, the estate ... has got crime ... 'cause people see it as a good area to come in and do crime, you know. I don't know where the people come from but certainly the people that come to the workshop, I can't imagine them standing outside and selling drugs so it's probably people from other areas seeing it as a nice quiet place with some alleys where they can start to build up their little business, you know.

Implying that it is the design of the area that has made it attractive to outsiders as a place to deal, Bill here assumed that this problem would dissipate when the area was rebuilt. As well as excluding dealers from 'the community', he also tends to equate the community with those people who come to public meetings. In addition, he associates outsiders dealing with unmanaged public spaces, again implying that disruption is something that occurs in public space, rather than something that is present within the community.

This assumption is also explicit in the way Bill talks about youths attracted to the shop from outside the area. Generalising, he describes the problems that arise around shops when there is insufficient density of population to sustain commercial activity and areas become unattractive to all but 'disenfranchised youths with nowhere better to go'.

> It's really common to, in the middle of those estates, a block of shops with the shutters ... all pulled down. ... You've got graffiti all over them and the space outside which was like a

community shopping place – where you met your neighbour and had a chat about how are you today, and that sort of thing – that then becomes the place where the disenfranchised youths with nowhere to go at night, that's the natural place for them to meet.

Young people are here associated with disorderly, unattractive, dangerous, dark places. Though less explicit about their involvement in crime, Bill contrasts their behaviour in these spaces with his utopian/ nostalgic vision of 'community shopping' areas. The purposeless or destructive activity of 'disenfranchised' young people around shops is contrasted with his vision of buzzing prosperity. Non-consumers, these young people are also non-community members who do not belong to that space and are constituted as out of place (Coleman and Sim 1998; Sibley 1995).

The constitution of community members as consumers, along with a tendency to draw out the similarity between their plans and residents' desires (for an attractive place to live and shopping facilities) is important to these private-sector understandings. Rooted in a conception of consumers as rational actors, there is a tendency throughout these accounts to make further distinctions between rational and irrational people and their demands.

The rational and irrational

This distinction is expressed in terms of differences in manner of speech and behaviour, though played down as quirks of personality, rather than problematic. Jack, for example, having drawn out the positives of the community, turned to the negatives. Relationships, he maintained, were strong, as evidenced in his experiences of consultation where there were few truly problematic people. However, his examples hint at some distinctions.

> I don't think intrinsically there are problems with the community. There is a few people who are clearly more brusque in their approach and more confrontational than others, and there's a few wily old codgers that are street-wise and stuff, but ... the quality of life is a problem not the quality of the community.

Though playing down the importance of these quirks, he is more critical of their impact on the consultation process; confrontational, brusque or 'wily old codgers', he implies a stubborn resistance.

Inherited antagonism

The distinction between irrational and rational behaviours is more apparent when discussing residents' involvement in the consultation process. Bill, for example, praised the ability of the Residents' Steering Group to put their personal agendas aside and represent the community, and so I asked him if he felt they were representative. Conceding that it was difficult to be sure, he thought they were, but continued:

> Inevitably there are some people who will not want to, because it's seen as an 'Us and Them' situation, they always want to side with the Us, 'cause we're seen as Them and no matter what kind of rational or logical argument you put to them they'll never agree because ... it's about victories and unfortunately that's, you know, some people will have that view whatever you do. So I think the Residents' Steering Group is probably representative of the traditional, rational members of the community.

The irrationality of the few is demonstrated by their confrontational approach to the process, by their refusal to see things differently. Antagonistic (and negative) from the outset, they cannot be reasoned with through 'rational and logical' argument and will never reach agreement. However, these are the exception. The majority, represented by the Residents Steering Group, is not only 'rational' but also 'traditional'. The antagonistic minority is thereby not only irrational, it is also excluded from Bill's notion of the 'traditional' (authentic) community who belong, thus de-legitimising their views.

In contrast to the reasonable, cooperative community, the irrational minority is associated with noise and aggressiveness. Bill continues (from above),[2] 'They come in just shouting off because they enjoy that process and they're just being antagonistic for the sake of it in certain circumstances.' Their behaviour is the result of '20 years of being disregarded ... by the City Council and they view this whole process with extreme cynicism', he explains, but it is an inherited antagonism that frustrates him and that he finds difficult to deal with. Though he seemed resigned to never being able to reason with such people, this reflects an assumption of his role as persuader, as selling the developers' ideas to residents.

Fear of the unknown and unfamiliar

Despite this assertion of the rationality of the majority, all these private sector professionals attempt to find an explanation for an apparent widespread distrust of their proposals. As well as an inherited scepticism, they also explain residents' anxieties as a fear of the unknown and unfamiliar. These fears of change are hard to soothe and make residents' reactions to plans difficult to understand and anticipate. Having tried to be accommodating, they tend to attribute residents' continued objections to these irrational fears and a lack of understanding. Jack, for example, talked about residents' desire for only one move of residence (though two would enable rapid redevelopment) and for a traditional house, rather than a flat, as natural but inherently irrational.

> You know, I think the desire to have one move is a natural, natural human one. I think the, the fight to try and get a traditional home is a natural one as well and I think that's a lot to do with fear of change really. I mean, it may be at the end that they do all move into their traditional homes equally, but we would still like to think that when people start to see what we're building they will suit a lot of people and they'll adopt it anyway.

He uses the example of an elderly woman who does not use her first floor at all but is insistent that she wants a house not a flat, because that is the environment to which she is accustomed and fears leaving. This is seen as an emotional, irrational reaction and a fear of change that these professionals imply is echoed in the responses of other residents. Inherently privileging the professional knowledge of 'good architectural principles' upon which the design is based, they cherish the hope that when the development is completed these fears will be allayed and that sense will prevail.

Shared goals

When I interviewed these developers towards the end of the consultation process for the master plan, they were all distressed by charges that they had not listened or responded to residents' views, and keen to stress the ways in which they had. However, they described the demands of 'rational' residents as being for the same basic amenities as any person living anywhere and therefore the same as their own. Jack exemplified this as he explained how residents' perspectives had been incorporated in the model of the development, in front of which we were standing.

> Although that may not look like any of the people's ideal, you may not realise it but it includes lots, a lot of the ideas

and principles and wishes ... They're not direct references, but things like, er, you know, they'll get sun, there'll be shops with people walking past all the time ... So therefore it's safer.

Residents' wishes coincide with the design principles upon which the plan is based. He implies that these are universal conceptions of an attractive place to live. If they differ – over houses or the number of moves – residents' demands tend to be regarded as irrational or unrepresentative.

Community is here partly constituted in relation to participation in the design process and tends, as a result, to constitute members of that community as rational, cooperative participants. Developers constitute the majority as rational consumers with the same desires for shops, services and safety, and the same image of community, as themselves. Though many residents may simply be fearful, others' stubborn refusal to compromise is seen as a lack of understanding or downright obstinacy and destructiveness. The views of this 'other' group, as with the 'bad apples', 'disenfranchised youths' and drug dealers, are all implicitly excluded from a constitution of a reasonable community with whom the developers can work. Those problems of the past, if not already cleared out by urban managers, are expected to be resolved by redevelopment. It is hoped that the anxieties of those residents who have participated and cooperated will be allayed in future, if they have not been already, by the developers' ability to sell the development to them upon completion. Part of an overall image-making process, this description of the estate and its residents is imbued with overtones of wilful optimism explicitly promoting the area. This binds its nostalgic appeal to community to a utopian vision, divorced from the day-to-day problems that other urban managers, and residents, confront in their accounts.

Fostering community and governing conduct

What is striking throughout these professional understandings is a tendency to equate 'the community' with the majority, even if hidden or fearful, and an equal propensity to distinguish them from a minority of problematic people, defined by their criminal, destructive or irrationally aggressive behaviour. This minority is implicitly excluded from their constitution of a cooperative community likely to participate in local governance. The minority represents those ungovernable or uncooperative residents, who disrupt processes of fostering community and regeneration.

Community is in essence constituted as unproblematic, orderly and perhaps most importantly, supportive of the work of these agencies or of the changes they hope to achieve. They share common goals and basic values. They are the reasonable, the responsible, the self-disciplined and committed. Amongst police and housing/regeneration understandings they represent a moral community, defined in contrast to a conception of risky/dangerous 'others' constituted along lines of moral conduct. This minority tends to be described through exclusionary discourses of disgust, identifying them as a danger to the well-being and purity of the moral community (Douglas 1992). Their conduct is both risky and morally deficient (Hacking 2003). This hybrid immorality and risk is tied to a notion of moral responsibility and culpability. An intractably 'risky' individual who does not change their disruptive ways, despite help or threat, and appears unwilling to take responsibility for themselves, may be seen as both blameworthy and risky. This redefines a notion of the 'undeserving' through a language of 'risk' that has a veneer of moral neutrality but constitutes such people as ungovernable in the short term. In effect, this limits a concept of citizenship to one 'conditional upon conduct' (Rose 2000: 335) and justifies incapacitation and dispersal of those perhaps not bad but ungovernable, on behalf of the majority.

The blurred lines between the outlooks of housing professionals and police may reflect new legal responsibilities for partnership-working within a crime and disorder partnerships, and mutual tendencies to categorise groups in terms of governability in order to legitimise coercion (Ericson and Haggerty 1997; Haworth and Manzi 1999). Equally this similarity may reflect some broader changes in the local governance of security, which seek to both 'responsibilise' citizens and restore faith in the effectiveness of local governance (Garland 1995; O'Malley 1992). This dual, contractual emphasis on encouraging compliance with a latent community and the control of an ungovernable minority (Crawford 2003a) legitimises the use of state agencies' coercive powers against the 'irresponsible'. Drawing lines of citizen/non-citizen, deserving/undeserving, this is a utilitarian conception of governance 'for the majority' (Hudson 2001), though presented as the symbolic embodiment of a moral voice (Etzioni 1993).

Though private sector perspectives tend to be less morally loaded, they are equally suggestive of normal, rational behaviour amongst a majority. They assume shared goals and normal rational desires despite irrational fears that lie in accordance with their own priorities, legitimating the demolition, rebuild and repopulation of the area. Regeneration, presented as the shared goal and vision of both residents and other partners in local governance, is also presented as a common good, in the interests of the success of which a minority may need to be removed. The 'moral voice' of community (Etzioni 1993) is in this way linked, through a concept of creating a balanced, sustainable housing market, to a conception of 'the community' as rational consumers with normal demands for an attractive and safe place in which to live. However, if people's demands are not in accordance with these shared goals and values they tend to be de-legitimised as unrepresentative of the 'rational' or 'responsible' community. This has enormous implications for the way in which residents and their knowledge are constituted as legitimate, constructive and part of a 'community' within a process of participation, which Chapter 9 now explores.

Notes

1 These disputes are described in similar terms to incidents of domestic violence where victims may not pursue cases and can lose credibility if there is multiple reporting (Merry 2003).
2 I prompted this with a repetition of, 'You think they are irrational.'

Part IV

Conclusions

Chapter 9

Participation?

Parts II and III make apparent the importance of relationships between residents and authorities in an area of social exclusion. Poor relationships can reinforce residents' sense of insecurity and powerlessness while limiting authorities' capacity to address local concerns and problems. Relationships that have been strained during decline are made fraught when brought suddenly into intensive contact during a period of consultation. Repairing these relationships, garnering the support and including residents in decisions about changes to the area is central to the local governance of the area, both in its physical regeneration and in the governance of security. This fundamental quandary for governance, of the need for good relationships while preserving a capacity to coerce, which can damage those relationships, is key to an emphasis on citizen participation in local governance. Citizen participation has become an almost unquestionable good in local governance. Whether within criminal justice sanctions, service delivery or redevelopment, the involvement of local people has become well nigh mandatory for bids for funding and as a means of achieving reform. However, the widely varying understandings and experiences that residents and professionals bring to such processes can make their likely outcomes unpredictable. Where the preceding chapters have outlined some of these perspectives, this chapter now attempts, by way of conclusion, to explore some of the outcomes of the clash of these world views during consultation. In this I am returning to the core questions of the book, unpacking the ways in which residents and professionals interpreted their own and each others' activities in participatory processes through their 'habituated' world views.

The chapter is divided into four sections. The first of these outlines some of the hoped-for benefits of participation in areas of social exclusion and some of the factors undermining those hopes. It stresses the need to question the unforeseen outcomes of these communicative processes, rather than be concerned solely with the technical difficulties they raise. The second draws lines of resonance and dissonance between residents' and professional understandings outlined in Parts II and III and the contribution the concept of 'habitus' makes in making sense of processes of participation, and identifying possibilities for dialogue between outlooks. The third section illustrates the exclusionary effects and miscommunications endemic to participation, drawing on observational material of meetings between residents and regeneration staff. These short exchanges are used here to provide a glimpse of the effects of a tendency for participants to talk past one another. They provide a brief insight into the effects of 'habituated' assumptions and exclusionary practices within participatory dialogues. The final section then sums up the unintended outcomes of the process.

Hopes and contradictions

Empowerment, engagement and trust

'Participation' can signify many different initiatives that hope to engage people in activities within their local area or with governing agencies. By capacity building and empowering the community to self-govern, take part in local governance, organise community events or bid for money, it is hoped that communities will build the strength to prevent spirals into decline, support one another and create links with government agencies. Participation is seen as an aid to better decision-making and effective, efficient, responsive and accountable governance (Bloomfield *et al.* 2001; Raco and Flint 2001). It is hoped that initiatives that are otherwise top down and liable to produce policies that fail upon implementation, or simply reproduce inequalities, will be more sustainable when based on local knowledge. Participation is presented as a means of tackling social exclusion, both from mainstream institutions and wider social networks, by building social capital and trust within and between communities and governing agencies (Kearns 2003). In these terms participation is constituted as mutually beneficial and, like community, is both a means to an end and an end in itself.

The confusion between means and ends within policies based on communitarian notions of community is exemplified in the hoped for benefits of participation and social capital. Professionals are encouraged to draw on local social capital and at the same time be involved in building it. It is the resource that poor communities are seen to possess and yet, if it is not working, to have lost. This understanding makes significant demands on professionals to build relationships and acquire local knowledge as well as to find ways to increase the willingness, confidence and level of participation of residents in local governance. The purpose of this participatory work is, however, made less clear by this confusion over means and ends and participation seems to become more and more emphasised as an end in itself.

Giving voice to the powerless

In particular, participation has been presented as a means of breaking down the divide between the powerless and powerful on the premise that participation with government agencies acts as a means of giving often powerless voices access to a decision-making arena. However, an assumption within participatory strategies that stakeholders can be brought together on an equal footing and form agreements that are fair and reasonable to all fails to take account of the disparity in power, not least between professional and lay *knowledges* (Mosse 2001; Young 2000). The power dynamics created by this difference in the knowledge claims of participants are particularly important in establishing that the capital at stake in this field is not social capital but cultural. What provides position may superficially be who you know / have access to, but the legitimacy of knowledge claims is the capital at stake. The minimal material resources, if any, that communities bring to bear in participation also weakens their position in discussions (Hastings 1996), especially where state bodies may themselves wield limited financial control. The degree to which the agenda for change had been predetermined by central government bidding processes, managerial targets and auditing procedures and the involvement of private sector property developers can severely curtail the degree to which community members are able to participate on an equal footing with professional partners (Atkinson and Cope 1997).

In order to differentiate between the degrees to which there is any real transfer of power or control to community groups scales of participation have been suggested. Arnstein (1969) put forward an eight-rung ladder, later expanded by Burns, Hambleton and Hoggett

(1994) to 12, even then simplifying what they admit to be a complex reality. However, these scales, other than suggesting the range of variation between participatory processes, offers some rather limited questions that focus on the techniques used within such processes rather than looking at more fundamental questions of their overall effects (Kothari 2001).

This dichotomy of powerful and powerless is of course over-simplified, ignoring internal power dynamics and diversity amongst powerless groups. Such divisions may be unintentionally compounded by participation if they go unrecognised (Kothari 2001; Young 2000) and simply reinforce the inequalities that participation hoped to overcome. Such an over-simplification also fails to consider the various competing understandings amongst citizens and practitioners, an absence which consideration of these 'habituated dispositions' hopes to address. I want here to highlight some of the dangers, implicit in a search for a united community, of a failure within participatory processes to recognise diversity of experience and perspectives on local problems and their solutions. All sides came to this process with preconceptions of who and what constituted 'community' that could simply be reaffirmed by the process and reproduce existing positions and inequalities.

Finding a community

Certain explanatory narratives amongst residents resonate more closely with professional scripts than others and may be accepted as exemplifying a more legitimate 'community' voice while others are excluded. An apparent coherence between them can reinforce a sense of agreement with professional understandings and undermine dissent. In addition the capacity to determine the legitimate participation of some residents over others is not confined to professionals but also forms part of the discourse of 'community' amongst residents themselves. The difference in power between communities and agencies within participation may thereby be more complex and nuanced than a discourse of 'empowerment' might imply. At what level participation benefits those whose views, or inclusion, are de-legitimated becomes less clear (Kothari 2001). Rather than focusing attention on the degree to which such processes fulfilled these hopes of empowerment, Kothari and her colleagues (2001) point out, it is as important to look at what the outcomes actually were in a range of participatory contexts. There are processes of exclusion at play within a process of apparent inclusion which it would be naive to ignore (Schneider and Ingram 1997; Young 2000).

I have stressed these exclusionary effects within professional and residents' accounts throughout Parts II and III. Professionals tend to present their knowledge of local problems and solutions as incontestable. A dominant and shared narrative of localised 'spirals of decline' precludes certain criticisms, constituting problems as those of the behaviour of a minority. Equally, participatory practices constitute 'the community' as those who participate constructively, cooperatively and reasonably within the process. Consultation practices are in this sense constitutive of the very community to whom professionals claim to be responding. This endeavour may break down some of their preconceptions about residents but can, equally, confirm them. Non-participation or cynicism implies, at best, uncooperativeness, at worst, destructiveness.

Building consensus

Ironically this exclusionary effect is in part a product of an assumption amongst professionals, that it was a normative alliance that was sought, based on shared values and goals of security and prosperity. Tacit understandings and funding requirements for 'consensus-building' undermined a rationale of acquiring local knowledge and diminished recognition of diversity (Tully 1999; Young 2000). This represents a communitarian commitment to a majoritarian governance and a conception of 'public good' which leaves little room for consideration of the rights or views of demonised minorities (Hudson 2003). There is also a tendency to make assumptions that 'community' perspectives endorse exclusionary and punitive responses. Such assumptions may be compounded by a search for consensus that encourages finding resonance and stigmatises dissonance between narratives.

If, as proposed in Chapter 8, professionals tended to see the community as having predictable 'demands' (for a safe, attractive place to live) and 'values', then the purpose of consultation is bound to be seen as primarily about building trust and institutional relations built on personal contact, rather than political empowerment. There is little scope for dissent or debate about possible solutions when professionals are understood to be simply responding to predetermined priorities. The purpose of participation is rather open to question if the proposal of solutions is understood to be a professional role as well. The role of residents is limited to a definition of priorities (sometimes through surveys) for bureaucratic delivery rather than democratic deliberation.

There are two important implications of an understanding of 'habitus' for making sense of processes of deliberation and participation that I want to explore, in the following sections of the chapter, through a brief analysis of the consultation process for the regeneration of this estate. Firstly, I want to consider the contribution of a conception of the impact of habituated assumptions on processes of communication and their embodiment in practices of inclusion and exclusion. Secondly, I want to address the implications of diversity, position and power dynamics within processes of participation (Young 2000). I will explore the overall communicative effects of practices that do not acknowledge diversity and instead reaffirm lines of 'desert' (Schneider and Ingram 1997) and 'belonging' that may compound people's conceptions of themselves as citizens or non-citizens (Tully 1999).

Communicating between habitus: finding resonance

The considerable differences in outlook amongst residents and professionals outlined in Parts II and III stand as a warning against assumptions of unity, common values and goals between partners in local governance. However, such preconceptions increase the significance of resonance between narratives as people seek assurance of agreement as well as mutual understanding during participatory processes. Most professionals were keen to stress their desire to listen and believed themselves to have gained insight into the lives of residents. To suggest that their overriding sense that residents agreed with them (outlined in Chapter 8) was a matter of wilful self-deception would be too simplistic. Residents also mirrored this tendency to see what they were expecting to see. Their various outlooks, I have suggested, reflect 'habituated' understandings. Their accounts are structured by conceptions of causation assumed to be shared and mutually comprehensible, though in reality rooted in widely differing life experiences (Bourdieu 1999, 2000a; Bourdieu and Wacquant 1992; Young 2000).

Though these accounts are habituated in relation to position they all draw on discourses and causal understandings that find points of coherence with others, though they may also mask dissonance. What I want to draw out here is the way in which residents' and professional understandings resonate in such a way as to confirm each other's preconceptions. I want, in particular, to briefly draw out points of coherence (and dissonance) in conceptions of community and otherness throughout the accounts outlined in Parts II and III that have particular implications for participation.

Conceptions of community and otherness

Decency and common values

Housing and regeneration officials' accounts find particular resonance with narratives of 'decency' amongst residents, with which they share a constitution of otherness along lines of moral behaviour and connect external appearances with moral worth. The accounts of residents who described themselves as the 'decent' portion of the estate also echoed a search amongst professionals for a 'moral voice' of community, both stressing 'family values' and responsibility. Residents expressing these sentiments tended to associate themselves with a wider national moral community amongst whom they counted professionals. Resonance with a notion of a moral community was coupled with an assumption of similarity to and sympathetic response from agencies without the antagonism or confrontation implicit in narratives structured by notions of 'us' versus an official 'them'. However, ironically, those voicing these understandings of isolated respectability could see other residents as threatening. They blamed those around them for decline and were the most in favour of the exclusion and punishment of disruptive neighbours, reaffirming professionals' impressions of support for such measures. However, these professional perspectives, being rooted in a constitution of community as similarity and minority as disruptive difference, tend to overlook experiences of exclusion from community.

Commitment and belonging to place

Other residents' accounts find resonance with professional conceptions of an authentic, committed community belonging to place. These discourses of belonging mutually reinforced an impression of a surviving community and were of particular appeal to those who described themselves as 'born and bred' in the area. Nostalgic stories of a lost community resonated with professional explanations of spiralling decline that also associated decline with outsiders and others brought into the area. This resonance between stories of a lost or surviving community confirmed the position of established residents and those who felt 'known', but focused claims to legitimacy around notions of an 'authentic' community voice. Again, this was exclusionary of relative newcomers or those conscious of being seen as 'other'. This resonance between residents' understandings of the 'deserving/decent' and of a 'surviving community' and their own assumptions gave staff the confidence to express their explanations of decline as common sense, shared by all.

Professional understandings of community fail to incorporate diversity. This is particularly apparent in the absence of minority ethnic groups within their conception of the local community other than in bringing disruption or change. An interpretation of a widespread demand for the exclusion of a disruptive minority, as a response to problematic conduct affecting the 'majority', represents an exclusionary discourse to many whose conduct could be in various guises constituted as 'other'. For those whose experience of the estate was of 'being other' the appeal of a nostalgic narrative of a lost community, used amongst professionals, was limited. Those residents' accounts that I characterised as expressing an 'independent fatalism' tended to be sceptical about the likely impact they could have on consultation and, distancing themselves from the estate, there was little occasion for resonance with professional conceptions of a current community. Though appealing to some, a discourse of 'community' could be potentially repressive.

United goals, constructive engagement

The emphasis on unity reinforced scepticism about the process amongst residents across the board. Though they hoped to accommodate diverse tastes and encourage a sense of ownership of the design process, a private sector emphasis on the similarity between agency and community goals, in particular, somewhat precluded the inclusion of diverse or oppositional voices and could in turn be perceived as irrelevant, co-opting or patronising. Likewise, understandings of professionals as 'other' contradicted private sector assurances of similarity and could be seen as irrationally entrenched positions of us and them. A professional focus on community as unity also de-legitimised and devalued the participation of those who questioned assumed common values and goals through noisy opposition. Potentially seen as destructive and unreasonable, there was an implicit exclusion of dissonant voices from participation. Such assertions of difference tended to be read as a product of lack of trust and past history and, if not amenable to persuasion, not constructively engaged.

For those critical of policy or suspicious of the motives of authorities, the emphasis on similarity, support and consensus could be understood as silencing. This was most marked amongst outlooks that could be stigmatised by association with protecting criminality, such as those of 'not grassing' or concerns for rights rather than security. Equally, expressions of a need to include demonised 'others', such as young people, could be overlooked and undermined as 'unrepresentative' of a fearful community. Similarly an emphasis amongst residents on their rights (to inclusion) could be poorly received or reinterpreted as an expression of a desire to exclude others. Although these processes of exclusion and reinterpretation were in part the product of exclusionary practices (see below) they were also a product of this attempt to find similarity rather than recognise difference, in order to reach consensus.

Rights, belonging and desert

The resonance between a professional understanding of community and belonging to place or a 'decent' majority implicitly limits the rights of those who do not 'belong'. While residents argued for the punishment of others and the protection of themselves, attempts to seek agreement could appear to endorse this limitation of rights of variously constituted 'others'. Highlighting the dangers in a notion of access to rights based on belonging to place, community or even nation (as exclusive and bounded rights), this majoritarian strand within communitarian politics resonates with equally exclusionary dynamics of 'defended' communities (Bauman 2001; Castells 1997; Hudson 2003) and of the constitution of 'local problems'.

This implied conditional nature of citizenship disappoints expectations of equal rights, particularly amongst those already uncertain of the degree to which they will be upheld by a biased system. Residents' conceptions of rights to social justice often refer to the gulf between an ideal and their experiences of the inequality which favours the already favoured. While those who saw themselves as deserving of this favour appeal to and resonate with a professional conception of their rights as a deserving majority, other narratives constitute their relationship to the state through this notion of unfulfilled rights. For those whose sense of belonging, or position in relation to authorities, was fragile, the implicit exclusion of those whose behaviour was ungovernable from community, communicated limited rights and the potential to be, as usual, defined as undeserving while 'yuppies' saw the benefits of this future (Ewick and Silbey 1999; Schneider and Ingram 1997). Complicated by a process of negotiation with private sector bodies as well as public, where roles, let alone lines of accountability, are unclear, an understanding of participation of citizens in a democratic process is further undermined by constitution of residents as consumers. This appeal to community and common values, demands or goals mitigates against an appeal for inclusion on the basis of equal rights.

Implicit professional understandings of community and desert mirror a liberal conception of rights limited within a community, which limit defence to 'our own' or assumes that some deserve more protection than others (Hudson 2003). Allowing the sacrifice of the few for the many, this majoritarian conception of the 'common good' undermines defence of the rights of minorities and offenders (Hudson 2003; Young 2000). Consensus is to be built around community, belonging and who to exclude in the interests of security. A resonance between public sector conceptions of otherness and those amongst residents who describe themselves as 'decent/deserving', I suggest, acts discursively to legitimate this identification of 'problematic/risky' people and confirm assumptions of popular punitiveness. It serves, alongside other exclusionary practices, to reproduce 'degenerate policy design' (Schneider and Ingram 1997) that distinguishes between the 'deserving' and 'undeserving' despite participation. The emphasis on building consensus and finding common ground for decision-making only compounds this process, communicating and reproducing inequality that does little to alter the outlooks or position of any. The next section relates some of the exchanges that took place in early meetings of the Residents' Steering Group, in order to illustrate some of the ways in which these effects are played out in practice. These examples are used here to outline the implications of the ways in which people using habituated understandings can talk past one another and find resonance in a way that reaffirms existing positions, privileges punitive discourses and excludes the already excluded, even if they are sitting at the same table.

Implications of miscommunication for participation

Though originally intended to be *selected* by council officers, the Residents' Steering Group (RSG), after protests from residents, was established by *election* with six elected representatives from the estate, whom I have named Pat, James, Rob, Deb, Henry and Margaret,[1] who worked closely with two regeneration professionals; Claire's role was to help them work as a group, while Christine, much more senior, liaised between them and the steering group of private developers and other professional partners meeting separately. This separation reflected, some residents felt, an exclusion from the arena in which decisions were really being made, but also a distinction between the forms of specialist professional knowledge brought to bear on the regeneration process and that of lay members. It was the dominance of this professional knowledge that in particular undermined and recreated residents' subject positions within this process.

Although there were important practices of what Iris Young (2000) calls 'external exclusion' (that excluded certain groups from access) in the formation and structure of the Residents' Steering Group (particularly excluding minority ethnic voices due to the claims of representativeness of the elected RSG), I want to focus on the 'internal practices' of exclusion that Young suggests hinder the development of processes in which lay perspectives are taken seriously even when included. These internal practices are implicitly tied to the ways in which residents and professionals tried to make sense of each other, to their differences in world view and differing basis for knowledge claims. These internal practices illustrate some of the ways in which an attempt to communicate between habitus creates problems of miscommunication. Most importantly I want to use some examples of these miscommunications to explore their wider effects on the process and its outcomes.

This section will, first briefly outline the ways in which professionals and residents conceived the purpose of participation and the implications this had for the position of residents within this new 'field' of partnership with professional bodies. This in particular explores the capital at stake in the process. Secondly, I will use some examples of exchanges within these meetings to illustrate the ways in which debate was inadvertently stifled and problems raised reinterpreted by professional staff through their own habituated understandings. These exchanges also illustrate the role of resonance, dissonance and silence in creating an impression of agreement with professional perspectives. The final section of the chapter outlines the effects and wider implications of miscommunication for processes of participation that seek consensus in this way.

Partnership with community

Professional partners and specialist knowledge

Intrinsic to the practices of 'internal exclusion' was a 'symbolic violence' as Bourdieu (1999) terms it, by which residents were assumed to need to acquire professional language and understandings in order to be included in a field in which that was the capital through which position was negotiated. Professionals tended to talk about the RSG as if they were a budding professional body as well as representatives of a community. Rather than a political process through which issues could be debated and new ways of addressing them sought, the process tended to be conceived as one through which residents could express either their needs (housing and regeneration) or consumer demands and aspirations/tastes (private developer). There was an intention throughout that the RSG would in the future develop into a body incorporated into local governance of the area and the emphasis was on their conduct and development as a semi-professional body with good, trusting working relationships with other professional bodies.

Professionals assumed common goals and that they knew both what the problems had been for residents and what the solutions were likely to be. This limited the scope for discussion of what problems they hoped to address and undermined any sense of taking local knowledge about them seriously, fuelling fears amongst residents that they were being co-opted. The RSG tended to be described as a 'go-between', communicating information to the community and feeding back their responses to professionals. However, the dominance of professional language and knowledge undermined residents' position both in the partnership and amongst fellow residents as they so clearly lacked the capital at stake in the process to be able to exert an authoritative voice. As professionals tended to conceive of the community as in close contact and united there was little debate as to how communication could be structured, particularly to include minority views. Public meetings were thereby held with a wider group of residents but were again conceived as occasions for informing residents and receiving 'feedback', rather than a forum for debate or expression of more diverse perspectives.

There was an implicit assumption amongst professionals and, as this language dominated, amongst residents, that residents needed to acquire specialist knowledge to participate in the project rather than, for example, wider skills of negotiation and organisation (Mohan 2001). This domination of professional knowledge, particularly that of planning and physical development, and the emphasis on the professionalisation of the RSG, reproduced positions in the participation process, making this a very one-way learning process.

Private sector developers, in particular, saw this lack of specialist knowledge as a stumbling block to productive consultation and argued the need for the education of communities prior to such processes.[2] Bill, for example, was full of praise for the way in which the RSG had acquired an understanding of the issues 'but they were enrolled probably twelve months before' the public meetings were held so they had had 'time to develop a knowledge base about what we're talking about. Now they've been through the learning process,' he continued, they were working well together and it was a shame that they would not be working with that community again:

We could buy up developments all over the place with that community because they understand exactly what's involved now ... and they'd be fully, fully on board and we could pull nearly everybody together.

Bill's description of the RSG as professional colleagues reflects an assumption of successful working relations as those of consensus and unity.

Resident standpoints: a steep learning curve

However, residents on the RSG were conscious of their lack of this cultural capital. They expressed feelings of being overwhelmed by the amount of information but also made requests for more, in order to feel able to make informed decisions or, if so inclined, to expose 'hidden interests'. These residents were disposed to come from the two perspectives that I characterised as seeing themselves as 'deserving' and of interpreting decline as the product of 'wilful neglect'. Margaret[3] and Henry, seeing themselves as deserving, were concerned not to be 'tarred with the same brush' as other residents. Rob, Pat and James, involved in starting the Tenants' Association, were all disposed to see decline as a product of the Council's 'wilful neglect'. Though Rob had some common understandings with Henry of a wider decline in 'values', his search for 'hidden interests' had more in common with James and Pat. A sixth member of the steering group, Deb, bridged some of these divides. From an 'old Millton family', she did not include Pat in her conception of belonging but shared some of her and James's concerns to defend 'the community' from exploitation or exclusion. Margaret and Pat had had considerable experience as local activists but while the former was often used as an example of commitment, Pat was referred to as from a 'problem' or 'criminal' family and as intimidatory or unrepresentative by local authority staff. Having faced legal action for slander in the past (having accused the Council of making money at local expense) she was cautious about what she said in meetings. Increasingly alienated she resigned under protest early on, saying that she could do more for the area by concentrating on her work with a network of voluntary and community organisations by whom she was supported.

Though these residents were differently disposed to the process they all described a similar sense of being in a subject position, constantly reinforced by the language used and knowledge required. For those disposed to see themselves as 'deserving' attention (whether by virtue of moral values or belonging) there was a sense of being listened to for the first time, but they too became disillusioned as the process progressed. All the residents in the group expressed feelings of being looked down on or assumed to be stupid. Their most frequent complaint was the way in which the use of professional jargon and acronyms acted in a way to disadvantage them in discussions. Deb, for example, complained that they had had to 'learn all these big words and you sit there thinking what does that mean? I haven't got a clue what they're on about.' Though she had expressed these concerns to staff their response had been to assure her that she would learn in time rather than that professional conduct should change. With professional knowledge so clearly the capital that gave position and authority, residents' representatives were constantly undermined, no matter how many times they were assured equality.

Deb felt that staff pretended to see them as equals when they did not.

> As much as they try – 'No, we don't, we know what you know, we're on your level' – They're not on our level, they're not. They're not friends of yours. I said this to [Bill[4]], I said, '[Bill] I don't care what you say or anyone says, that's how they look at us, you're off a council estate and that is it ... with your university degrees and all this, that and the other.'

Referring to staff's difference in terms of university degrees and claims to know what residents want and understand them on 'their level', she implies the status of their knowledge distinguishes them and diminishes residents. She found assertions of friendship and equality patronising, especially when they tried to convince her of their point of view, 'Then there's this, then there's that and ... They undermine your intelligence, you know, some of the things that they say, and I say to 'em, 'I'm not daft.'

Residents' lack of a position of authority in the process contradicted repeated assurances that decisions were open to negotiation and that the Residents' Steering Group could decide what it wanted, with no preconditions. Such unrealistic promises only heightened convictions that decisions were being made elsewhere. This situation precluded a discussion of the rules of the game, that might have addressed expectations of exclusionary or deceptive practices, and thereby limited its legitimacy in residents' eyes (Tully 1999). Assurances of inclusion in an equal partnership also limited their capacity to argue the exclusion of their perspectives or to expose different interests and thereby criticise policy (Schneider and Ingram 1997).

This dominance of professional language and promises of inclusion and equality only confirmed the suspicions of those disposed to look for 'hidden agendas' that they were being duped and co-opted. Continually trying to read between the lines, they saw offers of training schemes, like-for-like homes, computers and trips to other schemes as attempts to bribe or blind them to the reality that they were being subtly pushed out of the area or into a ghetto on its edge. Pat's scepticism about promises of parity of housing quality between private and rented housing exemplifies these attempts to expose deceit:

> It's all right saying, 'Oh you can have the penthouse or you can have this or you can have that', but have the [housing association] got the money to buy these houses, to rent them to us? I don't think so. I don't think so, no. They've not pulled the wool over *my* eyes.

In a process dominated by professional knowledge, residents' positions could only be reproduced, expectations of exclusion confirmed and ability to express their concerns or objections limited. Ironically, it exacerbated a wary scepticism amongst residents anxious not to be proved gullible. However, residents' positions were modified by resonance and dissonance between their understandings and those of professionals, which tended thereby to privilege particular voices and silence others. The following section outlines some of the effects of this coherence between perspectives and the practices that contributed to creating these effects.

Seeking consensus and finding resonance

Calming conflict and building trust

Tacit assumptions amongst professionals about residents' responses, and conditions of funding requiring consensus between partners, created an emphasis throughout meetings with residents on calming conflict and building consensus around common goals and values. Implicitly understood by staff as a means to move away from expressions of personal interest or individual anecdote, an emphasis on common goals and values was also understood as an expression of the growing professionalism of the RSG. Claire exemplifies this, illustrating their transformation through their adoption of a 'code of conduct'.

> They're such a professional group that they do, erm, you know, in the code of conduct they have to say that they've got those

issues with that person or they've got a personal interest ....
There has been a few problems in the past but I think they've
been ironed out and ... they see that ... they've got a job to do
... So everyone's got the same aspirations and the same end
goal, but just different ... ideas of how you get from here to
there.

Unified by common aspirations and a common goal, the group have
put aside their differences and begun to work as a team to get a job
done. That differences were diminished as personal, while agreement
given greater significance, masked the wide disparity in outlooks
amongst the residents in the group. This emphasis on commonality
precluded recognition of diversity of experience and instead focused,
particularly in the early meetings, on the conduct of representatives
within and outside the meetings, which some residents saw as a
means of silencing or limiting their capacity to express opposition.

A characterisation of those who were included in a concept
of community as fearful, and of more confrontational voices as
unrepresentative and even intimidatory, was an added dimension
to professional responses. Concerns and suspicions about exclusion
and deception could be interpreted as destructive. Distrust and anger
interpreted as the product of Council failure, needed to be assuaged
by building trusting relationships conducive to reaching amicable
agreement. There was therefore a repeated tendency for professional
staff to dismiss as irrational or negative expressions of concern about
residents' power to affect decisions or to try to prove that action was
being taken to increase their faith in agencies. However, this often
silenced discussion of problems without addressing suspicions of
exclusion, which only reinforced a sense among residents of being
co-opted.

Silencing and steering debate
The focus on supposedly uncontroversial bureaucratic details and a
code of conduct in order to build trusting relationships during this
tense period heightened the sense of being co-opted amongst those
disposed to expose exclusion and hidden interests. Attempting to
focus on decisions and visions for the future there was little time
given to discussing what problems the area currently faced. There was
no arena for battling out what residents variously thought the 'real'
issues were, though there had been some heated exchanges expressing
frustration at not doing so. However, professionals' attempts to calm
these by demonstrating their awareness of problems also contributed

to a tendency for staff to dominate discussion and silence debate by *telling* residents what the problems were. This could also have the effect of shifting concerns raised to reflect professional interpretations of local problems.

So, for example, an apparently simple plea from Pat for empty houses to be secured more rapidly initiated a discussion that exemplified this reinterpretation of a problem and the effect of resonance and silence in producing an appearance of agreement. Pat's request was echoed by Deb in relation to the now closed and vandalised shop, which sparked expressions of sympathy for the shopkeeper from others. Christine intervened to bring the discussion back to the point, explaining the background to the problem of empty houses and the shop, as she saw them. While Pat's focus was on the dangers posed to children climbing into them, Christine assumed a common understanding of a problem of 'squatters displaced from the centre of town because the police are not working citywide'. With poor relationships between the community and the police, she continued, their involvement in the regeneration partnership could wreck the process.[5] Still continuing uninterrupted, she shifted on to why the police do not patrol the area, fail to confront young people or just chase them away, unconsciously reverting to a tendency to link policing, crime and young people. She brought her explanation back round to *children as a danger*, exemplifying the gulf in outlook between her and Pat, who had raised this issue as *a danger posed to children*.

Not only did Christine silence this concern for young people by shifting the discussion towards her more punitive stance, but also the resonance between her understandings and those of Henry and Margaret played an important part in allowing an impression of agreement with her to persist, when they joined in to agree with her assertion of a need for more 'bobbies on the beat'. Indeed, although with different notions of legitimate policing, all agreed with the need for more of it and the discussion ended in silence. However, this also effectively silenced the expression of concerns about the protection and inclusion of young people, and the vulnerability of the shopkeeper and the need to board up empty properties quickly went by the wayside.

A similar tendency amongst private sector developers to lecture in public meetings, in an effort to show awareness, had some equivalent effects of silencing debate and reinforced the impression that developers were trying to sell the development to residents. These attempts undermined the potential for dialogue as professional knowledges dominated their stories of decline and were presented as both authoritative and unequivocal (Kothari 2001; Young 2000). They allowed no exploration of some of the subtleties and dilemmas presented by residents' understandings of local problems. This had the effect of both determining the issues addressed and, in finding resonance with understandings of 'decency', privileged more punitive views amongst residents.

Determining relevance and response

Similar exchanges and a tendency for professional staff to restrict, on an ad hoc basis, what they felt was relevant to discussion tended to highlight those problems prioritised by professional agendas rather than those of residents. Issues raised by James, Pat and Rob about repairs not being done were initially dismissed from the agenda as 'personal', though months later were admitted once they were described as 'strategic issues' and backed by the housing association which was keen to establish good relations with future tenants. Residents also raised concerns about rights to compensation if residents moved of their own accord, without waiting for notice. However, as a result of using a poignantly persuasive story of an elderly couple isolated and frightened in an empty block, this issue of generalised rights to compensation was reinterpreted by officials as a concern for vulnerable elderly people needing emotional support.

In contrast, the 'clean-ups' organised by Margaret and Henry in conjunction with an environmental voluntary organisation were enthusiastically encouraged by professionals, who organised demolition work to help and widely publicised their efforts. Resonant with professional understandings of 'taking back control', 'clean-ups' also accorded with a desire to demonstrate action (Flint 2002; Mosse 2001). A professional tendency to assume that they knew what action was desired when problems were raised meant that not only did problems go unexplored but their solutions were not discussed. For example, when the continued problem of young people hanging around the now derelict shop was raised by Henry and Margaret, it was taken on board as a current problem but, without discussion of what should happen, the shop's demolition was organised. Coming soon after attempts by other residents (some of whom were on the steering committee) to informally raise money to help the shopkeeper repair and reopen, this response was inadvertently insensitive and the demolition became symbolic of the death of the estate.

Proposals raised by staff, such as the introduction of neighbourhood wardens, were also accepted with surprisingly little debate, though only Margaret, Henry and Rob expressed any enthusiasm for them. There was no discussion of crime and disorder on the estate. During the short debate, James alone muttered that the wardens would simply be 'like red rags to a bull' but, such comments going unexplored, others only voiced their scepticism after the meeting. As no one adamantly objected, Claire seemed to take silence as agreement.

Some time later, James explained his comment further. Assuming these schemes would be coming 'further down the line' he considered them a good idea for the future (yuppie) estate but they were not for now.

> Honest to God, neighbourhood wardens, putting them on this estate now, they'd get ripped apart! (JK: Why?) They would not like the idea of people spying on them, right ... I can't tell them [officials] that but ... don't forget the new area, hopefully'll have a lot of money coming to the area and they've got to be seen to be protected or seen to have some security the police haven't provided yet.

Seeing wardens as a form of private security, instituted for the benefit of future wealthy residents, he anticipated hostility to another form of policing in the area but, significantly, felt unable to express such concerns in the meetings as he might be construed as defending criminality. The lack of discussion and exploration of dissent exposed this process to such instances of assumed consent, particularly around

The shop after demolition

issues of security. Although residents were keen to take advantage of resources they could get, insufficient attention was paid to the way they could be introduced without aggravating local sensitivities to policing and surveillance, to negotiating their legitimacy. The resonance with the perspectives of those who saw themselves as 'the deserving' was particularly undermining and silencing of those more inclined to express concerns for residents' rights, especially of those demonised or seen as undeserving or risky.

Discourses of rights and responsibilities
Of all the shifts in meanings caused by this resonance between narratives the most significant were during discussions over the policy of residents' right to return to the estate upon rebuild and whether there would be 'criteria' for eligibility for rehousing. The 'right to return' was first raised by residents and there was surprising agreement between them, all agreeing that it should be backdated to the announcement of regeneration plans, two years earlier. In the following meeting, with the head of housing management, their expectations were surpassed with an agreed date predating the one they had expected to fight for. As soon as the date was announced, the tension lifted enormously, the battle no longer needing to be fought.[6] The tension between residents also lifted during this meeting with their attention focused on a unanimous concern to ensure rights for residents rather than on the rules governing the group.

This coherence over generalised rights of all residents reflected a common language through which they could represent residents without being de-legitimised as driven by personal interest. This right to inclusion was an issue over which they, at first, showed remarkable unity and a concrete focus for negotiation. It suggests some wider benefits to a legal discourse of rights as a basis for deliberation capable of promoting inclusion (Hudson 2003; Young 2000).

Pat and James first raised the issue of 'criteria' amongst fears that current residents would be barred from return. Usually at loggerheads with them, Margaret too asked for assurance that 'nothing would be forced on us' in this regard. However, Claire, interpreting their fears as of a readmittance of 'problem families', suggested they look to having a Community Agreement. This shifted the language away from a right to return to what behaviour they would not tolerate and the limits placed on that right. Ironically, this moved away from a consensus about rights towards disagreements about tolerable behaviour, and from concerns about inclusion and justice to exclusion in the name of security.

In later interviews Henry and Deb expressed approval of the introduction of criteria that would 'get rid of the riff raff', but Rob, Pat and James warned of the potential abuse of such powers for 'hidden interests'. Rob, for example, stressed the need to give people a chance to return and was concerned that a set of very 'high' criteria would exclude many, instead of whom 'they'll get all yuppies in, won't they.' However, these three residents also expressed a wider concern about policies that could create ghetto areas to which those excluded would be moved. Rob expressed this most clearly.

> What happens if you can't move back on it? ... The policy's wrong 'cause you go on about all the villains and all them who don't look after their houses. You've got to put them somewhere ... so where are you gonna put them all? All on one estate? What would it be like there? So you know what I mean ... You've got to give them a chance to live to that criteria, you know ... Give 'em a chance to meet it, and that's the only way you'll improve things, init? You couldn't say, 'Oh, you can't live on there 'cause you're not good enough.' You're a second-class citizen straight away, aren't you?

This reflects a strong sense amongst those residents disposed to expose hidden interests that they were defending the rights of the vulnerable and the potentially stigmatised and excluded. It contrasts greatly with the precautionary trend amongst public sector managers. However, such views were rarely voiced in meetings, these concerns for rights and inclusion being continually stifled.

Though united around rights, the subsequent focus on conduct reinforced a division in outlook between residents, privileging those presenting themselves as decent and authentic members of the community, an exclusionary trend not lost on those less certain of being characterised as such. In the 'brave new world', James thought, a lot of behaviour would not be allowed and people would be excluded through Anti-Social Behaviour Orders penalising behaviour the 'decent' residents thought reprehensible. A man coming home drunk with his trousers fallen down, for example, 'might be fuckin' hilarious' to him 'but yuppies, middle-class people would complain and campaign to clean up the estate ... for drunken behaviour. Now that might be anti-social to them but it won't be to us.' Through Community Agreements, he worried, people were 'signing away a lot of basic rights'. The divisive effect of the professional emphasis on limited entitlement was apparent in the stifling within meetings of these expressions of concerns about inclusion and justice alongside security (Hudson 2003), concerns which were silenced by fears of being written off as protecting criminality. This effectively privileged more punitive outlooks. Rights were, through this focus on responsibilities to the community, limited to a 'club good' conceived in terms of conduct (Crawford 2003a; Rose 2000). The changes to the area augured well for the exclusivity of the area rather than its inclusiveness. Despite such concerns, four months later the discussion recorded in minutes of the RSG meetings, was focused on altering the terms of a 'good neighbour agreement' to be more stringent and exclusive.[7] This gave the impression of consensus where perhaps they had simply found resonance and silence.

Re-entrenched positions

These misunderstandings and controls on the issues under discussion meant that many of the suspicions and divisions between residents persisted throughout the process. With no alteration in position of participants, which could only have been achieved by altering the capital at stake in the process (Bourdieu 2000a; Bourdieu and Wacquant 1992), there could be little hope of a change in outlook amongst either residents or professionals. The process confirmed for professionals, through resonance and domination, that the priorities they expected were also those of the community. Equally, the suspicions of those who feared co-option and hidden agendas were reinforced, while the hopes of those who saw this as an opportunity to be heard tended to be disappointed. It was noticeable that some of the residents more experienced in local politics gradually distanced themselves from the process, if participating at all. Even those who believed that they 'deserved' to be and would be heard became more and more disillusioned, while the process offered little to counter more fatalistic expectations of this process as a mere 'talking shop'.

Privileging punitiveness, confirming exclusivity
Though this process did not promote a change in outlook amongst participants, it did have some important effects as a result of the continued dominance of professional understandings. Professionals found confirmation of their outlook in its resonance with similar notions of belonging to place and conceptions of otherness (along lines of behaviour and external appearances) amongst residents. This

had the effect of privileging punitiveness, strengthening the legitimacy of their more exclusionary responses.

Not only silencing other perspectives more resonant with concerns for rights, these exclusionary discourses and the policies they justified reinforced expectations that undesirable residents would be evicted/never allowed to return. Conscious that they might not be considered desirable for various reasons by other influential residents or professionals, many expressed a heightened sense of vulnerability and anxiety about the implications of regeneration for them. Those who felt their rights had not been upheld in the past had no reason in this context to expect any different, compounding expectations of inequality.

Punitive and exclusionary discourses and practices only confirmed expectations that residents would be ignored, played with, duped or co-opted and heightened fears of future ghettoisation or being driven out. This could only exclude from the process the already excluded and reaffirm suspicions that there was little point in participating in it as the future was 'not for us'. Attendance at public meetings gradually tailed off and was reduced to a core of four or five regulars; at the final public meeting, in fact, there were more professional staff there than residents.

Playing the numbers game

Discussions were dogged by expressions of the conviction that residents were being driven out. This was apparent in a 'numbers game' (Young, 2000) between developers and the RSG: over the number of houses (rather than 'yuppie' flats) to be built; where they would be sited (in the centre/on the edge); the number of times people would be moved (whether they would be 'decanted' out of the area altogether, move once within the development or intend to move back and never do so). Much of these discussions were expressions of a consciousness of relative powerlessness. Conscious that in the future they would be in a minority (10 per cent social housing) they were anxious not to become an even smaller number, nor be less well served or valued. Moreover, these were all issues that involved them in conflict with the development company who began to fundamentally question the capacity of the RSG to speak for the majority of residents on these issues. As a result these conflicts came down to a tussle over who could convince the other that they were representing the views of a greater number of residents.

The ability to play this numbers game came to a head in a dispute over the assertion by the developers' team that many residents were willing to move twice if they could return to live in the centre of the site. Since a declared majority would justify 'decanting' residents and speed up the rebuild, developers were keen to establish agreement and a survey was proposed to establish evidence on which to base discussions. The wording of the survey, which took the form of an information sheet weighing up the pros and cons of two moves, was heavily weighted to an agreement to two, and carried out after being seen by only one of the RSG, resulted in their unanimous resignation. The RSG were painfully aware that where such decisions appeared to be made elsewhere, non-negotiable or weighted against them, they could only be a means of legitimating decisions.

This consultation process could only confirm this sense of being co-opted and re-entrench positions on both sides. Developers were confounded by these fears of ghettoisation that they could only interpret as a lack of trust inherited from past Council failure and residents' failure to grasp the concept of 'pepper-potting' people in mixed communities. Bill was worried that residents' assumptions 'that they would all be living in one of the blocks' … 'might produce the very effect they had been trying to prevent'. He hoped that more would in the end come round to living in the flats once they were built, creating that mix. However, residents on the RSG expressed almost identical concerns about a failure to mix, but their focus was on a concern that there would be too few houses and so all would be filled with social housing tenants and clearly identifiable as such. Never getting beyond residents' concerns about exclusion and stigma, if all houses were filled by social housing tenants, and private sector desires to retain high density by building apartments instead (hence the reluctance to increase the number of houses), the process hit stalemate and collapsed.

Credibility, legitimacy and capital

Accusations of unrepresentativeness involved the RSG in a numbers game which they did not have the resources to undertake. Their only credibility was as representatives of a moral or authentic community, reinforcing exclusionary understandings of belonging and limited rights. Undermined by an official discourse of responsibilities to the community, as opposed to rights, and challenged about their ability to represent the majority/community, a concern to defend minorities and denigrated groups fell by the wayside. So early concerns about and desires to include children, young people and confront issues of health and drug addiction were given little priority, if not precluded from discussion, as not relevant at this stage.

The dominance of professional knowledges and a restricted conception of participation as the expression of preferences or needs within a specific project, focused around planning and marketing priorities, reproduced the subject position of residents within a process in which they had no cultural capital. Without an attempt to discuss their perspectives on local problems, and acceptable responses to them, there was little scope to give credence to what knowledge they had. No amount of social capital in such a situation could improve their bargaining position in a game so clearly stacked against them.

Questions of the role, power and inclusion of residents in consultation, though raised early on in the process, were never thoroughly addressed, undermining the legitimacy of the entire process in the eyes of residents. Compounded by practices of external and internal exclusion (Young 2000), it reproduced subject positions and exacerbated the alienation of those residents already sceptical of their capacity to influence local governance. In effect this participatory process had two important outcomes: privileging and endorsing punitiveness and policies of exclusion; and confirming residents' suspicions and expectations of authorities and their understandings of the nature of inequality. These meetings thereby came across to many as simply an attempt to sell residents something that was 'not for us', that would favour the already favoured (Ewick and Silbey 1999). At the expense of a recognition of diversity of experience and complexity of conceptions of local problems the search for a moral, united community implicitly went about creating consensus around who to exclude to the detriment of the rights of demonised minorities and criminalised 'others' (Hudson 2003). This was never at the forefront of discussions with private sector partners, though it was apparent in the practices of local managers, and so heightened a sense of being a shady undertone to changes taking place. Chapter 10, by way of conclusion, will begin to outline a more inclusive approach to local governance and participatory processes, addressing some of these issues of communicating across habitus and taking account of the ways in which problems are constituted.

Notes

1 Their perspectives are outlined below.
2 One of their number argued this same point in a talk given at a national conference for people involved in regeneration (Urban Summit 2002).

3 Margaret refused to be interviewed, in part because of my association with Pat, whom she saw as threatening and disreputable but her outlook and Henry's were often similar during these meetings and more informal conversations.

4 On the private developers' team.

5 Police were not brought into discussions until well after I finished my fieldwork over two years later.

6 Unfortunately, later inconsistency and lack of clarity about this date put residents back on the defensive.

7 I was not attending these later meetings so cannot comment on the progress towards this change. No mention of concerns about exclusion was recorded in minutes.

Chapter 10

Towards a governance of just sustainability

I have, throughout the book, presented multiple experiences and explanations of the changes seen on this estate. Though variously constituted, community was amongst all used as a vision of a state of untroubled stability and security, contrasted with the reality with which they were faced (Bauman 2001). Differing explanations for the failure to produce that imagined ideal, or for its disappearance, I have suggested, say as much about those voicing them and their (dis)position as the problems they identify. Although differing in important ways, not least in how they attribute blame, these accounts all pivot around accounts of the failure of the local state, exposing notions of legitimate governance. For residents, it is the poor relationships with local authorities, as much as within the community, that many associate with decline.

Crime, disorder and the decline in the appearance of the area are often used by residents to highlight problems beyond their capacity to control that have gone unchallenged by local agencies. For many it is not simply a failure to tackle local problems but to fulfil their rights as tenants and citizens and a reflection of wider inequality. These narratives of neglect reflect not just a lack of faith in governing bodies' capacity but a loss of legitimacy. Local governance falls short of a justice ideal of equal treatment, most glaringly in their failure to provide residents with basic security, let alone fulfil their duty of care. It was this loss of legitimacy, as well as a fear of retaliation, that contributed to residents' reluctance to report. Authorities' responses could prove as useless and potentially as damaging as the offence, upholding a 'grassing' taboo.

From the perspectives of officials this reluctance to report was crippling local governance and much of their energy was spent on enforcement in an attempt to encourage it. However, these lay narratives re-emphasise the need for governance in areas of social exclusion to be engaged in a dialogue about the legitimacy of their responses, not simply attempting to reduce fears. In areas or amongst groups whose experience has undermined a sense of unbiased response they are essentially engaged in a renegotiation of legitimate authority, in being held to account. Although it is in this light that local participatory processes are, of course, conceived and encouraged, in practice they have the potential to produce some rather different outcomes.

My chief concern is that a belief that punitive and exclusionary measures will restore faith in the capacity of governing agencies may have the counter-productive effect of alienating those least likely to report or engage in local governance, while bolstering the position of those already well disposed but least able to provide informed opinions as to the ways to confront problems. Moreover, as I have suggested, I see a danger of processes of participation privileging punitiveness, rather than promoting inclusion. There is too ready an assumption that resonance with professional understandings denotes representativeness and that, for example, a widespread call for more policing reflects a widespread punitiveness. The emphasis within participatory processes on building consensus and trust around common values and goals, along with an identification of risks to the community (tied to moral conceptions of responsibility), has the effect of simply creating consensus around who to blame (Douglas 1992; Hudson 2003).

Exclusionary practices and discourses undermine those aimed at inclusion, confirming worst suspicions, heightening anxieties and advising caution and distance from authorities. Responses need to demonstrate sensitivity to a sense of both need for and exposure to intervention rather than sheer ability to exert what can appear callous or threatening authority. After all, neglect and then clampdown has often been the experience of such areas, both in terms of policing and housing management. Responsiveness in this sense is not simply about responding to a demand for enforcement (to do something) but engaging people in a dialogue about the implications of potential responses to problems. It is about acknowledging the dilemmas people face in dealing with problems, appealing to inclusive intentions rather than exclusionary impulses and a reassurance of rights and inclusion, the fragility of which contribute to residents' sense of insecurity. To build a sustainable future for areas without the banishment of those considered other, disruptive or ungovernable, there needs to be a far greater concern for justice in local governance. Rather than a management of risks to ensure security or the wholesale regeneration of areas, in this all or nothing way, there is the potential for a more subtle mode of urban governance in a promotion of 'just sustainability'.[1] This reasserts the need for urban governance to be driven by concerns for equality, justice and sustainability as well as prosperity and security, recognising the damaging effects of too much of a swing to the latter. Such places might not seem as prosperous, nor as safe, but their future may prove more secure.

What I want, tentatively, to begin to outline here are some directions in which this more inclusive ethic of local governance might go, and parallel practices of participation that might engender its development.

Inclusionary responses to crime and disorder

Though there will always be the need for public protection, I see the precautionary trend in risk management, exemplified within local authority and police perspectives, as a slippery slope (Haggerty 2003). It derogates rights in the name of security (Hudson 2003). Crucially, exclusionary measures implemented in the name of security and future prosperity have the potential to be not only unjust but, ironically, unsustainable as they can simply compound the distrust with which authorities are viewed. Only by confronting problems of disorder in a way that communicates inclusivity can there be any prospects for a change in many people's willingness to engage in participatory processes or report problems, particularly about the range of activities around the illegal drug trade.[2] Equally, it is only when 'outsiders' or 'others' are, through such processes, accepted as 'insiders' that the prospect for the internal capacity to control becomes imaginable (Girling, Loader and Sparks 2000).

In order to rebalance questions of security and justice without diminishing concerns for safety, and move away from a demonisation of 'others' there is arguably a need for the endorsement of forms of justice promoting inclusion rather than banishment/incapacitation (Hudson 2003; Johnston and Shearing 2003). I would add that this is necessary for sustainable governance of urban areas where attempts to tackle social exclusion are undermined by the impact of insensitive criminal justice and risk management responses. It is beyond the scope of this book to outline what these might be but I feel that there is more scope for the use of responses, particularly to neighbour disputes and 'anti-social behaviour', that rely on concepts of dispute resolution that could be accessed without reporting to traditional authorities (Liebmann 1997; Wright 1996). Responses that do not bring the weight of local authority powers to bear on problems straight away perhaps have more chance of negotiating a more lasting peace without fear of retribution, particularly in areas where state authorities have an ambiguous legitimacy (McEvoy and Mika 2002; Johnston and Shearing 2003). Such approaches affirm a commitment to a future-focused sustainable, equally preventative, justice but less punitive than a risk management approach. Maintaining a distance from, but supporting, such interventions could potentially begin to ease some of the reluctance to report, minimise a 'net-widening effect' of enforcement (Cohen 1985) and communicate an attempt to promote inclusion without appearing to neglect or stamp on disorderly (and sometimes criminal[3]) behaviour.

Inclusionary participation

More directly in response to my observations of this participation process for regeneration and the marked lack of participatory involvement in and discussion of issues of crime and disorder,[4] I want here to suggest some moves towards more inclusive participatory processes that take account of the way in which problems are constituted and of a need to bridge between 'habituated' understandings.

Communicating between habitus

For a genuine inclusion of citizens in participatory processes, it is important that professional knowledge does not dominate agendas or communication. Participation that does not reproduce inequalities must not be geared around particular projects of regeneration or professional fields of expertise in which residents are at a disadvantage. Ironically, an understanding that communities can be included in *partnerships* with professional bodies on an *equal* footing actually limits their ability to challenge these power dynamics, particularly such internal exclusionary practices, other than by opting out. There is, in addition, a danger of conceiving of residents as equivalent 'experts' on their area. This exposes them to the challenge of the representativeness of their experience, to the 'authenticity' of their knowledge. Rather, residents bring to the table perspectives on problems that could not otherwise be accessed. An understanding of perspectives on problems leaves much more scope for the inclusion of voices of minority and demonised groups, not representative but with valuable experience to bring to bear in tackling local problems. This approach is more conducive to 'problem-solving' than one linked to zero-tolerance (Johnston and Shearing 2003). It also removes questions of representativeness from the creation of processes of participatory democracy (Young 2000). This is a more inclusive approach to participation than one anticipating representation of a majority, from which some are necessarily excluded and which endorses a tendency to blame 'others'.

Participatory processes present problems of bridging between different world views in a way that does not silence dissent or reinforce blame of 'others'. Widely different causal theories and preconceptions present problems for a conception of deliberation through rational persuasion based on common understandings/values which tended to characterise professional approaches. Iris Young (2000: Chapter 2) suggests that, instead, a recognition of narrative forms of communication can counteract the internally exclusionary effects of an emphasis on rationality within deliberative approaches. Acknowledging the wider significance of stories told, not as private interest or anecdote, but as expressions of nuanced understandings of the complexity of problems based on experience, however, requires a significant change in professional practice. Though there is potential for training in this regard, such a change would also require an incentive to take residents' understandings seriously, acknowledging professional understandings as partial (in both senses of the word). This would necessitate flexibility in policy and accountability to central government that managerial techniques and centralised 'steering' undermine (Crawford 2001).

The inclusion of divergent voices still presents the potential for problems of miscommunication and a tendency to blame 'others'. However, what was apparent in the early days of this process was the capacity that the resonance of rights discourses between residents' narratives had for bridging between their divergent positions. Rather than 'values', this language drew on common cultural conceptions of justice and injustice (Douglas 1986). More resonant with residents' conceptions of a justice ideal of legitimate governance, a rights discourse, on the basis of a more universal human or civil rights, offers a language and basis of practise that mitigates against the exclusionary and divisive effects of 'community' (Hudson 2003; McEvoy and Mika 2002). It offered a recognisably legitimating language for politicisation and participation beyond authenticity and belonging. However, a rights discourse had become equated with intransigence, confrontation and criminality, and a majoritarian emphasis on responsibilities to the community made defence and inclusion of minorities, denigrated and unpopular groups difficult (Crawford 2003a; Hudson 2003; O'Malley 2004; Rose 2000).

For this language of rights to regain its credibility in this context there needs to be a re-centring of a goal of achieving justice as well as security in local governance, refocusing on what kind of order it is hoped will be produced (Pitch 1995). This necessitates state endorsement, particularly from locally elected councillors, and enforcement to such ends (Hudson 2003). Without it residents' use of this language, and their attempts to present minority or unpopular perspectives, lose credibility.

Participatory democracy

The limitations presented by 'partnership' between professional agencies and community representatives (as consumers or local experts) suggest the need for a movement away from such an understanding of participation and instead to consider the role of local participation as a new level of participatory democracy linked more closely with representational democracy. Rather than attempting to mobilise communities' expressions of demands for services (such as to address crime and disorder) around solutions provided by specialists, there is perhaps scope for a politicisation and renegotiation of the remit of citizens' participation to enable a legitimate means by which new governing arrangements between public, private and civil sectors may be held to account. If to open policy directions to critique about privileged interests, unforeseen consequences and misconceived foundations, participatory bodies need to maintain a distance from, even if working with, public bodies.

However, as Bourdieu emphasises, to participate in any field players need to be convinced that the game is worth playing. Where experience has suggested co-option rather than capacity, processes can, as in the process described above, increase a sense of powerlessness and unwillingness to participate. A significant say in the allocation of local budgets may provide local public participatory bodies with the financial capital, as well as the symbolic, to hold partnerships to account and, rewarding participation with tangible influence, convince previously sceptical groups that this is a game worth playing.

Most importantly, such participatory structures need to have a demonstrable legitimacy, as well as capacity. They need to be capable of feeding into wider democratic and policy-making processes if governance is to go beyond a conception of problems as local and avoid competition for resources between areas. Without a link to representative democracy in this way, the capacity, and thereby the legitimacy and longevity of such structures, will be limited (Mohan 2001; Wainwright 2003). There is a need for local democratic structures to connect with other structures of representative democracy in recognition that 'problems' are by no means local.

Notes

1   I have borrowed this term from arguments promoting the need for governance to address inequality in resources as well as environmentally sustainable practices if lasting change to address climate change is to be effected (Agyeman and Evans 2004). Unsustainable consumerism and the increasing gap between rich and poor represent equally important implications for crime control as well as urban governance (see, for example, Hayward 2004) and is an important perspective from which to approach issues of inequality and security in a way that holds the rich responsible for harm as well as the poor. To this I have added an emphasis on the need for concerns for justice and rights in governance and within citizen participation, slightly altering the significance of 'just' governance.
2   Though officers reported the success of anonymous reporting through 'crimestoppers', for example, this perpetuates an understanding that reporting is illicit, that it is 'grassing'.
3   The issue of such processes dealing with incidents that could otherwise be dealt with under criminal law is one I do not have the space to go into here. Debates around these concerns are discussed at length in the vast and growing literature on 'restorative justice' approaches.
4   You may recall the local Crime and Disorder Partnership suspended such sessions until they could enforce effectively.

Appendix

Conducting interviews

Interviewing to access a sense of residents' 'habitus', I wanted to explore underlying causal narratives used within their accounts. My approach had much in common with narrative analysis and biographical interviewing, characterising people as storytellers, producing narratives that use causal logics and beliefs to maintain and create a sense of coherence and meaning to their lives (Josselson and Lieblich 1999; Linde 1993). I wanted to elicit peoples' life stories in relation to living in this place.

Conversations

I began each interview by asking residents, 'How have you come to be living here?' This was a deliberate invitation to tell me a story, and phrased to invite explanation through a description. This question elicited very different responses and immediately gave the interviews unique qualities. People began their stories at different times in their life, describing previous homes, life decisions, important events, life stories in relation to living there. Residents' life stories and their position in this place began to offer an insight into their sense of identity (Josselson and Lieblich 1999) and of their sense of their position in the world (Bourdieu 2000; Hall 2000), in particular, how closely their understanding of themselves and their own trajectory was tied to Millton or the estate. These stories provided a jumping-off point from which I could simply prompt further explanation or repeat words asking for explanation.

Eliciting stories and allowing people to lead the conversation minimised a sense of interrogation. Stories could expose the contradictions between expounded theories and the events as people described them (Hollway and Jefferson 2000) but it was often in identifying these contradictions that interpretation was fruitful (Willis 2000). Explanations, for example, of why people were safe, such as, 'I'm known', or 'People don't steal from their own', might contradict their experience of being burgled by people they knew but were important to their understanding of their position in the area. Relating stories were also a means of asking people to describe events that might be difficult or upsetting to explain. Responding to individual circumstances, responses, styles and what people said required sensitivity and willingness to adapt the interview to what I encountered (Lee 1993).[1] I had some standard questions as a guide (see examples below) but I hardly used them, as much as possible using less interrogative prompts. Often a simple 'um' or 'yeah'[2] was enough to encourage a continued description of whatever they were talking about or confirm understanding. Only when I felt we were wandering completely away from what I wanted us to be talking about, or when they came to a complete halt, did I ask questions.

I wanted to provide an atmosphere in which residents and professionals felt able to talk freely in their own terms without fear of censure. This was particularly difficult to achieve with officials who seemed less willing to let down a professional guard. However, I went out of my way to promote an atmosphere that broke down some of the power dynamics within interviews that could hinder a sense of shared understandings and acceptance (Lee 1993: Oakley 1986). To suggest that I was always in a more powerful position as regards communication with residents and less so with officials would be a gross oversimplification. I was as conscious of official anxieties about an academic study as I was that I would sometimes turn up on doorsteps on damp days and be invited in out of pity. As these were social events it was important to create, for myself as well as the participant, ease of conversation. In particular I handed over control of the recording equipment in order to distance the interview from some residents' experiences of being interviewed by police. Although some residents and professionals initially expressed alarm at the tape recorder, the conversational style distanced the interviews from this more official expectation.

Analysis

These interviews and observations of meetings produced unique and rich material but of a bulk and diversity that presented some challenges for analysis. Although each interview was unique to the person who produced it, there was a similarity of form across all, engendered by questions prompting an initial life story. I analysed the interviews as internally referential texts and cross-referenced sections through an analysis of language and of the narrative structure of the stories within them. In this sense each interview was treated as a case study and in part written about as such. However, what I have focused on is the similarity between accounts. Amongst residents I suggest four loosely defined narratives. By narratives I mean distinct ways of understanding the decline of the estate and relations with authorities, which are associated with particular causal explanations of social inequality and of 'habituated' disposition (Bourdieu 2000).

Sample interview schedules

Interviews with residents and staff were based on similar questions about the area and its problems, but tailored to the people being interviewed. I did not refer to the questions during the interviews, except to check that we had covered the issues I hoped to by the end. I have included two samples here, one for residents and one tailored to a housing strategy officer I had met before. These should not be read as if interviews followed their structure.

Interview with residents

How have you come to be living here?
What impression do you think people outside the area have of it?
When have you encountered this?

What was it like when you first moved here?
Has it changed?
How would you explain what went wrong?
Do you find people help each other on the estate?
Tell me about people you are close to.
Do you think it would be easy to move into the area (now and in past)?

What problems do you think the area has had? (Refer back to explanation of what went wrong.)
Do you think there has been a crime problem/drug problem? (If don't mention.)

Who do you think should have been dealing with the problems?
Have you ever tried to get involved in trying to resolve some of the problems? Anyone else?
Have you ever tried to intervene? E.g. talked to kids, their parents.

Would you report incidents and who to?
What do you think of the work of the police?
What do you think of other government agencies? E.g. housing, social services?
Have you come in contact with other organisations other than these?

Do you feel safe in the area? Why?
a) walking at night, in the day time, when talking to people who are not from there, when talking to others who live on the estate.
b) compared to other areas of Manchester, city centre, neighbouring areas
c) parts of estate where don't feel safe?
Have you done anything to make yourself feel safer or taken precautions to ensure your safety? E.g. staying in, alarms, dogs, walk with others (fostering relationships with others/agencies).

What do you think the estate will be like in five years' time? Will you stay?
What do you think about the regeneration of [the estate]?
If you ran the estate what would you do to sort out the problems?
Is there anything you would like to add that you think I have not asked you about or think that I don't understand?

Interview with housing strategy

Your job
Could you tell me a little about how you have come to be working in this field?
How did you envision your job when you started working on this project? Has that been your experience?
At what point did you become involved with the project?

The area

What was your initial impression of the area and has it changed?

Do you think the area has particular problems that are different from other areas?

What is you perception of [the estate] area compared to other areas of Manchester ?

What do you think relationships between people are like there?

What do you think relationships between **residents and agencies** are like?

What is your impression of relationships now and have they changed? How would you like it to be?

How do you feel in the area – safe? Compared to other areas? Been there at night?

Problems in the area

What do you think have been the main problems in the area? Why do you think they have resulted in so many voids?

Which of the problems do you think was most serious? Which was most difficult to deal with?

Do you feel it was the role of housing to deal with these problems?

How do you feel they should have been dealt with and who should have dealt with them?

Why do you think these problems existed?

Do you think the problems in the area have changed?

What impact do you think regeneration has had on the area?

Do you think crime and/or disorder is a particular problem in the area?

Dealing with problems

Looking back, do you think there was anything that could have been done to prevent the decline of the estate?

Do you feel there has been opportunity to approach any of these issues yet? Will they be approached during this period of build?

Do you have much contact with other agencies in trying to confront some of these problems?

Have there been any times when you felt it was the responsibility of local people to sort out a problem?

Do you think local people are willing to get involved in dealing with the problems?

Do you think the police should be responsible for dealing with the problems in the area?

What is your opinion on the use of anti-social behaviour orders/ eviction orders? (If mention.)

The consultation process
What were your expectations for this consultation process? Has that been fulfilled?
Would you have liked it to be any different?
Do you find consultation useful?
How do you feel your relationships with the residents' steering group is developing?
Has this consultation differed from other experiences you have had?
In your experience of these processes has this differed from others?

Working in partnership?
Has this differed from other projects where you have been working in partnership?
What impression have you gained of police, developer, regeneration company?
How are these partnerships coming together – any successes, frustrations?
Do you feel you have a part to play in any partnership in this area? Have you been encouraged to participate?
(If bring up.) Problems of trust? Feasible for you to gain trust of community at this stage?

Future
Do you have any fears for the future of the area?
How do you foresee the balance of housing sectors in the area? Any concerns?

Rounding up
What do you think the area will be like in five years' time?
Are there any problems that you have any concerns about how they can be tackled?
Is there anything you would like to add that you think I have not asked you about or think that I don't understand?

Notes

1   The most important example of this was with a girl who told me, at the outset, that she had just come out of hospital after her second suicide attempt. At such a delicate time I was very anxious not to distress her but also did not want to leave as she had seemed keen to do the interview. I was particularly careful to let her lead what we talked about and at the end made an effort to concentrate on the positive things that she had told me. I was relieved when a friend of hers arrived with whom I left her.

2   These are not included in the text as they interrupt the rhythms of people's speech.

References

Abrahams, R. (1998) *Vigilant Citizens: Vigilantism and The State*. Cambridge: Polity Press.

Agyeman, J. and Evans, B. (2004) '"Just Sustainability": The Emerging Discourse of Environmental Justice In Britain?' *The Geographical Journal*, 170: 155–164.

Anderson, B. (1983) *Imagined Communities*. London: Verso.

Atkinson, R. (2000) 'Narratives of Policy: The Construction of Urban Problems and Urban Policy In The Official Discourse of British Government 1968–1998', *Critical Social Policy*, 20: 211–232.

Atkinson, R. and Cope, S. (1997) 'Community Participation and Urban Regeneration In Britain', in Hoggett, P. (ed.) *Contested Communities*. Bristol: Policy Press: 201–221.

Atkinson, R. (1999) 'Discourses of Partnership and Empowerment In Contemporary British Urban Regeneration', *Urban Studies*, 36: 59–72.

Back, L. (1994) *New Ethnicities and Urban Culture: Racisms and Multiculture In Young Lives*. London: UCL Press.

Bauman, Z. (1998) *Globalization: The Human Consequences*. Cambridge: Polity Press.

Bauman, Z. (2001) *Community: Seeking Safety In An Insecure World*. Cambridge: Polity.

Baumgartner, M.P. (1988) *The Moral Order of The Suburb*. New York: Oxford University Press.

Beck, U. (1992) *The Risk Society*. London: Sage.

Bourdieu, P. (1999) 'Understanding', in Bourdieu, P. *et al.* (eds) *The Weight of The World*. Cambridge: Polity Press.

Bourdieu, P. (2000a) *Pascalian Meditations*. Cambridge: Polity Press.

Bourdieu, P. (2000b) 'The Biographical Illusion', in Du Gay, P., Evans, J. and Redman, P. (eds) *Identity: A Reader*. London: Sage.

Bourdieu, P. and Wacquant, L. (1992) *An Invitation To Reflexive Sociology*. Chicago: University of Chicago.

Bourgois, P. (1996) 'In Search of Masculinity: Violence, Respect and Sexuality Among Puerto Rican Crack Dealers In East Harlem', *British Journal of Criminology*, 36: 412–427.

Braithwaite, J. and Daly, K. (1994) 'Masculinities, Violence and Communitarian Control', in Newburn, T. and Stanko, E. (eds) *Just Boys Doing Business?* London: Routledge.

Brent, J. (1997) 'Community Without Unity', in Hoggett, P. (ed.) *Contested Communities*. Bristol: Policy Press.

Burchardt, T., Le Grand, J. and Piachaud, D. (2002) 'Degrees of Exclusion: Developing A Multidimensional Measure', in Hills, J., Le Grand, J. and Piachaud, D. (eds) *Understanding Social Exclusion*. Oxford: Oxford University Press.

Burney, E. (1999) *Crime and Banishment: Nuisance and Exclusion In Social Housing*. Winchester: Waterside Press.

Burns, D. Hambleton, R. and Hoggett, P. (1994) *The politics of decentralisation: revitalizing local democracy*. Basingstoke: Macmillan.

Bursik, R. and Gramsmick, H. (1993) *Neighbourhoods and Crime*. New York: Lexington.

Campbell, B. (1993) *Goliath: Britain's Dangerous Places*. London: Methuen.

Castells, M. (1997) *The Power of Identity*. Oxford: Blackwell.

Choongh, S. (1998) 'Policing The Dross: A Social Disciplinary Model of Policing', *British Journal of Criminology*, 38: 623–634.

Cohen, S. (1973) *Folk Devils and Moral Panics*. St Albans: Paladin.

Cohen, S. (1985) *Visions of Social Control*. New York: Plenum.

Coleman, J.S. (1989) 'Social Capital and the Creation of Human Capital', *American Journal of Sociology*, 94 (Supplement): 95–120.

Coleman, R. and Sim, J. (1998) 'From The Dockyards To The Disney Store: Surveillance, Risk and Security In Liverpool City Centre', *International Review of Law, Computers and Technology*, 12: 27–45.

Cox, K.R. (1993) 'The Local and The Global In The New Urban Politics: A Critical View', *Environment and Planning D*, 11: 433–448.

Crawford, A. (2001) 'Joined-Up But Fragmented: Contradiction, Ambiguity and Ambivalence At The Heart of New Labour's Third Way', in Matthews, R. and Pitts, J. (eds) *Crime Disorder and Community Safety*. London: Routledge.

Crawford, A. (1997) *The Local Governance of Crime: Appeals To Community and Partnerships*. Oxford: Clarendon Press.

Crawford, A. (2003a) '"Contractual Governance" of Deviant Behaviour', *Journal of Law and Society*, 30: 479–503.

Crawford, A. (2003b) 'The Pattern of Policing In The UK: Policing Beyond The Police', in Newburn, T. (ed.) *The Handbook of Policing*. Cullompton: Willan Publishing.

Davis, F. (1979) *Yearning For Yesterday: A Sociology of Nostalgia*. New York: Free Press.

Davis, M. (1990) *City of Quartz: Excavating The Future In Los Angeles*. London: Vintage.

Della Porta, D. and Diani, M. (1999) *Social Movements: An Introduction*. Oxford: Blackwell.

DETR (1999) 'Towards An Urban Renaissance. Final Report of The Urban Task Force, Chaired By Lord Rogers of Riverside.' London: The Stationery Office.

DETR (2000) 'Our Towns and Cities – The Future: Delivering An Urban Renaissance.' London: The Stationery Office.

Douglas, M. (1966) *Purity and Danger*. London: Routledge Kegan Paul.

Douglas, M. (1986) *How Institutions Think*. London: Routledge Kegan Paul.

Douglas, M. (1992) *Risk and Blame: Essays In Cultural Theory*. London: Routledge.

Duneier, M. (1999) *Sidewalk*. New York: Farrar, Straus & Giroux.

Elias, N., and Scotson, J.L. (1965) *The Established and The Outsiders*. London: Frank Cass and Co.

Ericson, R. and Haggerty, K. (1997) *Policing The Risk Society*. Oxford: Oxford University Press.

Etzioni, A. (1993) *The Spirit of Community: Rights, Responsibilities and The Communitarian Agenda*. New York: Simon and Schuster.

Evans, J. (2003) 'Vigilance and Vigilantes: Thinking Psychoanalytically About Anti-Paedophile Action', *Theoretical Criminology*, 7: 163–189.

Ewick, P. and Silbey, S. (1999) 'Common Knowledge and Ideological Critique: The Significance of Knowing That The "Haves" Come Out Ahead', *Law and Society Review*, 33: 1025–1041.

Feeley, M.M. and Simon, J. (eds) (1996) *The New Penology*. London: Sage.

Field, J. (2003) *Social Capital*. London: Routledge.

Flick, U. (1998) *An Introduction To Qualitative Resaerch*. London: Sage.

Flint, J. (2002) 'Social Housing Agencies and The Governance of Anti-Social Behaviour', *Housing Studies*, 17: 619–637.

Foster, J. (1995) 'Informal Social Control and Community Crime Prevention', *British Journal of Criminology*, 35: 563–581.

Foster, J. (1999) *Docklands: Cultures In Conflict, Worlds In Collision*. London: UCL Press.

Garland, D. (1995) 'The Limits of The Sovereign State: Strategies of Crime Control In Contemporary Society', *British Journal of Criminal Justice*, 36: 445–471.

Garland, D. (2001) *The Culture of Control: Crime and Social Order In Contemporary Society*. Oxford: Oxford University Press.

Giddens, A. (1991) *Modernity and Self-Identity: Self and Society In The Late Modern Age*. Cambridge: Polity Press.

Giddens, A. (1998) *The Third Way: The Renewal of Social Democracy*. Oxford: Polity Press.

Girling, E., Loader, I. and Sparks, R. (2000) *Crime and Social Change In Middle England*. London: Routledge.

Girling, E., Loader, I. and Sparks, R. (1998) 'A Telling Tale: A Case of Vigilantism and Its Aftermath In An English Town', *British Journal of Sociology*, 49: 474–90.

Griffiths, S. (1998) 'A Profile of Poverty and Health In Manchester', Manchester: Manchester Health Authority.

Hacking, I. (2003) 'Risk and Dirt', in Ericson, R.V. and Doyle, A. (eds) *Risk and Morality*. Toronto: University of Toronto Press.

Haggerty, K.D. (2003) 'From Risk To Precaution: The Rationalities of Personal Crime Prevention', in Ericson, R.V. and Doyle, A. (eds) *Risk and Morality*. Toronto: University of Toronto Press, 193–214.

Hall, S. (2000) 'Who Needs Identity?', in Du Gay, P., Evans, J. and Redman, P. (eds) *Identity: A Reader*. London: Sage.

Hall, S., Critcher, C., Jefferson, T., Clarke, J. and Roberts, B. (1978) *Policing The Crisis: Mugging, The State and Law and Order*. Basingstoke: Macmillan.

Hall, T., and Hubbard, P. (1996) 'The Entrepreneurial City: New Urban Politics, New Urban Geographies?', *Progress In Human Geography*, 20: 153–174.

Hammersley, M. and Atkinson, P. (1995) *Ethnography: Principles In Practice*. London: Routledge.

Hancock, L. (2000) 'Going Around The Houses: Researching In High Crime Communities', in King, R.D. and Wincup, E. (eds) *Doing Research On Crime and Justice*. Oxford: Oxford University Press.

Hancock, L. (2003) 'Urban Regeneration and Crime Reduction: Contradictions and Dilemmas', in Matthews, R. and Young, J. (eds) *The New Politics of Crime and Punishment*. Cullompton, Devon: Willan Publishing.

Harvey, D. (1996) *Justice, Nature and The Geography of Difference*. Oxford: Blackwell.

Hastings, A. (1996) 'Unravelling The Process of "Partnership" In Urban Regeneration Policy', *Urban Studies*, 33: 253–268.

Hastings, A. (1999) 'Analysing Power Relations In Partnerships: Is There A Role For Discourse Analysis?', *Urban Studies*, 36: 91–106.

Haworth, A. and Manzi, T. (1999) '"Managing The Underclass": Interpreting The Moral Discourse of Housing Management', *Urban Studies*, 36: 153–165.

Hayward, K. (2004) *City Limits: Consumer Culture and The Urban Experience*. London: Glasshouse Press.

Helleiner, J. and Szuchewycz, B. (1997) 'Discourses of Exclusion: The Irish Press and The Travelling People', in Riggins, S.H. (ed.) *The Language and Politics of Exclusion: Others in Discourse*. London: Sage.

Herbert, S. (2001) 'Policing The Contemporary City: Fixing Broken Windows Or Shoring Up Neo-Liberalism?', *Theoretical Criminology*, 5: 445–466.

Hockey, J. (2002) 'Interviews as Ethnography? Disembodied Social Interaction In Britain', in Rapport, N. (ed.) *British Subjects: An Anthropology of Britain*. Oxford: Berg.

Hollway, W. and Jefferson, T. (2000) *Doing Qualitative Research Differently*. London: Sage.

Hollway, W. and Jefferson, T. (1997) 'The Risk Society In An Age of Anxiety: Situating Fear of Crime', *British Journal of Sociology*, 48: 255–265.

Hope, T. (ed.) (1995) *Community Crime Prevention*. Chicago: University of Chicago Press.

Hudson, B. (2003) *Justice In The Risk Society*. London: Sage.

Hunt, A. (2003) 'Risk and Moralization In Everyday Life', in Ericson, R.V. (ed.) *Risk and Morality*. Toronto: University of Toronto Press.

Hunter, A. (1995) 'Private, Parochial and Public Social Orders: The Problem of Crime and Inequality and Incivility In Urban Communities', in Kasinitz, P. (ed.) *Metropolis: Center and Symbol of Our Times*. New York: New York University Press)

Imrie, R. and Raco, M. (2003) 'Community and The Changing Nature of Urban Policy', in Imrie, R. and Raco, M. (eds) *Urban Renaissance? New Labour, Community and Urban Policy*. Bristol: Policy Press.

Innes, M. (2004) 'Signal Crimes and Signal Disorders: Notes On Deviance As Communicative Action', *The British Journal of Sociology*, 55: 335–355.

James, A.L. and James, A. (2001) 'Tightening The Net: Children, Community and Control', *British Journal of Sociology*, 52: 211–228.

James, O. (2000) 'Melting Geography: Purity, Disorder, Childhood and Space', in Hollway, S.L. and Valentine, G. (eds) *Children's Geographies: Playing, Living, Learning*. London: Routledge.

Jessop, B. (1997) 'The Entrepreneurial City: Re-Imaging Localities, Redesigning Economic Governance, Or Restucturing Capital?', in Jewson, N. and MacGregor, S. (eds) *Transforming Cities: Contested Governance and New Spatial Divisions*. London: Routledge.

Jessop, B. (2002) 'Liberalism, Neoliberalism and Urban Governance: A State-Theoretical Perspective', *Antipode*: 452–472.

Johnston, L. and Shearing, C. (2003) *Governing Security: Explorations In Policing and Justice*. London: Routledge.

Jones, P.S. (2003) 'Urban Regeneration's Poisoned Chalice: Is There An Impasse In (Community) Participation-Based Policy?', *Urban Studies*, 40: 581–601.

Jones, T. and Newburn, T. (1998) *Private Security and Public Policing*. Oxford: Oxford University Press.

Josselson, R. and Lieblich, A. (eds) (1999) 'Making Meaning of Narratives', in Josselson, R. and Lieblich, A. (eds) *The Narrative Study of Lives 6*.

Kasinitz, P. and Hillyard, D. (1995) 'The Old-Timers' Tale', *Journal of Contemporary Ethnography*, 24: 139–165.

Kearns, A. (2003) 'Social Capital, Regeneration and Urban Policy', in Imrie, R. and Raco, M. (eds) *Urban Renaissance? New Labour, Community and Urban Policy*. Bristol: Policy Press.

Keith, M. and Pile, S. (eds) (1993) *Place and The Politics of Identity*. London: Routledge.

Kelling, G. (2001) 'Broken Windows and The Culture Wars: A Response To Selected Critiques', in Matthews, R. and Pitts, J. (eds) *Crime, Disorder and Community Safety*. London: Routledge.

Kidd, A. and Wyke, T. (1993) '[Millton]: The First Industrial Suburb', *Manchester Regional History Review 7*.

Kothari, U. (2001) 'Power, Knowledge and Social Control In Participtory Development', in Cooke, B. and Kothari, U. (eds) *Participation: The New Tyranny?* New York: Zed Books.

Lacey, N. and Zedner, L. (1995) 'Community In German Criminal Justice: A Significant Absence?', *Social and Legal Studies*, 7: 7–25.

Lee, P. and Murie, A. (1999) 'Spatial and Social Divisions Within British Cities: Beyond Residualisation', *Housing Studies*, 14: 625–640.

Lee, R.M. (1993) *Doing Research On Sensitive Topics*. London: Sage.

Lees, L. (2003) 'Visions of "Urban Renaissance": The Urban Task Force Report and The Urban White Paper', in Imrie, R. and Raco, M. (eds) *Urban Renaissance? New Labour, Community and Urban Policy*. Bristol: Policy Press.

Lewis, D.A. and Salem, G. (1986) *Fear of Crime: Incivility and The Production of A Social Problem*. New Brunswick: Transaction Books.

Lieblich, A., Tuval-Mashiach, R. and Zilber, T. (1998) *Narrative Research: Reading, Analysis and Interpretation*. London: Sage.

Liebmann, M. (1997) 'Community and Neighbourhood Mediation: A UK Perspective', in Macfarlane, J. (ed.) *Rethinking Disputes: The Mediation Alternative*. London: Cavendish.

Linde, C. (1993) *Life Stories: The Creation of Coherence*. Oxford: Oxford University Press.

Loader, I. (1996) *Youth, Policing and Democracy*. Basingstoke: Macmillan.

Loader, I. (1997) 'Policing and The Social: Questions of Symbolic Power', *British Journal of Sociology*, 48.

Loader, I. (2000) 'Plural Policing and Democratic Governance', *Social and Legal Studies*, 9: 323–345.

Loader, I. and Mulcahy, A. (2003) *Policing and The Condition of England; Memory, Politics and Culture*. Oxford: Oxford University Press.

Logan, J. and Molotch, H. (1987) *Urban Fortunes: The Political Economy of Place*. Berkeley: University of California Press.

Lund, B. (1996) *Housing Problems and Housing Policy*. Essex: Addison Wesley Longman.

Lupton, D. and Tulloch, J. (1999) 'Theorizing Fear of Crime: Beyond The Rational/Irrational Opposition', *British Journal of Sociology*, 50: 507–523.

Macleod, G. and Ward, K. (2002) 'Spaces of Utopia and Dystopia: Landscaping The Contemporary City', *Geografiska Annaler B*, 84: 153–170.

Manchester City Council (2001) 'Manchester's Corporate Housing Strategy', Manchester: Manchester City Council.

Manchester Housing (Oct 1999) 'Living On [The Estate]', Manchester: Manchester City Council.

Massey, D. (1994) *Space, Place and Gender*. Cambridge: Polity Press.

McEvoy, K. and Mika, H. (2002) 'Restorative Justice and The Critique of Informalism In Northern Ireland', *British Journal of Criminology*, 42: 534–562.

Merry, S. (1981) *Urban Danger*. Philadelphia: Temple University Press.

Merry, S.E. (2003) 'Rights Talk and The Experience of Law: Implementing Women's Human Rights To Protection From Violence' *Human Rights Quarterly*, 25: 343–381.

Mirlees-Black, C. and Allen, J. (1998) 'Concern About Crime: Findings From The 1998 British Crime Survey', London: Home Office.

Mohan, G. (2001) 'Beyond Participation: Strategies For Deeper Empowerment', in Cooke, B. and Kothari, U. (eds) *Participation: The New Tyranny?* London: Zed Books.

Mosse, D. (2001) '"People's Knowledge", Participation and Patronage: Operations and Representations In Rural Development', in Cooke, B. and Kothari, U. (eds) *Participation: The New Tyranny?* London: Zed Books.

Nelken, D. (1994) 'Community Involvement In Crime Control', in Lacey, N. (ed.) *A Reader on Criminal Justice*. Oxford: Oxford University Press.

New [Manchester] Ltd (2000) '[The Estate, Millton]: Stage 1 Development Prospectus', Manchester City Council.

Newburn, T. (2001) 'The Commodification of Policing: Security Networks In The Late Modern City', *Urban Studies*, 38: 829–848.

Newburn, T. (2002) 'Community Safety and Policing: Some Implications of The Crime and Disorder Act 1998', in Hughes, G., McLaughlin, E. and Municie, J. (eds) *Crime Prevention and Community Safety: New Directions*. London: Sage.

O'Bryrne, D. (1997) *Working Class Culture: Local Community and Global Conditions*. London: Routledge.

O'Malley, P. (1992) 'Risk, Power and Crime Prevention', *Economy and Society*, 21: 252–75.

O'Malley, P. (1999) 'Volatile and Contradictory Punshment', *Theoretical Criminology*, 3: 175–196.

Oakley, A. (1986) 'Interviewing Women: A Contradiction In Terms', in Roberts, H. (ed.) *Doing Feminist Research*. London: Routledge.

ODPM (2000) '[Urban] Villages and Sustainable Communities: Final Report', London: Stationery Office.

Payne, R. (2001) 'Gender, Race, Age and Fear In The City', *Urban Studies*, 38: 899–913.

Pitch, T. (1995) *Limited Responsibilities: Social Movements and Criminal Justice*. London: Routledge.

Power, A. and Tunstall, R. (1997) 'Dangerous Disorder: Riots and Violent Disturbances In Thirteen Areas of Britain 1991–2', Joseph Rowntree Foundation.

Putnam, R.D. (1993) *Making Democracy Work: Civic Traditions In Modern Italy*. New Jersey: Princeton University Press.

Quilley, S. (1999) 'Entrepreneurial Manchester: The Genesis of Elite Consensus', *Antipode*, 31: 185–211.

Revill, G. (1993) 'Reading *Rosehill:* Community, Identity and Inner-City Derby', in Keith, M. and Pile, S. (eds) *Place and The Politics of Identity*. London: Routledge.

Reynolds, F. (1986) *The Problem Housing Estate*. Aldershot: Gower.

Riggins, S.H. (1997) 'The Rhetoric of Othering', in *The Language and Politics of Exclusion: Others in Discourse*. London: Sage.

Rimstead, R. (ed.) (1997) 'Subverting Poor Me: Negative Constructions of Identity In Poor and Working-Class Women's Autobiographies', in Riggins, S.H. (ed.) *The Language and Politics of Exclusion: Others in Discourse*. London: Sage.

Rose, N. (2000) 'Government and Control', *British Journal of Criminology*, 40: 321–339.

Rydin, Y. (1998) 'The Enabling Local State and Urban Development: Resources, Rhetoric and Planning In East London', *Urban Studies*, 35: 175–192.

Sampson, R., Raudenbush, S. and Earls, F. (1997) 'Neighbourhoods and Violent Crime: A Multilevel Study of Collective Efficacy', *Science*, 277: 918–24.

Sampson, R.J. and Raudenbush, S.W. (1999) 'Systematic Social Observation of Public Spaces: A New Look At Disorder In Urban Neighbourhoods', *American Journal of Sociology*, 105: 603–51.

Schneider, A.L. and Ingram, H. (1997) *Policy Design For Democracy*. Kansas: University Press of Kansas.

Sennett, R. (1998) *The Corrosion of Character: The Personal Consequences of Work In The New Capitalism*. New York: Norton & Co..

Sennett, R. (2005) *Respect: The Formation of Character In An Age of Inequality*. London: Penguin.

Shearing, C. and Stenning, P. (1987) *Private Policing*. London: Sage.

Sibley, D. (1995) *Geographies of Exclusion*. London: Routledge.

Skinner, J. (2001) 'Taking Conspiracy Seriously: Fantastic Narratives and Mr Grey The Pan-Afrikanist On Monserrat', in Parish, J. and Parker, M. (eds) *The Age of Anxiety: Conspiracy Theory and The Human Sciences*. Oxford: Blackwells.

Skogan, W.G. and Maxfield, M.G. (1981) *Coping With Crime*. New York: Sage.

Skogan, W.G. (1990) *Disorder and Decline: Crime and The Spiral of Decay In American Neighbourhoods*. New York: The Free Press.

Smith, N. (1996) *The New Urban Frontier: Gentrification and The Revanchist City*. London: Routledge.

Smith, S. (1986) *Crime, Space and Society*. Cambridge: Cambridge University Press.

Stanko, E. (1990) *Everyday Violence: How Women and Men Experience Sexual and Physical Danger*. London: Pandora.

Stone, D. (1988) *Policy, Paradox and Political Reason*. Glenview, IL: Scott Foresman.

Suttles, G.D. (1972) *The Social Construction of Communities*. Chicago: Chicago University Press.

Taylor, I. and Jamieson, R. (1996) 'Fear of Crime and Fear of Falling: English Anxieties Approaching The Millenium', in Akerstrom, M. (ed.) *Crime, Culture and Social Control*. Stockholm: Carlssons Forlag.

Taylor, I., Evans, K. and Fraser, P. (1996) *A Tale of Two Cities: Global Change, Local Feeling and Everyday Life In The North of England*. London: Routledge.

Tully, J. (1999) 'The Agonic Freedom of Citizens', *Economy and Society*, 28: 161–182.

Tylor, T. and Boeckmann, R. (1997) 'Three Strikes and You Are Out, But Why? The Psychology of Public Support For Punishing Rule Breakers', *Law and Society Review*, 31: 237–265.

Valentine, G. (1996) 'Children Should Be Seen and Not Heard: The Production and Transgression of Adult's Public Space', *Urban Geography*, 17: 205–220.

Van Dijk, T.A. (ed.) (1997) *Political Discourse and Racism: Describing Others In Western Parliaments*. London: Sage.

Vaughan, B. (2002) 'Cultured Punishments: The Promise of Grid Group Theory', *Theoretical Criminology*, 6: 411–431.

Wainwright, H. (2003) *Reclaim The State: Experiments In Popular Democracy*. London: Verso.

Walkerdine, V. (2001) 'Safety and Danger: Childhood, Sexuality and Space At The End of The Millenium', in Hultgvist, K. and Dahlberg, G. (eds) *Governing The Child In The New Millennium*. London: Routledge.

Walklate, S. (2002) '"I Can't Name Any Names But What's-His-Face Up The Road Will Sort It Out": Communities and Conflict Resolution', in McEvoy, K. and Newburn, T. (eds) *Criminology and Conflict Resolution*. London: Palgrave.

Walklate, S. and Evans, K. (1999) *Zero Tolerance Or Community Tolerance? Managing Crime In High Crime Areas*. Aldershot: Gower.

Ward, K. (2003) 'Entrepreneurial Urbanism, State Restructuring and Civilizing "New" East Manchester', *Area*, 35: 116–127.

Wetherell, M. (2001) 'Debates In Discourse Research', in Wetherell, M., Taylor, S. and Yates, S. (eds) *Discourse Theory and Practice: A Reader*. London: Sage.

Willis, P. (2000) *The Ethnographic Imagination*. Cambridge: Polity Press.

Wilson, J.Q and Kelling, G.L. (1982) 'Broken Windows: The Police and Neighbourhood Safety', *Atlantic Weekly*, March: 29–38.

Wright, M. (1996) 'Justice Without Lawyers: Enabling People To Resolve Their Conflicts', in Wright M. (ed.) *Justice For Victims and Offenders: A Restorative Response To Crime*. Winchester: Waterside.

Young, I.M. (2000) *Inclusion and Democracy*. Oxford: Oxford University Press.

Young, J. (1999) *The Exclusive Society: Social Exclusion, Crime and Difference In Late Modernity*. London: Sage.

Young, J. (2001) 'Identity, Community and Social Exclusion', in Matthews, R. and Pitts, J. (eds) *Crime, Disorder and Community Safety: A New Agenda?* London: Routledge.

Index